IF
YOU'RE NOT
DEPRESSED
YOU
OUGHTA BE IN
THERAPY

CONTENTS

iv

DEDICATION

This book exists because of a woman I met on March 1, 1986. I remember the date with such certainty because the woman, Carol Rosin, a year and a half later, became my wife. —We met on the steps of Los Angeles City Hall; a location selected as the launch site for The Great Peace March. She was the president and founder of a non-profit based in Washington, D.C. called The Institute for Security and Cooperation in Outer Space (ISCOS). This institute was a think tank thinking about how to prevent the weaponization of outer space that had been officially promulgated by the Reagan "think" tank in 1983.

That fateful day, Rosin was in Los Angeles to walk the first ten miles with the 5,000 peace marchers who were to walk from L.A. to D.C. Although, at the time, I was marginally involved in the so-called peace movement through my membership in an organization, now defunct, called Beyond War, the real reason I was standing on the steps of City Hall was that my then friend, actress Jane Alexander, had asked me to come to meet a woman who would clue me in on nefarious Reagan proposals for outer space, that is to say The Strategic Defense Initiative (SDI), (aka "Star Wars").

The next day, March 2nd, Rosin visited my house in Sherman Oaks and proceeded to "brief" me for four hours on why the SDI was a "dumb, dangerous, unaffordable, unworkable, untestable, and destabilizing idea," followed by her alternate vision for the peaceful uses of outer space, the real estate situated 80 miles (and up) above all our heads. That March afternoon, she hauled an enormous number of thick documents out of a huge old-fashioned briefcase and spoke endlessly of space farms, hotels, space elevators (!), hospitals, explorations and so on and on. I understood very little of what she said. It all seemed farfetched to my earthbound imagination. I mean, what holds up the upper end of a space elevator was pretty much all I could think about.

When she had finally finished and was about to leave, at least I thought she was about to leave, she asked me if I had ever heard of the drug Ecstasy. I had. It so happened that a week or two before, a friend of mine had experienced an astounding opening of her heart on that very drug and she had left a message on my machine extolling its considerable virtues. Now here was this stranger holding a tablet of the very same in her outstretched hand. She claimed it was as pure as the proverbial snow because it came from the National Institutes of Health, no less. So, "Why not?" I said to Self and popped the little fellow. An hour later, I found myself lying on my bed upstairs gazing deeply into this stranger's eyes with what I presumed was Love, since it was certainly beyond anything I'd ever experienced before that moment.

The next day, Rosin proposed marriage and was quite offended when I declined while expressing my opinion that she was certifiable. (In case it is not apparent in this account, the Ecstasy had, by this time, worn off.) Nevertheless, not to be gainsaid, this irrepressible woman moved to Los Angeles and we began to live together. After that, my life was daily inundated by the copious contents of that colossal briefcase and I began to live in the vision this extraordinary woman held for the possibilities of a peaceful global future.

One night after we had been together for a while, I composed five limericks in a dream. Upon awakening, I remembered them and wrote them down. Before that time, I had had no relationship with that poetic form at any time in my life. But Carol Rosin is a very powerful woman, a very psychic woman, and I have always had the sneaking suspicion that she snuck into my head that very night. And, subsequently, these 33 years later, has refused to leave.

INTRODUCTION

Today, as we are embarking on 2019, the United States still suffers the consequences of the Second Gulf War foisted on a gullible people and a craven Congress by morally bankrupt men. After two hundred thousand American troops swept over Iraq's borders, employing in the exercise thousands of tons of bombs, missiles, tanks, bombers, and assorted other weapons of high strangeness that raised big dust in the desert, here we are once again still bombing the new Bad Guys just because they're kinda failing to appreciate all our good works: ISIS/ISIL. Yippee, the game continues.

Insanity is oft defined as continuing to do the same things over and over while expecting different results. So here we are again: the war wagon rumbles on, the drums rum tum, flags flap, troops cheer, and its hip-hip hooray for the USA.

- *This book was written in the black ink of depression. It was edited with the burning pen of cynicism and proofed by rage.*

During a Republican presidential debate back in '99, one of the moderators asked the seven or eight hopefuls to name their favorite political philosopher. The only answer I recall was George, Jr's: "Jesus Christ."

You know, Jesus Christ, the Prince of Peace, the Lamb of God, the Light of the World, the Proponent of turning the other cheek, of resisting not evil, of happily handing over your vest when a bad guy steals your coat...that Guy. Ah, but there I am sinking once again into the grease trap of cynicism. And black skepticism. Disbelief. A shame you can't patent bullshit. (Or can you?) Well, finally, it really doesn't seem to make much difference who's president. Past and present, all those good Christian gentlemen emerge from church of a Sunday clutching the Good Book and the wife on the way back to the White House to order the next round of carnage.

War and its ravages are not astonishing. They've been with us a long, long time. What is astonishing is that we take them for granted and, like deer in the headlights, we stand in the middle of the road waiting for the impact. Seems famed author, Jean Paul Sartre, was right when he entitled his book, *No Exit.*

I believe, if you accept the seemingly universal thesis that war is inevitable, you are, by definition, depressed. And it must then follow, if you're not depressed, you are either dead or in serious denial. Given the world we've created, the killing, the pollution, the extinctions, the millions of orphans, the legions of displaced people, the intention to "weaponize" the moon and space, the continuing manufacture of nuclear weapons, and the constant drumbeat now for "pre-emptive" War on Terror, if you're not depressed, you need to urgently find yourself a good shrink.—

Because, Baby, you really oughta be in therapy.

1

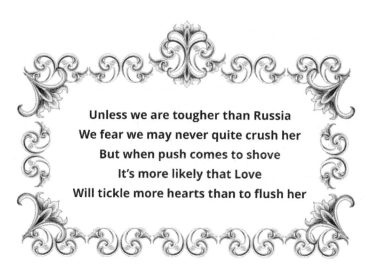

Unless we are tougher than Russia
We fear we may never quite crush her
But when push comes to shove
It's more likely that Love
Will tickle more hearts than to flush her

It's 2015, 28 years after I wrote this first limerick, and we've done the deed: taken the Soviets to the mat. And we did this by simply announcing our intention to place weapons in space, causing those dumb Russkies to spend themselves into penury to try to keep up. Kind of the equivalent of a huge military potlatch. It was STAR WARS that done it! That, anyway, is the myth of The Great Reagan Legacy; kind of the Republican equivalent of scouring those well-known stables.

- *And what exactly have we achieved by this statesmanlike coup?*

For one, by "defeating" the USSR and Iraq (twice), we've spent ourselves into oblivion as well. Depending upon with which accounting scam it is viewed, the U.S. Federal Debt is now around 20 trillion dollars and skyrocketing daily, a sum which can never be repaid, making it certain that generations of Americans will remain forever yoked, like a nation of donkeys, to the great tax wheel.

But the fiscal aspects of the "defeat" of the USSR and Iraq are small potatoes compared to the social fallout threatening to poison our planet as sure as Chernobyl, Hiroshima, Nagasaki, and now Fukushima. The dumb game of brinksmanship, played for half a century with the USSR, forced us to become nuclear thugs, insane bodybuilders piling mountains of nuclear, chemical, biological, and "conventional" (don't ya just love that word?) muscle atop muscle, in endless displays of useless power. We were toughs. We became tough. And now we're constantly playing Godzilla proclaiming ourselves the world's only superpower; arrogant enough in our enormous self-absorption to unilaterally abrogate international treaties, pull out of full participation in the World Court, refuse to sign on to the Ottawa Convention banning the use and sale of land mines (hey, business is business), diss the Kyoto Protocols on the environment, and...well, you get the idea

- *And we did it while going to church Sundays and prattling about Jesus, and love, and lambs. You know, Jesus, Prince of the Pentagon. Him.*

And Iraq? In smithereens. And around the corner, Afghans await the massive aid promised to rebuild their ravished country. We busted the Taliban but, sorry George, they're back and the warlords are putting in the poppy crop. It's tough guys, but after 9/11 we had to dump you on the back burner. Too busy saving Iraq from the Nasty Guy. Too busy poking around looking for those incredibly elusive Weapons of Mass Destruction (darn, we know they're there, it's just that devilishly clever Nasty Guy hid them so well). Meanwhile, in these years now after the World Trade Center, Iraq has descended into chaos. Good stuff for the nightly news but not too cool if you're in full battle gear getting blownup, shotup, fuckedup in a 130° cauldron on extended duty in the asshole of the universe getting fingered daily by millions of really pissed Iraqis. And let's not forget our use of Depleted Uranium weapons that will forever be the toxic calling card we've left behind. Oh, your babies are being born with terrible malformations, with cancer? Your land is poisoned for a loooong time? Sorry, folks, it's called war. And hey, we had to do something with all that toxic shit. Didn't want it around here. I mean, that stuff is bad for your health.

Sorry Russkies, we only had the shekels to destroy you. But don't take it too hard. Remember, your plight was our goal all along. And even if we wished to help, we couldn't. We're broke, Baby. Blew the family fortune stockpiling all that junk. But never mind, no problem. Broke or not, our current Commander in Chief is not reticent. Donny loves war, too, just like every good, red-blooded American boy. And, as we plunge headlong into 2018 there seems to be a chance that Trump will hump North Korea's Little Rocketman allowing us to remove those dusty nukes from cold storage and really get a good rumble rolling. And there is no doubt congressional stooges, those stalwart guardians of our national treasure, will feed the kitty.

PS: Not that I would ever presume to question the efficacy of Reagan's grand, statesmanlike *tour de force* with the Star Wars gambit, but it is interesting to note that, back aways, A&E aired a tape of Paul McCartney's '05 appearance in Red Square. Interspersed with the songs were brief interviews with older Russian musicians and other fans of The Beatles. Interesting none of them seemed to know that Star Wars was the reason for the collapse of their country. Not one. In fact, they were under the odd impression that the reason the country tanked was because of the subversive influence of the Fab Four who had been banned all those years. Of course, by banning the boys and the sale of their records, the bureaucrats turned Paul and John and Ringo and George into the hottest item in town. And, despite the threat you could get packaged and FedExed to Siberia for doing it, young people found a way to buy and to listen to that delicious, smuggled contraband. At times, during the Red Square concert, the camera looked around at the audience and found tears streaming down the cheeks of many of the older people who said they were deeply moved that Paul could actually be singing *Back In The USSR* in, of all unimaginable places, Red Square.

PPS: End of 2017, we've had terrorist attacks all over the place. ISIS is grinning and, jeez, imagine you lost your kid in Iraq for nothing. For nothing, Cheney. For nothing...

2

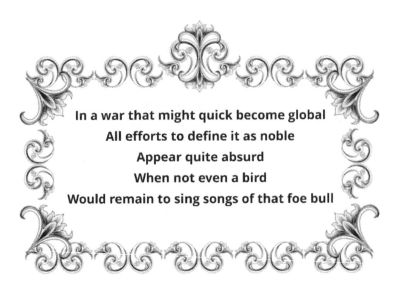

In a war that might quick become global
All efforts to define it as noble
Appear quite absurd
When not even a bird
Would remain to sing songs of that foe bull

We've been slipped a mickey. We were just staring at the TV one day and next thing we knew we woke up with needles in our arms, tubes up our collective noses and hate dripping slowly in our veins. Occasionally, a politician drops by and speeds up the drip or slows it down, depending, but the drip is always going day, night, round the clock. Eventually, of course, the poison kills us one way or another.—

We've been listening to the foe bull so long, so relentlessly, the Big Lie has been so perennially instilled, it seems inconceivable it is just a lie. But the truth is there are no enemies. There are only other sick people, poisoned by the same bullshit in translation. Arabic, German, Chinese, this tribe, that tribe, this sect, that sect, makes no difference: same lies spouted by the same song and dance men in spiffy worsted suits or long white dresses and funny hats. I mean, you can't play the deadly game without an enemy. It's the USSR, then the USSR is Ok. Whoops! Well, how about China? Yeah, maybe China works. But China's big and strong and has nuclear pecs. Besides, there're big bucks in China buying refrigerators and cars, so China's Ok. Wait a minute, here's one. How about Iraq? But we're gonna need a backup 'cause Iraq's gonna dive too quick. Hey, no problem. Backup's Afghanistan.

I ran into a guy I knew in Greenwich Village once. Washington Square. Greek guy. A homeless, self-described "bum" and a drunk. I liked him. I said, "Hey, Greek, come home with me, I had a party last night and I got half a gallon of Gallo red left." He said, "Nah, there's no hurry, let's just sit here in the sun for a while. I haven't had so much security in a long, long time." If you're addicted to wine, it's nice to know there's half a gallon waiting. If you're addicted to war, knowing you're never going to run out of enemies has to give you a nice warm, comfy feeling.

For fifty years, the USSR and the U.S. played the heavy in each other's productions. Worked out nicely for both of us. We were well-cast, enthusiastic players willing to spend incalculable fortunes on unusable stuff to scare the living popo out of each other with a policy of nuclear deterrence that would have been hilarious if it hadn't been wacko. We each willingly rolled the dice with the aptly-named Mutually Assured Destruction (MAD).

If it comes down to it, we were told, we could always square off in a nuclear showdown and win. You know, win! The truth, pointed out to us by innumerable scientists and people of simple common sense, was that the Big Boom (as opposed to the Big Bang that created the Earth) would, if unleashed, uncreate the Earth. And yet most of us were willing to swallow the lie that we could "win" such a war, so we hunkered down and went along with the loopy game of Cosmic Chicken. Each of us saw the other as, in the immortal words of The Great Communicator, "the evil empire." And, you know, if the other guy is Evil you must be Good which kinda makes the whole wack job sweetly religious. And, if God is on your side, well, then the Cause, the Crusade, must be noble so probably it's OK to fry the planet after all. (Yeah, Bush, Jr. actually used the word "crusade" in his last State of the Union address. Great word, very descriptive, except it seems the A-rabs, for some inexplicable reason, were a bit touchy about it.)

And, apparently, our moral monitors (who are always lining their pockets with those trillions for "defense") didn't care their progeny weren't going to be around to hear the nightingale sing on a summer's night.—

And so what, huh? These days who knows what a nightingale sounds like anyway?

I mean, are there still nightingales?

3

By shifting to subtler criteria
Thus allaying our fears and hysteria
We might find a font
Of real detente
Pretty swell, lots like smelling wisteria

The thing is you can't sell people *The Lie* if they're thinking rationally. Rational people don't undertake genocide, mass rape, or MAD. Thus, the first task of the *Big Liar* is to stupefy the citizenry, numb our brains so they can transform neighbors into enemies and timid chickens into warrior hawks. I've read that before 9/11, the loonies in the administration were sighing about the fact they needed another Pearl Harbor to fire up the engines of war. And, whaddya know, they got one.

There's a psychologist who presented at a peace conference I once attended in San Francisco (I can't recall his name) who studied how governments contrive to manipulate people to fear and hate other people. Among other things, he showed slides of propaganda posters from the two World Wars populated with garish caricatures of "the enemy." For example, an American poster depicted Tojo, a Japanese general, as a hideous monster eating children, his huge teeth bared in a leering, satanic smile with a dead child bleeding in his maw.—

And, of course, there are the simple lies: sometimes euphemistically referred to as "disinformation" or, currently, "fake news." When well executed, these lies pose as the sternest truths. For example, before hostilities broke out in the First Gulf War (aka *Desert Storm*: hey, shoulda been on the Weather Channel!), a young woman tearfully testified before the U.S. Congress that she had witnessed Iraqi troops tossing babies out of bassinets and incubators in Kuwaiti hospitals in order to take those items back to Iraq, a nation clearly short of them in its own hospitals. This fable was widely reported in the U.S., drumming up a great deal of animosity towards Iraq, making it a good deal easier for Americans to go to war to kill such monsters. And shortly thereafter we did. Bad guys tossing babies in the dumpster works real good.

The only problem with the testimony was that it was not true, a fact which only emerged after we had, in the delicate words of daddy Bush, "kicked Saddam's butt." The young woman who had testified before Congress was, in fact, the daughter of the Kuwaiti ambassador to the U.S. She later admitted she'd been lying and had been coached by a PR firm. After seeing it, I wondered why the film *Wag the Dog* didn't do very well at the box office? Because it was brilliant. Of course, the reason it slumped is, who needs to go to the movies to see a president create a war in order to distract the country from his problems when you can see him do it live on TV—for free?

Got a problem with "soft on defense"? Hey, send in the Rangers or the Seals to whack Bad Guy Bin Laden. Never mind he's unarmed and there are women running around, whack him anyway, throw him in the chopper and dump him in the ocean so there won't be a grave and a headstone where bad guys can come to kneel.

- *You're a hero. No more soft-on-defense for you.*

So did we learn? Nah. Bush the Second and his team of Olympic Bullshitters carpet bombed us with fabrications to push us into another war: *Iraqi Freedom.* (Now that's a title for a war!) Saddam has oodles of WMDs just waiting to be launched on 45 minutes notice, a bunch of chemical labs in mobile trucks (see the pretty satellite photos), Iraq is harboring Al Qaeda terrorists, Iraq is responsible for 9/11, the Bad Guy kills his own people so they'll

8

welcome us and, even without allies, we can do it on the cheap; it won't cost us a penny 'cause Iraqi oil'll pick up the tab.

- *Quick, plug in the Air Wick.*

We need to be damn skeptical next time we're told there's a Bad Guy in town. While there are certainly bad guys around, the point is the war industry *needs* bad guys, there's open casting on bad guys year 'round. And there's no question, when it serves their purpose, the nut jobs are ecstatic when new bad guys show up to star in the next production. And, let's be honest, if there's no heavy around when we want to try out our new toys, we can always create one. I mean, we *did* invite Iraq, through our ambassador, April Ashby, to invade Kuwait. In other words, the First Gulf War was a setup, a sucker play, making everybody who played, by definition, a sucker. And Ms. Ashby? Well, she walked off into the sunset after performing her role in *Desert Storm, The Movie.*

And, when the stench of his lies became intolerable, Deaf Sec Donny Rumsfeld himself ambled after Ms. Ashby into the aforementioned sunset.—

And where is the young woman today who testified before Congress about babies and bassinets? No idea. But if I had to, I'd guess she was comfortably recumbent somewhere in daddy's palace inside Kuwait sipping a nice, cold lemonade.

Cut! Print!

Slim white missiles when poised like erections
Can hardly be viewed as protections
For torching the earth
Provides minimal mirth
And more pain than a man feels who sex shuns

The great psychiatrist Wilhelm Reich had the idea that modern Western society has built a muscular "armor" into the physical bodies of its citizens in order to suppress and redirect the natural flow of sexual energy. Without this "armoring," he pointed out, we might not be disposed to become the robots we're supposed to become. We might even stand firm in resisting all the things robots are supposed to do, like commuting two hours a day in heavy traffic to punch a time clock to work incessantly in order to be able to consume all the vitally important stuff we're supposed to consume. If we were slipping around inside each other with the kind of deep, orgasmic transcendence Reich said "primitive" peoples feel, having to sacrifice our lives to the state, the corporation, and the bank might make us a bit cranky. Reich was not terribly popular with the U.S. government. In fact, the gov threw him in Federal prison where he died. And, lest any of his ideas survived, it also burned all his books, files, and equipment.

- *Good thing he fled Hitler to pursue his research and write his books in a free, open society!*

On a continuum which, at one end, has a village of glistening, painted, naked tribal people pounding their bare feet into the dusty earth in a transport of sexual foreplay and, at the other, a stockholders meeting of GE, not much question at which end of the continuum industrialized societies hang out.—

Something as irksome as sex, however, is not easily swept under the cultural carpet. It tends to pop up. But can one really imply that, as a culture, we suppress sexuality? After all, we're inundated with it: porn is the hottest thing on the internet—worldwide. And prostitution is a multi-billion-dollar business. Scantily clad women are employed to sell everything from movies to hardware (no pun intended). But that's the point. Pornography and the ubiquitous sexual sell are not sexual intimacy. Anyway, we're all too exhausted running two jobs or trying to find any job before the extended unemployment insurance runs out again, paying too many taxes, keeping too many insurance policies afloat, trying to save the house to go for anything more than a possible quickie.

Oh, yeah, need that little blue job to pump the ole pecker? Hey, when they started selling Viagra, they had old farts like Senator Bob Dole fessing up (or maybe "up" is the wrong word?) that he could no longer slap the smile on Elizabeth without the assistance of the Little Blue Pill. But have you noticed that lately the Little Blue Job is being peddled by muscular 35-year-old athletes striding into the locker room on a sunny Sunday morning sporting that special smirky smile?

- *"Something's different about you this morning, Billy Bob. New haircut?"*

The phallic nature of our missile program has been described all too well by famed anti-nuclear physician Dr. Helen Caldicott in her famous book *Missile Envy*. So I'll simply state my belief that a powerful case can be made connecting our suppression of real sexuality to its symbolic manifestation in the huge missile programs we men have embraced.

- *Nah, nah, my missile is bigger than your missile. And can shoot further.*

But, while the load a man drops at orgasm delivers pleasure and the potential of the consummate creativity of conception, the load our missiles will deliver when they're ejaculated from their concrete wombs in which they've been nestled (in Mother Earth, no less) are designed to bring only incomprehensible grief.

- *Or did you really think your heart attack was from ice cream?*

5

A lady from old Nagasaki
Who survived staying looped on hot *sake*
Stated barbecued flesh
Especially when fresh
Is splendid when done Teriyaki

A wizened crone is living on the outskirts of Nagasaki. —One day the sun falls. —Or is it the sun? —Perhaps it's a gigantic meteor. Something has happened. —She does not know what. All she knows is there was a blinding radiance, tempestuous winds, hot fires all around, houses burning, collapsing. Was it an earthquake? She does not know. She is very thirsty, but there is no water. She drinks *sake* instead. Hot from the bottle. Her mouth burns. The air is tangible and dense, electrical. She is drunk now and lost, reeling in the streets. Nothing is familiar. The air is an inferno. She does not know what is happening. Others stagger past like lost denizens of Hell. Is it possible she is already dead? —Night comes and she is drunk and very hungry. But there is nothing to eat.

- *To smoke a city in a second—now we're talkin' efficient!*

6

If Teller's yer feller then tell her

"Farewell and God bless you," don't sell her

The SDI lie

As pie in the sky

'Cause then you're even dumber than Teller

In 1992, because I was playing a Marine general on the sitcom *Major Dad* and everyone assumed I was, by definition, a conservative Republican, I was invited to deliver the opening address at the U.S. Space Foundation's annual meeting in Colorado Springs. My wife, Dr. Carol Sue Rosin, a leading opponent of "Star Wars," calls this "the gathering of the six hundred greatest hawks in America." The Strategic Defense Initiative (SDI), subsequently renamed Ballistic Missile Defense, National Missile Defense, etc. is the largest R&D project in history. Announced by Reagan in 1983, it is ostensibly a scheme to protect the U.S. and its allies from enemy bad things falling out of the sky by encircling the earth with space-based weapons. In my remarks to the Space Foundation, I suggested the SDI was a useless, flawed idea from many points of view. I suggested it is an unaffordable, untestable, unserviceable, politically destabilizing weapons system that would essentially be run, not by humans, but by computers with a four second lag time in which to decide whether any launch was threatening, accidental, or benign and what should or should not be done in response.—

Moreover, and perhaps most damning of all, I pointed out that the proposal was frivolous (if not ludicrous) in the extreme because an infinitely more likely scenario for the delivery of a nuclear device to U.S. shores would be by what is known in the trade as the "Satchel Charge Strategy." This describes, as the name rather poetically implies, a scenario in which a nuclear weapon (and some are the size of a softball, capable of taking out an area as small as Yankee Stadium) is spirited into this country in a "satchel," perhaps in parts smuggled in by several people at different entry points who then contrive to meet, assemble, and arm the weapon. Against this scenario or others like it (for example, a weapon secreted aboard a ship docked in New York harbor), there *is* no defense. Since 9/11, the question of the validity of the SDI is urgent. —Because, when I see politicians and armaments experts interviewed on TV these days, they seem to be in agreement that it is not a question of *if* we will be struck by a WMD, but *when*. We have already spent a fortune attempting (and failing) to create a workable anti-missile technology in preparation for the actual emplacement of space-based weapons. Billions more will be spent in pursuit of the realization of this doomed dream...or is it a Dream of Doom? Never mind 3,000 physicists pronounce the dream unrealizable, Bush and his cohort and now Trump have committed to dreaming it. And me? I just think about all the hospitals and all the schools we could build in all the cities in all the countries that are dreaming a different dream.

- *They dream a dream. We research a nightmare.*

Directly following the aforementioned address, I was summoned to the general's office by my friend and sponsor at the convention, then Lt. Col. Stan Rosen. He was alarmed by my suggestion that the Satchel Charge Strategy was an infinitely more likely possibility for the U.S. to face than a nation attempting suicide by launching an ICBM at us. Obviously, the sole reason I'd been invited to speak was because I would tell fun stories about *Major Dad* or *Hill Street Blues*, (the latter series was one in which I played the Chief of Police for seven years). So, once I arrived in his office, General X attempted to reassure me in no uncertain terms that our military was, at that very moment, in the process of designing sophisticated equipment that would be able to detect and interdict nuclear weapons at our borders even when hidden in a satchel. "But sir," I said, "we can't even keep

15

out Mexicans, never mind what they've got in their luggage!" Politically incorrect but I knew I had made the point when he became apoplectic.

I met Edward Teller at that meeting. The late Dr. Teller was the "father of the hydrogen bomb" and a leading proponent of the Strategic Defense Initiative. In fact, Teller was the advisor who sold President Reagan on the feasibility of space-based weapons. At the Space Foundation convention, Teller was a superstar. A short, gnomish man, he was at that time in his mid-80s. I have been told he was an accomplished classical pianist. And he was obviously brilliant in a certain way. But when I met him, I could not help thinking that a mind devoted throughout the span of a lifetime to the greater destruction of masses of other people was scary wacko. Einstein understood the terrifying implications for humankind of what he had helped to create. In his famous 1956 statement regarding the new reality posed by the advent of nuclear weapons, "Everything has changed except our way of thinking and we thus drift towards unparalleled catastrophe," he implored us to awaken to the roar of the rapids boiling ahead.

By contrast, there was old Ed Teller, ancient, decrepit, bushy brows hanging like awnings over glinting eyes, basking in the plaudits of the war players, still pitching the same game

- *As we indeed drift, wittingly, towards Einstein's shattering caveat.*

7

Binges of deadly exchanges
Singe eyeballs and bees and endangers
Both heroes and roses
And so war disposes
Of Brahms, of Romance, and Lone Rangers

The thing about playing "heigh-ho" with the planet is it means saying goodbye to everything. When we contemplate the idea of nuclear attack and retaliation (and don't sling the crap about "limited nuclear war" which is nothing if not an entirely new definition of the word oxymoron) it means the absolute end of civilization as we have lived it. But what does this actually mean?

Despite repeated assurances from the War Department, (yeah, that's what it was called when I was a kid until they decided the name made us look like maybe we were prone to violence so they changed it to the Defense Department) that we're just protecting ourselves from people who "envy our way of life" and that nuclear war is survivable and winnable, the merest glimmer of imagination suggests the opposite. It is not survivable. Its unsurvivability is clearly the reason the Bush Boys, in their leaked "Nuclear Posture Review," asserted their determination to build a whole new generation of smaller nuclear

17

weapons, so-called "mini-nukes" and "bunker busters." —Which makes sense. Obviously, the big nukes couldn't really be used because they worked too well. —So now we're gonna have in our arsenal Cute Nukes that can take out smaller pieces of real estate or penetrate deep underground to kill Bad Guys who may be lurking down there smugly sipping sweet tea. Yeah, even "evildoors" (Bush had trouble pronouncing the word) have a sweet tooth. Never mind such a weapon will hurl tons of radioactive dust into the air, it allows us to crow "gotcha" which is vital if that's the only way you can imagine handling the world's troubles.

In any case, the very concept of "winning" a nuclear war is somewhere between lunacy and bullshit. There will be only protracted, inconsolable grief for the unfortunate survivors and the gradual dying of the world we have known. It will not be a rerun of World War Two even at its most devastating. Vast areas of the planet will be rendered instantly uninhabitable for tens of thousands up to a quarter of a million years. That is five times as long as the accepted history of "civilized" human habitation on the earth. That figure encompasses several ice ages. It is five Great Years (25,000 years) which is the time it takes the sun to revolve around *its* sun. And this does not include the well-known Carl Sagan concept of "nuclear winter" or the mass destruction of bees and other little guys necessary to pollinate a great deal of earth's vegetation.

I'm thinking now of Rupert Brooke's lovely poem *The Great Lover* which he wrote before his death in World War One. Here's a portion of that great poem. While reading it, one need only imagine that all of it is gone. All of it. Irrevocably gone.

"...These I have loved:
White plates and cups, clean-gleaming,
Ringed with blue lines; and feathery, faery dust;
Wet roofs, beneath the lamp-light; the strong crust
Of friendly bread; and many-tasting food;
Rainbows; and the blue bitter smoke of wood;
And radiant raindrops couching in cool flowers;
And flowers themselves, that sway through sunny hours,
Dreaming of moths that drink them under the moon;
Then, the cool kindliness of sheets, that soon

18

Smooth away trouble; and the rough male kiss
Of blankets; grainy wood; live hair that is
Shining and free; blue-massing clouds; the keen
Unpassioned beauty of a great machine;
The benison of hot water; furs to touch;
The smell of old clothes; and other such-
The comfortable smell of friendly fingers,
Hair's fragrance, and the musty reek that lingers
About dead leaves and last year's ferns...

Dear names, and thousand others throng to me!
Royal flames;
Sweet water's dimpling laugh from tap or spring;
Holes in the ground; and voices that do sing:
Voices in laughter, too; and body's pain,
Soon turned to peace; and the deep-panting train;
Firm sands; the little dulling edge of foam
That browns and dwindles as the wave goes home;
And washen stones, gay for an hour; the cold
Graveness of iron; moist black earthen mould;
Sleep; and high places; footprints in the dew;
And oaks; and brown horse-chestnuts, glossy-new;
And peeled sticks; and shining pools on grass;
All these have been my loves. And these shall pass.
Whatever passes not, in the great hour,
Nor all my passion, all my prayers, have power
To hold them with me through the gate of Death.
They'll play deserter, turn with traitor breath,
Break the high bond we made, and sell Love's trust
And sacramental covenant to the dust.

Oh, never a doubt but, somewhere, I shall wake,
And give what's left of love again, and make
New friends, now strangers...

But the best I've known,
Stays here, and changes, breaks, grows old, is blown
About the winds of the world, and fades from brains
Of living men, and dies.
Nothing remains.

19

Dear my loves, O faithless, once again
This one last gift I give: that after men
Shall know, and later lovers, far-removed
Praise you, 'All these were lovely'; say, 'He loved.'"

And no Lone Ranger? The Masked Man, whose exploits thrilled and dreamed me huddled under the covers as a child listening past my bedtime to the radio from 7:30 to 8pm, is replaced after the first nuclear exchange with the next version of Ollie Oop who may turn out to be a swell guy but who will not, for sure, have "the great horse Silver" between his loins and a secret mine for the manufacture of silver bullets.

- *And no Brahms? No mail? No snails? Best we think on this one.*

8

My warheads are many he figgers
With scarier, hairier triggers
So like it or not
When I tell 'em to squat
They'll do it 'cause I've got the big Grrrs

You can always know how scared someone is by the size of their muscles. When I see men who've stacked mountainous muscles atop muscles, I think, "Inside, that's one scared puppy." The muscle may, of course, be metaphoric, as in the case of those empire builders who find it exciting to metastasize endless quantities of money and power. Or a nation with a zillion useless weapons stacked to the heavens.

That we are the "greatest, strongest, richest country on the face of the earth" has been repeated to us here in the U.S. so often, the assertion seems to have the same kind of axiomatic truth like *quad erat demonstrandum*: that's what you write after you've proved that an isosceles triangle has two equal sides. And it's clear the idea of being the greatest also includes being the biggest, strongest, meanest, kickass sonofabitch on the planet. We in the U.S. are told endlessly that we're the Last Remaining Superpower and that means nobody kicks sand in our face. Those old enough may remember famed bodybuilding guru Charles Atlas, who made a fortune selling his system of "Dynamic Tension" to "90 lb. weaklings" who were determined to never again let any well-built hunk "kick sand in their faces" and steal their girlfriends.

While apparently appropriate for a muscular nation to kick sand in other's faces, for example in Cuba's face, in 90 lb. weakling Grenada's face, in Panama's face, in Nicaragua's face, in Iraq's face, in the Philippine's face, in Native American's faces, in Libya's face, Afghanistan's face, to name just a few faces in which we've kicked sand, the U.S. considers it very bad form for others to kick sand back. Of course, it happens occasionally that some little pipsqueak nation, unaware of its place in the grand scheme, does just that. For example, a tiny ragtag militia in Somalia kicked a few grains in our face and we skedaddled, but that was one of those embarrassing places where muscles didn't seem to properly impress the locals. Like Vietnam.

Flexing only works when the other guy buys into the game. Those pesky Viet Cong never bought into it and they blew us over. While the USSR did buy into it, making them the perfect adversaries. The U.S. and the USSR squatted facing one another across the planet for the better part of half a century, spending trillions pumping iron and *Grrrring* mindlessly at each other like two scared, nasty old pit bulls. It would have been a lot cheaper if we had done it like those old National Geographic stories about New Guinea warrior cosmetologists who laid on fierce-looking face paint, put enormous sheaths around their wee wees, tied the sheaths around their necks to make themselves appear perpetually erect (every real man's not-so-secret dream) and rushed at their playmates shouting insults and rattling their spears without the intention of inflicting any grievous harm. The whole charade being more of a macho minuet than a real war, permitting a day of dress up and allowing the boys to burn off some of that annoying Big T.

- *If only we'd been as smart as those boys, we'd at least have had some splendid exercise and a lot of good fresh air.*

22

9

A lady who loved Hiroshima
Planted flowers and said, "I'm a dreamer,
When men stop their killing
My mums will be thrilling"
Never dreaming what finally would cream her

She died quickly at least. Poof. Gone. And her mums? No, they never bloomed nor would they ever…

- *There are those who plant and there are the others.*

10

The scum of the earth are in charge
The apocalypse now is writ large
Two hundred elephants
Murdered by celebrants:
Guillotined kings sans La Farge

O, what the AK47 has done for us. Think of the old days: tribesmen plotting an attack on a herd of elephants, their spears waggling; clever little buggers because they've actually learned how to cut one of the great pachyderms out of the family herd, bring him down and portion him out, light a fire, dance and feast and, who knows, maybe even thank the big fella's spirit, as they say Native Americans used to do when they hunted long ago. Pretty, if you're not a vegetarian, but definitely low-tech.

Now I read a tiny item in the New York Times informing me that 200 rotting elephant carcasses have been discovered in the Congo by a waterhole. They've been slaughtered with automatic weapons and their tusks sawed off. This is clearly capitalism at its most efficient: small investment, large payoff, no troublesome paperwork, low overhead and capital requirements, powerful cash flow to the bottom line.

Sort of the animal equivalent of clear cutting. No time wasted culling and sorting and assessing. Just take 'em all. In and out. And, come to think of it, really, how are these Congolese businessmen any different from the fabulously wealthy entrepreneur who was, as I wrote this, about to clear cut the last great stand of virgin redwoods in the world in northern California? I should say not different at all. Of course, he "owns" the 60,000 acres of redwoods he plans to "harvest." But then I suspect our little African merchants could have made an excellent case that they owned the elephants they harvested. —They and their forebears have, after all, if Leakey is correct, been harvesting around those parts for a million years or thereabouts. Their claim is strong. And, far from condemning them, we should I think celebrate our celebrants for so rapidly assimilating the message of universal capitalism we so urgently peddle to the world.

Let's dry our eyes. No mourning for our fallen brethren, those trumpeting kings of the veldt, those giant aristocrats of another age. No! Rather bid them a fond adieu, smiling, as they say Madame LaFarge did, as the fairest heads fell to the guillotine. Like her, let's kiss a noble age goodbye. And, far from grieving, let us welcome our new venture capitalists into the councils of Industrialized Mayhem as we declare the elimination of yet another species, albeit they were, ah, magnificent.

- *Progress.*

11

Our George, who had muscles like bustles
Felt safe 'cause when he heard rustles
To keep his heart calm
He flexed his huge arm
Thus evading, he hoped, the real tussles

We are all literally dying to love. The heart aches to blossom into a rose of delight and spread its luscious fragrance. Fear counsels caution. "Don't be rash," says Fear. "Wait! Don't trust." (The old joke: How do you say "Fuck you" in Hollywood? Answer: "Trust me"!)— The bud remains tightly wrapped upon itself, its scent stifled. Fear is a perpetual winter, nothing blooms. And, like winter, fear lies hard and frozen in the body. We build tight, chronically tense muscles, we become living monuments to the ego, the false Self: "hard bodies," that most coveted appellation. But as we do this, as we assiduously struggle to immure ourselves in the physical equivalent of solitary confinement, love begs to be set free. To silence this call, we seek solace in drugs or hunting or sex or slapping the wife and kids around when they seem unwilling to accept our ice cold shut heart. We are like Coleridge's Mariner, awash in a sea of love, afraid to imbibe.

26

There is, on the part of virtually every segment of our society, a monolithic commitment to keep us afraid at all times. I remember being herded with 350 mostly Jewish guys from Brooklyn into a huge auditorium at Fort Dix, New Jersey soon after being inducted into the Army in October of '53, the Korean War still reverberating through the world. It was serious.

The purpose of the assemblage we soon learned was to read the Uniform Code of Military Justice to us. This document informed us of several things: we were no longer citizens; we were soldiers. We were no longer protected by the Constitution of the United States; we were soldiers subject to the Uniform Code. We were not to think but to obey. If we did not, we could be executed. Seemingly every Article of the Code ended with the resounding thud of a gallows trapdoor: "Maximum Penalty...Death." The message was get scared fast and stay that way, snap shit or die. —And a thousand young bellies hardened that day as we imagined the ordeal that lay before us.

- *The end of innocence.*

And lest you breathe a sigh of gratitude you were not conscripted along with us, with Roy Bush and Joe DiPiazza and Seymour Passman, think again. For we have all of us been sitting breathlessly, silently, in a vast auditorium before an endless stream of terrifying presenters. The American Medical Assoc. after all has told the public and physicians alike we must do it their way. If we do not, Maximum Penalty...Death. Physical death or professional death. But death. The IRS demands we reveal all: Maximum Penalty...Financial Death. The Peer Group, the Judge, the Deodorant commercial, the Insurance Company, the Condo Association, the Moral Majority, all remind us that failure to toe the line must be considered a very, very bad idea. I mean, what we hear now from politicians, authorities, popes, experts, ads, infomercials, the nightly news, you name it, makes the Universal Code of Military Justice sound like Little Bo Peep.

Against this onslaught of Fear, it would seem reasonable to erect a bastion of defense.

- *But, sorry, Georgie boy, it ain't muscles.*

27

- *Maybe money?*

- *Figure it out.*

12

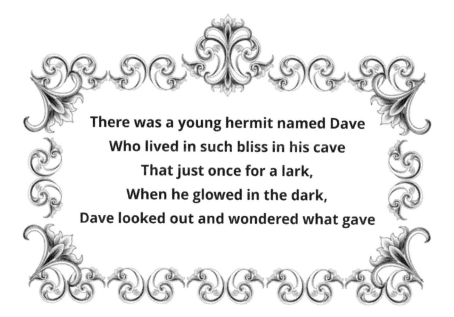

There was a young hermit named Dave
Who lived in such bliss in his cave
That just once for a lark,
When he glowed in the dark,
Dave looked out and wondered what gave

Hey, Baby, if you've decided keeping track of the condition of your navel is your path up the mountain instead of going after the bastards ("Personal salvation is all one can achieve anyway!") it's OK. But just remember, Dave, when you start to glow in the dark and your kid is shitting in the sink, like the kid in that indelible glimpse of the Apocalypse, the movie *Testament*, it's gonna be too late for "shouldawouldacoulda." —And remember also, if you finally decide to peep outside on that final night to check out what happened, there won't be anyone around to fill you in. Wolf Blitzer will not interrupt this program to bring you important Breaking News because there won't be any program to interrupt.

- *No Wolfie either.*

13

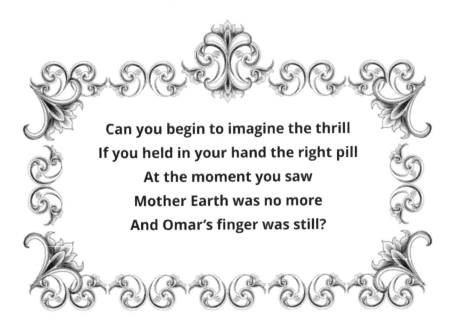

Can you begin to imagine the thrill
If you held in your hand the right pill
At the moment you saw
Mother Earth was no more
And Omar's finger was still?

The verse to which I've alluded is, of course, from *The Rubaiyat of Omar Khayyam* in the famous Edward FitzGerald translation:

> "The Moving Finger writes; and, having writ,
> Moves on: nor all your Piety nor Wit
> Shall lure it back to cancel half a Line,
> Nor all your Tears wash out a Word of it."

Sometimes Fate grabs you by the scruff of the neck and whispers hoarsely in your ear, "This way." Maybe you knew in your heart She was lurking and, because you were afraid, you held your breath and did nothing. Maybe you were defiant, despite warnings She would come. But, if you've smoked two packs a day for thirty years, you don't get to act surprised when you feel Her icy hand. If you've sat by in docile approval while madmen prepared for, even welcomed The Last Act ("Proves the Good Book was right, don't it?") you may realize it's a trifle late to grouse when She at last hurls you over the precipice.

I once saw a piece about young Tamil Tiger rebels in Sri Lanka. All of them were issued and carried around their necks a capsule of cyanide to be used as a kind of Instant Checkout the moment they realized capture and torture were inevitable. —Possession of the capsule made them fierce fighters.

Frequently, I wonder why more of us do not fiercely fight to free ourselves from the slavery of manipulation and deceit to which we are perpetually indentured. Is it because we're cynical? Jaded? Hopeless? Unimaginative? Docile? Stupid? Are we obediently lining up on the station platform waiting for the next boxcar, baskets packed, hoping against hope it's a picnic because one cannot imagine the alternative? After all, holocausts, both the gas chamber and mushroom cloud variety, are relatively rare, so, hey, it really could turn out to be a picnic

- *Couldn't it?*

Slavery or Death? When faced with capture, the Tigers chose the latter. Are we so chicken we choose the former?

It's 2017. The U.S. has just kicked ISIS out of Iraq. (Some nice condos available in Mosul and Raqqa if you're not too troubled by total devastation.) And we're planning to do the same for the fortunate citizens of Afghanistan. And the fact that it's taken 17 years and counting? Only shows when we make a commitment, it's a commitment.

What's that you say? Perhaps a million killed or maimed, thousands of U.S. soldiers bite the dust, many thousands more wounded and suffering severe psychological disorders…the famed PTSD. And, wait a sec, you're saying the "T" stands for "Traumatic."

Jeez, Louise give 'em a pill, help the poor slobs forget what they've done, what they've seen. And are there enough pills for those who seem somewhat less than appreciative of our efforts to save them from themselves? Inexplicably, they seem burdened by the misconception

31

that, in some incomprehensible way, we're to blame for the fact they're suffering.

What? No weapons of mass destruction? Iraqi oil didn't pay for the whole shindig? U.S. on the brink of economic extinction? Three wars. Lies up the wazoo. Bush, Cheney, Rumsfeld et al walking around free men? No way. You gotta be kidding.

The great psychiatrist Dr. Eric Berne wrote a lot about winning and losing. He said, "Losers plan what they'll do when they win; winners plan what they'll do in case they lose."—

- *Sorry "Mission Accomplished" Georgie Boy, Dickhead, Donny Rumsfuck, you're losers. Big Time.*

But, pssst, hey guys, any time wanna score some a them Tamil Tiger Check Out Pills, I'm your boy.

Citizens of Iraq, of Afghanistan, of...well, you name it. Waiting for apologies?

- *Piece of advice: don't hold your breath.*

And did we learn? Oh, excuse me, I have an announcement.

- *Ladies and gentlemen, the Man of the Hour, the President of the United States of America, our new Commander-in-Chief...Donald J. Trump.*

14

You have to admit men are funny
On the one hand their natures are sunny
On the other they'll sell
Their fellows to Hell:
Armegeddon for contracts and money

A manufacturer contrives to dump his waste in an estuary; medical societies forcibly resist methods to cure and relieve suffering they perceive might challenge their own bottom line (witness what they did to homeopathy in the late 19th century and what they tried to do to chiropractic in the '50s); top executives of giant tobacco companies swear before Congress, right hands aloft, their product is neither poisonous nor addictive even as they plan campaigns to drive their coffin nails through the palms of younger and younger children. These disgusting slobs make the fired postal employee hurrying to his former workplace, the serial killer, the rapist seem ridiculously inefficient by comparison.

Columnist William Safire once wrote an op-ed piece in the N.Y. Times promoting a theatre missile defense system for the U.S. under the scenario that some impoverished, desperate Russian officer with the key to the woodshed where nuclear missiles are stored sells one to a Terrorist State for a pretty piece of change. When Bill Safire writes about it, you know it's on the minds of the Establishment. But Bill, where were you when tens of thousands of these weapons were being stockpiled? Had you nothing to say to your rich friends while they were making billions from this obscenity? —At least the starving Russian officer has the excuse of trying to put borscht on the table.

The international arms dealer steps onto his yacht; the serial killer steps finally, all appeals exhausted, into the gas chamber. Is there a difference? Sure. One wears a cheap suit.

There was a joke going around when I was studying to be a Marriage, Family, and Child Counselor that went, Mickey Mouse takes Minnie to court to get a divorce. The judge examines the case and declares his verdict: "Mr. Mouse, having examined your suit, the court finds no evidence that Minnie Mouse is insane." "No, your Honor," says Mickey, "I didn't say she was crazy, I said she was fucking Goofy."

On occasion, when my fellow interns and I would come out of a session with some particularly dysfunctional family, we would roll our eyes at one another and pronounce our diagnosis: FG.

- *You men, you nations, you corporations selling weapons, cigarettes, your deadly poisons, yes, all of you who perpetrate your various forms of mayhem on a needy, hurting world, rich and powerful though you may be... FG.*

15

A Guy in the sky named Jehovah
Exclaimed to Himself, "This ain't clover,
Those schmucks down below
Forgot or don't know
That war on their Mom means its over"

The moment in the past when we decided God was of the male persuasion was the moment it all went *gaflooey*. And if that wasn't bad enough, we made Him an extraterrestrial by removing Him from Mother Earth and plopping Him up on a cloud. And then making Him a white Guy to boot. Caucasian Guy up on a cloud, long white beard in a white bathrobe who knows everything.

- *New definition of fruitcake—*

Besides, if there is a "Great Spirit" (Native Americans knew what to call Her) and It happens to have a gender and the gender happens to be male for some unfathomable reason, I'd find it impossible to believe He could forget His soft, fierce, feminine "better half," our Mother, sensuous Gaia. In the few languages I know, the romance languages, the Earth is a Lady: *La Terre, La Terra, La Tierra.*

- *Pacha Mama.*

And as for Her creatures, if we use husband as a transitive verb, to husband, the word means to care for, to manage prudently: thus, we are to husband our fellow creatures with loving kindness as we are our own families. It may come as a great shock to some, but we're not supposed, ever, to kill animals for sport and stuff them for the parlor, hang their heads over the fireplace, or turn their skins into bedspreads or carpeting. Bears do better with their heads and skins attached caring for their babies and Mama never meant for the heads of the Noble Elk or King Lion to be used as interior decoration. This, of course, will not be a popular assertion among that group of yahoos who yearn to crash through the woods on the first day of the "season" with their silly Abercrombie & Fitch plaids and their high-powered rifles, in desperate search of their masculinity. Or who poach out of season for that matter. Or by headlights at night that capture the startled eyes of their prey for the deadly shot.

- *Anything for a kill.*

I lived in the boonies in Vermont for two years. Believe me, I've seen them. Sad cases.

And let's consider for a moment "scientific" experimentation on animals for the so-called benefit of so-called humans. I mean, if you think it's virtuous to strap monkeys down, or subject any animal to the routine mayhem they are forced to endure, I suspect there ain't nothin' I can say to change your mind. I do, however, ask myself how you can, if you're a sadist, oh, I'm sorry, I meant to say "scientist," participating in such "experiments," how you can, I wonder, look that little creature in the eye as you impart your deadly stroke, how you can listen to that terrified being wail its anguished plaint to Gaia? How you can, I wonder, sleep?

I had a girlfriend once who was an alcoholic and went to AA meetings. At the end of the meeting, the assembled penitents would join hands while one of them would lead the rest in the Lord's Prayer. One night this duty devolved upon my girlfriend and, because she was tired of God always being a man, she decided, just for a lark, to ask everyone to join hands and she began, "Our Mother which art in heaven, hallowed be Thy name…etc." What she got from the group afterwards, men and women alike, was pure rage. She was flabbergasted.

Nah! She was naive.

Why are we so angrily committed to God as a man? The answer is so obvious it's almost not worth saying. God is a man because men said He was. And if you don't like it, you just might end up as a medical experiment.

- *So, Sister, whaddya gonna do about it?*

(Some may note that I've capitalized all the God words throughout this short piece. Hey, just playin' it safe, people, 'cause I've heard God gets pissed off if you don't capitalize His Name…er, I mean, Her Name.)

16

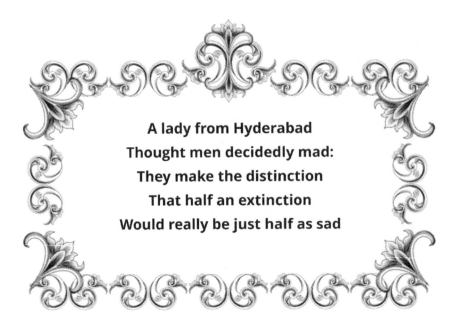

A lady from Hyderabad
Thought men decidedly mad:
They make the distinction
That half an extinction
Would really be just half as sad

People who talk about winning and surviving nuclear war have, I fear, severely limited imaginations. To consider nuclear war and then talk about winning and surviving it means you're not seeing it in your mind's eye. And if you're not seeing it, you're not feeling it. Because if you were seeing it, you'd be feeling it and the feeling that would be choking you would most probably be unfathomable grief. Greater sadness than you would have ever experienced because you would *feel* the death throes of Mother Earth Herself.

I saw a special on hurricanes on The Learning Channel one day. After one of the virulent storms they covered, people emerging from their shelters were stunned by the devastation they saw around them. One woman said she now knew what nuclear devastation would be like.

- *Seriously?*

I mean, was she kidding? Didn't she know that after a nuclear event she wouldn't have emerged? Didn't she know that after a nuclear event she wouldn't have been able to rebuild her precious home, even if by some miracle she had emerged. And didn't she know that, in any case, she would rapidly sicken and die of radiation poisoning? Didn't she know that no National Guard would roll into town to help out as they had after the hurricane? That there'd be no psychiatrist to help survivors get over their grief, no neighbors with whom to weep, no food flown in, no lumberyard or hardware store, no birds, no trees, no insurance, no nothing? She didn't know. She couldn't see it.

- *Winnable? Survivable? Even if it were, Pyrrhic Victory takes on a totally new definition.*

17

Contemplate times in the past
With opposing armies amassed
If one had The Bomb
Now all would be calm
And certain the first would be last

There's a strong tendency these days to think, because Russia and the United States have destroyed some of their stockpiled nuclear weapons and the bad old days of the Cold War are supposedly over, the nuclear threat has been miraculously stuffed back into Pandora's Luggage. This is nonsense. Pakistan, India, Israel, China, North Korea, Iraq, South Africa and many others have added or are rushing to add that nice touch of nuclear panache to their arsenals. Sooner or later, unless this metastasis can somehow be stopped, every nation, large and small, will have some nuclear capability. Imagine the idiocy. Uruguay? Ethiopia?

- *Get real!*

In fact, only Switzerland will be nuclear free. But even she will be busy counting the money and praying the winds don't change.

When I wrote the above verse, I was thinking of the all-time Hit Parade of great Military Moments. For example, the Battle of Agincourt, a turning point in the course of military history and, of course, a battle memorialized in Shakespeare's *Henry V*. —Every time I read or hear those immortal lines from Act IV, Scene III, I am filled again with fervor hearing Harry pump up his troops for the coming battle:

> "...And Crispin Crispian shall ne'er go by,
> From this day to the ending of the world,
> But we in it shall be remembered,
> We few, we happy few, we band of brothers;
> For he today that sheds his blood with me
> Shall be my brother; be he ne'er so vile,
> This day shall gentle his condition:
> And gentlemen in England now a-bed
> Shall think themselves accurs'd they were not here,
> And hold their manhoods cheap while any speaks
> That fought with us upon Saint Crispin's Day!"

It's just the best stuff. And the story is greatness itself: 5,000 bedraggled, hungry, bone-weary English bowmen defeat 75,000 fresh, well-provisioned, crack French knights, the cream of French manhood. Great plays are made of this stuff. Prologue says at the beginning of the play,

> "O, for a Muse of fire, that would ascend
> The brightest heaven of invention!
> A kingdom for a stage, princes to act,
> And monarchs to behold the swelling scene!
> Then should the warlike Harry, like himself,
> Assume the port of Mars; and at his heels,
> Leash'd in like hounds, should famine, sword, and fire,
> Crouch for employment..."

- *I mean, old Bill had to know he had the elements of a big hit with this story. And he pulled it off.*

I thought, too, of the famous photo of the raising of the flag at the great battle of Iwo Jima in World War II. If you were American, that

41

photograph brought tears to your eyes. I suppose it also brought tears to your eyes if you were Japanese, though possibly for different reasons. Because I played a Marine general on the sit-com *Major Dad* for four years, I was invited to Marine Corps Birthday Balls and Scholarship Balls every season and the man who took that famous photo, Joe Rosenthal, then quite old, was there once signing his famous photograph for those who wanted one. He was treated with great reverence by the highest-ranking Marines and former Marines for the miracle he had captured on film all those years ago on a tiny atoll in the Pacific Ocean when opposing armies were massed on an infinitely greater Agincourt.

But then, when my blood is all fiery with pride and I'm clenching back tears, and I'm ready to march into hell behind snare drums and skirling bagpipes, I think, had either side had The Bomb back then, there would be no deathless words commemorating those 5,000 heroic English yeomen. There would have been no historic photo of any flag raising. In fact, if both sides had had The Bomb, there would likely be no history. —We forget war is only heroic if someone's still around to thrill to the pipers and tell the tale.

When we waggle our nuclear arsenals at one another, what we actually threaten is the demise of history. We say essentially to the infinite generations that would have come after us:

"The end is now. You will never weep to the songs of war. You will never gaze into each other's eyes to the strains of 'I'll be seeing you in all the old familiar places...' that magnificent Irving Kahal and Sammy Fain anthem of World War II that captured all the bittersweet poignancy, the terror and romance, the delirious, enthralling sweep of that great world event."

To those billions who would have followed us, we simply say instead—

- *"Curtain!"*

18

Sipping Chablis when Vesuvius
Blew its top was hardly the grooviest
In the next war, Pompeii
Will seem child's play
And remains for the Louvre? Dubious

The good news about volcanic eruptions is, unless you happen to be in the wrong town when they occur, they usually don't make much difference. I say "usually" because sometimes they do. Sometimes they're so big and throw so much volcanic debris into the atmosphere that weather patterns around the world are affected for a year or more and that can turn out to be pretty mucky if you're counting on a crop to make the house payment. But then, after a while, things get back to normal. Of course, if you *are* in the wrong town when a volcano pops its cork, it might be too late to set up that Revocable Living Trust.—

- *The good news about the next big war is it'll probably be The Last War and we won't have to go through all that Sturm und Drang ever again.*

- *The bad news is that afterwards there won't be any good-looking, suntanned archeologists in khakis from Banana Republic poking around looking for chochkies for the world's museums.*

19

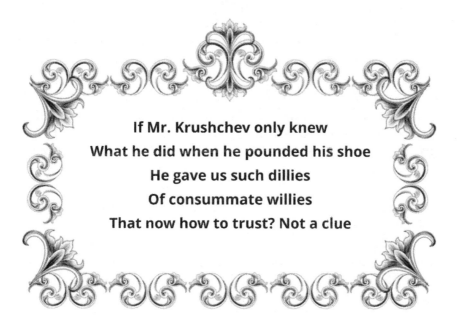

If Mr. Krushchev only knew
What he did when he pounded his shoe
He gave us such dillies
Of consummate willies
That now how to trust? Not a clue

It was October 12th, 1960. Nikita Khrushchev, at that time the head honcho of the USSR, was in New York along with big shots from every other U.N. member nation to address the U.N. Senator Lorenzo Sumulong, the head of the Philippine delegation expressed astonishment that the Soviets could be concerned about Western imperialism when the USSR itself had swallowed all of Eastern Europe. Mr. K., outraged by this exchange, famously whipped off his shoe and pounded his desk with it. Considering a day or two before he had proclaimed, "We will bury you," at the Soviet Mission on New York's Park Avenue, this wild gesture scared the living bejeezus out of the West. He, and by extension his country, seemed to Western nations like raving maniacs, totally out of control. Khrushchev's gesture instantaneously made a splendid case for the arms buildup we were embarked on anyway. If we were afraid of this unknown, malevolent power before, the image of this nutcase banging his shoe on our grave as we suffocated, buried alive underground, never a popular notion under any circumstance, was the capper.

Heretofore, the Cold War had seemed somewhat distant and unreal. Now, on the instant, it was made palpable to all. We were to be buried alive. Like Pompeii. Not that all had been cozy with the USSR before Khrushchev, but the shoe was that unexpected blow precipitating a crisis of trust that is then virtually impossible to get past.

Trust is hard won and easy lost. If I reach for your face 10,000 times to bestow a caress, you trust the $10,001^{st}$ time I reach for you will be the same. If I punch you instead, however, the following 10,000 times I reach for your face, you will each time wonder which it will be: the feather or the fist.

Marriage counselors know that, by the time couples decide they might need some help with their marital problems, they've usually beaten one another to a pulp, emotionally if not physically. Reestablishing trust, even if possible, can be a long and arduous process. In the same way, while The Cold War officially ended when the Berlin Wall came down sending Russia and the U.S. into counseling, there are those skeptics on the right who still, all these years later, cannot trust that Russia will not turn on us if we ever drop our guard and trust again. There are a number of esteemed members of Congress who believe and have stated publicly that the entire collapse of the Soviet Union was a charade staged to lull us into a state of unpreparedness.

The scaredy cats, struck once, will never trust again. We are thus condemned to that well-known "eternal vigilance" which, though I know it is supposed to be the price of my liberty, actually just makes me feel tense.

I would think the path beyond the constant tension of distrust, as with people, has to be blazed with the reassurance of a sincere apology on both sides. It sometimes works for people. They fight, they say or do nasty things to one another, they apologize, and then sometimes they stay married for another three decades. But nations (their politicians) cannot apologize. Occasionally, of course, one will. Japan, for example, did apologize to the people of South Korea for pressing their young women (known then as Comfort Women) into sexual service for Japanese troops during the Second World War. But, before offering it, the apology required extraordinary debate in Japan and fifty years to get it said! Somewhat tardy. For tight-assed, frightened people apologies are a sign of weakness. And God forbid the U.S. should ever be caught looking weak.

When the Smithsonian Museum attempted to mount a commemoration of the 50th anniversary of the atomic bombings of Hiroshima and Nagasaki, unyielding forces in the U.S. vociferously opposed even the merest suggestion that our decision to use The Bomb was morally wrong. Wiping out the innocent civilian populations of two major Japanese cities would "save American lives" and was, therefore, *ipso facto*, moral. And an apology? Stop right there, Boyo. We're the good guys. Good guys don't apologize.

- *Problem is everybody wants to play the Good Guy.*

- *But a sincere apology takes a Big Guy.*

20

Everyone moans, "Where O, where, O
Will we ever find a true hero?"
But who needs a savior
From Greece or Batavia
If next war the score's zero zero?

We talk about "win/win solutions" in which all players win. Its opposite obviously is "lose/lose" where all lose. A "zero sum game" is a game in which the sum of the winnings and losses of the various players is always zero. In meteorology "zero zero" means "atmospheric conditions characterized by zero visibility in both horizontal and vertical directions."—

- *Read that again! Has anyone ever defined war and politics more accurately?*

No Achilles. No Lord Nelson. No Sgt. York. No Teddy at San Juan Hill. No statues in the park.

- *Sound like a lose/lose to you?*

48

21

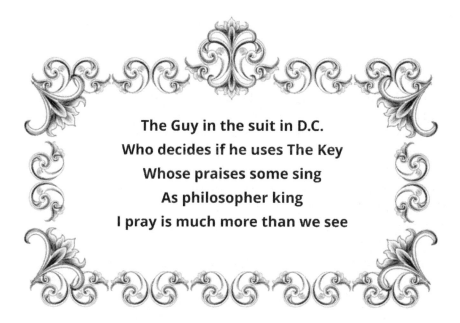

The Guy in the suit in D.C.
Who decides if he uses The Key
Whose praises some sing
As philosopher king
I pray is much more than we see

I wrote this when Ronald Reagan was president and was universally hailed as "The Great Communicator." Watching him I, an actor, always knew I was watching an actor acting. The question for me was: did *he* know he's acting? I thought he did. Then one day I *knew* he did. At a press conference he held towards the end of his second term, a press conference I was watching, the president, in his warm, inimitably avuncular way, stopped abruptly and said something like, "Ladies and Gentlemen, thank you very much, but Helen has informed me my time is up." Helen Thomas was the lady from United Press who, as the senior White House correspondent, apparently performed the duty of timing the press conference. The president then turned from the microphones to leave but, just before the networks cut away, I heard him say as he turned— "I'm on the wrong set."

Now to me, and I dare say to every other person in film work who was listening, this was amazing. Because in that one sentence the man had confirmed my deepest suspicions about him over the previous

49

years of his presidency and before. Namely, that he had played some kind of central casting version of a president, speaking well-crafted words other people had written for him but who had never stopped *thinking* of himself as an actor.—

Only people who've worked in the film industry know what the phrase, "on the wrong set" means. Assistant directors use it to announce to cast and crew that filming has been completed on the set they're on and they are now to consult their daily call sheet and move to the next indicated location. If the location happens to be a distance away, then it's necessary to break everything down: electrics, sound, wardrobe, makeup, cameras and get the whole shebang on the road. "Ladies and gentlemen," they announce, "we're on the wrong set."

Writing this, I still get the creeps I got the day I heard Reagan say it. He had completed the "Press Conference Scene" and now the company was pulling up stakes and moving to the Oval Office or wherever the next scene was on the call sheet. What fun. He had been in makeup and hair no doubt for the TV cameras, he had donned wardrobe, rehearsed it and shot it. And in every scene throughout the day, every day, he starred. —And everyone is eating it up and calling you "The Great Communicator" to boot. An actor's dream. The problem is you're in the real world and you've got The Key in your pocket and there's no next scene on your call sheet.

- *Tell me that's not weird. And I'm an actor!*

I've spent years playing what they call "suit parts" – rich, evil lawyers, senators, rich evil husbands, Chief of Police (*Hill Street Blues*), Marine General (*Major Dad*), CEOs, that kind of guy – the kind of parts where you flick your French cuffs a lot on your custom made shirt. And so I watch the suits in D.C. to see how they handle it. Clinton, Dole, Bush, Nixon, Obama...all of them: "empty suits." I can't include Carter because I always had the suspicion there was actually somebody inside the suit. The problem, however, is not with the suits, the problem is with us: we *want* empty suits. We *elect* empty suits. When, on those rare occasions we actually find somebody inside the suit, we tear them apart: Eugene McCarthy writes poetry and sounds like a philosopher; Edmund Muskie sheds a tear of rage in defense of his wife; Adlai Stevenson is really smart but has a hole in the sole of his shoe, Carter admits, in the famous Playboy interview, that he's had lust in his heart and he's hesitant to wipe Iran off the face of the earth to get our hostages back.

Talk about naïve. Imagine! We turn the fate of the planet over to con artists and scavengers, turn it over willingly to bad actors. Is it even remotely possible then that things could be other than they are?

- *Hey, people, could it be that all of us are shooting our cuffs on the wrong set?*

22

They say the Lord God on High
Is calling the show from the sky
But I'd like some proof
S/He's there in the booth
'Cause if not, in the last act we die

Sooner or later, it's difficult to avoid the notion that we are indeed engaged in a cosmic battle between the forces of good and evil. In fact, in most cultures this is supposed to be what's going on. All that internecine pie throwing in Greek mythology, God and the Devil, Arjuna and the bad guys...all of it has the forces for good fighting the forces of evil for control of our souls. Campbell's "Hero with a Thousand Faces" fighting on all fronts. It's an idea I can get behind, maybe even on a literal level. Who knows what unseen armies clash beyond our dreams?

My problem is not with the idea of an epic battle, but rather that the bad guys seem to be winning on every front. In "spiritual" circles much is made of the fact that God allows us Free Will and we are thus responsible for our actions. We are also told God is all-powerful, omni-everything, which should mean S/he's capable of prevailing in the battle of good and evil but has simply chosen to sit this one out.

It occurred to me that our lives can be seen as a vast, unending dramatic spectacle played out over and over again. It's a hit. A long run. Cults, cultures, religions, whole peoples, languages, civilizations come to the fore, dominate the action for a while, and then are swept away by the story line. And the big Stage Manager in the sky is up there in the booth in front of a bank of monitors calling the cues. It's a TV series. Probably a soap opera.

On the other hand, if there is no God, no producer, no White Brotherhood in the Himalayas, no Koot Hoomi, no teleprompter, no script, nothing cosmic about it, if it's just us forever seeking our own self-interest, improvising as we go; if there will never be a *deus ex machina* to tie it all up neatly at the end; if it's just us after all is said...

But let's just for a moment assume there is a Director. Scripted the whole show. Well, I can buy that. S/he's just like us (we're made in the same image, right?): gets bored, likes a bit of shoot'emup and mayhem, the occasional tearjerker. A channel surfer. I mean, it's perfect: God's on a heavy production schedule, up at dawn, long days, sometimes 'round the clock, no family life, always worried about the Nielsens, heavy stress. When S/he comes home after a long day, S/he just wants to get comfortable and veg out in front of the new big screen TV. Regular cloud potato.

- *So whadya think? — Rewrite or close this turkey?*

23

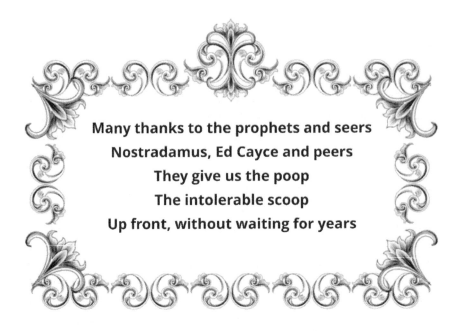

Many thanks to the prophets and seers
Nostradamus, Ed Cayce and peers
They give us the poop
The intolerable scoop
Up front, without waiting for years

Concerning prophesy, I find myself enthralled but unconvinced. There used to be a guy in New Hampshire named Gordon Michael Scallion. (Why am I always suspicious of guys with three names? I mean, when Bill Clinton went to William Jefferson Clinton after he got elected the first time, could you buy that? Lyndon Baines Johnson! Gimme a break!) Scallion publishes a newsletter containing his prophesies on coming earth changes. He keeps score for his subscribers on his predictions regarding earthquakes and volcanic activity around the world. By his own admission, he's very successful.

He sells a map depicting what the United States will look like after the cataclysm he predicts will dump California into the drink that has you bidding on beachfront property someplace around Denver. Allowing the continuity of Western Civilization after earth changes of such magnitude, this could be considered a long-term investment

54

of rare potential. The fact I don't feel inclined to rush to Colorado to tie up some tasty properties, however, suggests to me I'm perhaps a tad skeptical about it all.——

My grandfather, in whose house I grew up, used to play pinochle with a friend of his named Max Land. One night, as my grandfather told it, Max said to him, "Herbert, you wanna put some money into my son's invention? He just came up with a camera that develops the film inside the camera." My grandfather said, "Sounds crazy! Who needs a camera to do that?" Yeah, Granpa, the Polaroid Land Camera.

I ask myself, is Scallion my Max Land? Let's remember Edgar Cayce, the granddaddy of contemporary seers, also predicted California would fall in the ocean around the end of the 20th century. I don't live in California anymore, but I have to admit, when I still lived there, I used to occasionally wonder if my last thought before I went down for the third time wasn't gonna be something about missed deals on beachfront property?

- *Glub, glub——*

24

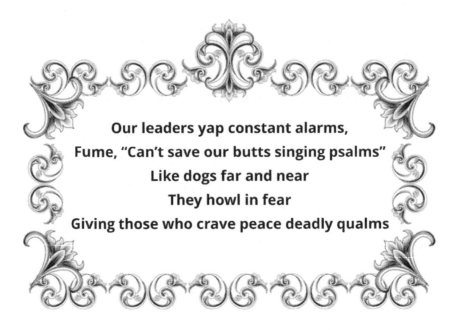

Our leaders yap constant alarms,
Fume, "Can't save our butts singing psalms"
Like dogs far and near
They howl in fear
Giving those who crave peace deadly qualms

Painful to admit perhaps, but we in the U.S. were guilty of sounding contrived alarms during the off-the-charts arms buildup of the 1980s. Highly exaggerated CIA intelligence reports regarding the USSR's military capabilities and intentions hoodwinked the U.S. Congress and the American people into accepting the necessity for plunging the nation into a financial abyss to pay for new generations of weapons we were going to need just to stay abreast of our enemies. The Soviets, reading these fallacious assessments of their capabilities and intentions, assessments they obviously knew to be false, felt impelled to actually try to achieve what they were said to already have in order to stay competitive. Since they knew the Pentagon and the CIA were lying to the Congress and the American people, how could the Soviets trust the U.S. not to use the weapons it was planning to build? After all, if we weren't planning to use them, why build them? Clearly not to counter capabilities Moscow possessed because they knew we knew they did *not* have such capabilities.

Nazis had it right. Control communication, then repeat the lie often enough until it becomes the truth. Witness Big Dick Cheney and Iraq's WMDs. Man, that same old National Security crap works every time. And that sick, sad MF is, many years later, still singing the same tune. Hitler killed six million; The Dick only a million. Hey, guy's a Bush leaguer, ain't so bad after all. I remember watching The Dick on one of the talk shows. Since things weren't going so well in Iraq at the time, the host asked him some questions about the veracity of the intelligence that led us into that country to take down its boss and ferret out his Weapons of Mass Destruction. Probably a nice guy, Cheney. Probably loves his family. Probably worries about his stents and his pacemaker. But, man, I'm watching this guy lie through his teeth. Still lumping Hussein with bin Laden because of a supposed meeting sometime before 9/11 between a high-ranking Iraqi muckamuck with an al-Qaeda operative in Hungary or Bulgaria or someplace. Never mind even the CIA has disavowed this putative encounter, makes no difference, say it anyway. Say it and if it proves to be false in the future just say, like Big Dick, "I misspoke."

It's close to midnight. Many try to sleep. Others huddle around the cold flame of the television screen. Across the street, the dog barking at the chemtrailed, drone-filled sky offers us five alternatives: wake the owner, feed the dog, poison the dog, learn to sleep despite the barking...

- *or maybe just make friends with that lonely pooch?*

25

Our lust for more bombs is not bravery
Only think and realize it's knavery
To have thrice what we need
To accomplish the deed
Is a creed beyond dumb, Sir, it's slavery

There's a great Gary Larsen (*The Far Side*) cartoon depicting the hold of a Viking slave ship: wretched, starving men at the oars, huge Viking warriors overseeing them with their horned helmets and whips. One emaciated little oarsman has lifted his pinky to attract the attention of his brutal master. "Yoo hoo," he calls out, "I've got a blister!"

Unlike our brave little hero, we could get out of our cartoon by simply refusing to pull those oars. But to do that we would first have to recognize and then be willing to flee our enslavement. We'd have to stop pulling the oars and hold our pinkies up to the scary guys in the bear skins: the politicians and demagogues brandishing their whips. Problem is, those of us alive today have never known a world outside the ship's hold, chained to the heavy oars of the Warfare State. In our lives, there has been only war or the preparation for it.

Terry George, an Irish writer and director of the film *In the Name of the Father*, talked about the failed peace process in Northern Ireland in an op-ed piece in the N.Y. Times of July 17, 1996:

"Those precious months of peace were squandered partly, I believe, because we failed to recognize the psychological legacy of the previous 30 years. There are not two but three cultures in Northern Ireland: Protestant, Catholic and the War. In a warped twist of history, the war culture manages to cross the sectarian divide. Seventy years of division and 30 years of conflict have so institutionalized many people that they find themselves best defined by the war...The IRA cease-fire (now broken) and the peace process threw both communities into confusion. Peace beckoned, but no one properly took into account the war culture's addictive hold. Of course, people don't say they are for the war, any more than they could say they are for cancer. Yet the politicians and the paramilitaries can be examined on their actions over the last year and separated into factions: the war faction and the peace faction..."

So we abide in our addiction. And who can blame us? Been addicted a long, long time. —Ah, but the 800 billion or so that we'll pour into the bottomless sewer of military preparedness for the 'war on terror" in 2016 could, if not for our addiction, provide infinite jobs to feed, clothe, educate, and heal the world.

It's easy to say, "Give up the addiction, lay down the oars." —But to do that, to leave the darkness of the hold to climb up onto the wide deck would mean incurring the wrath of the guys with the horns on their helmets, finding a BAND-AID for that pinky blister, and getting our eyes used to the sun.

- *knave [neyv]* **noun** *An unprincipled, untrustworthy, or dishonest person.*

- *Sound like any public servants you know?*

26

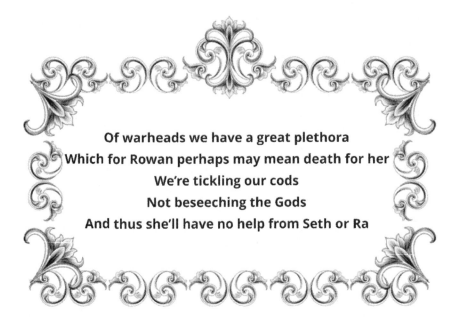

Of warheads we have a great plethora
Which for Rowan perhaps may mean death for her
We're tickling our cods
Not beseeching the Gods
And thus she'll have no help from Seth or Ra

Back on September 29, 1996, there was actually a story in the N.Y. Times on page A8 on the decree issued by then Russian President Boris Yeltsin transferring control of Russia's nuclear arsenal to Prime Minister Victor Chernomyrdin while he, Yeltsin, underwent open heart surgery. In the same edition we were informed, this time by a front-page headline, that "Gulf War Veterans in Navy Unit Tell of an Iraqi Chemical Attack...Troops Stories At Odds with Pentagon Account." And on page A11: "British Call Halt to Cow Slaughter Demanded by European Union." This following the previous day's announcement that Switzerland would "cull" (read "slaughter") 250,000 animals from its herds, all in an effort to halt the spread of dreaded "mad cow disease."

Stories like these, especially when they conveniently appear all together, make me think I'm reading satire from a newsletter put out by the inmates of a maximum-security psychiatric facility.

Believers in reincarnation tell us we continue to return to this earthly plane over and over until we learn our karmic lessons. Sounds real good until you consider that that scenario makes all the people on this planet right now assholes who haven't learned their lessons in mucho previous incarnations. You know, souls still working through various stages of duh. In other words, all the human beings alive today are people who haven't yet gotten with The Program. Because when you do get with The Program, you're sent off to graduate school someplace else. I should mention here that, occasionally, a few advanced souls like Buddha, Jesus, Mohammed and some lesser known graduates do get it and actually choose to *return* to Nutsville to help suffering humanity, a choice even we inmates can see is an act of tremendous self-sacrifice.—

So, we might call Earth "The Holding Planet." If you're really a wacked-out sociopath in some other universe, they cull you and send you down here to get your head straight...a kind of intergalactic concentration camp for psychiatric Basic Training. The problem is all the rehab is voluntary and most of us never find out it's even available until checkout time.

And then there's the Gulf War on The Holding Planet: hey, your troops are sick because they got a dose of nasty chemicals? No problem, deny it. Cheaper that way. Or Yeltsin's goin' in for open heart surgery? Don't denounce The Bomb with what may turn out to be your dying breath, nah, give the key to some other inmate so he can exterminate millions of defenseless humans. And is it way too much to expect us inmates to get the connection between how we treat animals and how we treat each other?

And of the old gods, Seth or Ra (in case you didn't know, both sun gods in early Egyptian religion), we known nothing. Although it sometimes may console the spirit (the one that's here wandering around looking for rehab) to remember that once such entities were familiars. And if once they were, could they be once again? With luck or faith, one might hope, sooner rather than later, that the old Gods and Goddesses will relent and rise again to awaken us from the scary dream in which we've been lost for eons.

- *Perhaps even save one's kid, Rowan, from this idiotic Looney Toons cartoon we're trapped in.*

27

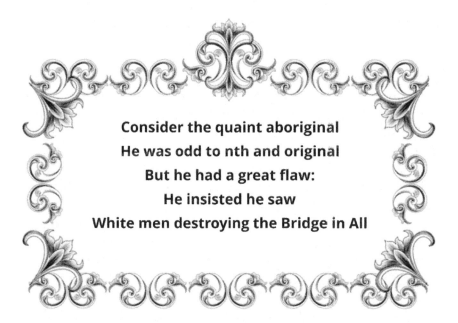

Consider the quaint aboriginal
He was odd to nth and original
But he had a great flaw:
He insisted he saw
White men destroying the Bridge in All

It's Saturday, 10:30 in the morning. When I finish writing this, I'll shower, dress, and take the subway from 72nd St. and Broadway down to Times Square, 42nd St. I'll walk north up Broadway a couple of blocks and turn left on West 44th St. to the Shubert Theatre about halfway down the block towards 8th Ave. I'll make this trip six days a week, every week until the show I'm doing closes: a show called *Big, The Musical*, based on *Big*, the movie.

Because it's New York and not Los Angeles where I live, instead of taking the subway, I sometimes walk down Broadway from 71st St. (where I'm subletting a friend's condo) all the way to 44th, a walk that would be considered unimaginable in L.A. because later you'd have to walk back again. But walking gives me time to think about what the city must have been like before we "bought" it from the Native Americans. I look at it now, walk in it now, look in the faces of the street vendors, the shopkeepers, the tourists in their thousands, from all over the country, all over the world and I am sometimes filled with sadness. Sounds gooey, I know, but deer browsed here, bear scratched their backs against the trunks of trees, foxes flicked their bushy tails, beaver gnawed tasty trunks in pursuit of their immemorial feats of engineering. I've never seen a bear or a fox or a beaver and I don't really know too much about them, but they were here. Right here.

Back when I was doing *Big*, there was a lot of talk in the theatrical community about the "Disneyfication" of Broadway (meaning, of course, the whole theatre district not just the street). Disney turned its hit animated film *Beauty and the Beast* into a stage musical and brought it to Broadway. Since it was a big hit, Disney said to its corporate self, "Wow, there's big money to be made on the Great White Way." So Disney led the charge to basically shut down raunchy, wonderful 42nd Street and upscale it. One of New York's most notorious stretches of real estate, the street had been home for decades to porn theatres, tourist traps, drug dealers, prostitutes, fleabag hotels, and the weary human wreckage washed up on the shores of major cities around the world.

But once it had been different. When I played Julian Marsh in the musical *42nd Street* at the Shubert Theatre in Los Angeles for a year, a story that takes place in the '30s, every night at the end of the show, left alone on stage, I sang, "Come and meet those dancing feet on the avenue I'm taking you to, 42nd Street." In those days, the theatres on the street were filled with plays and musicals. No porn.

Disney took a look at all those old theatres just waiting to be filled with Mouse lovers and whistled "Heigh Ho, heigh ho, it's off to work we go." It bought and renovated the once glorious New Amsterdam Theatre on the south side of 42nd St. It's a tall building with floors for offices above the theatre and has a small rooftop theatre in addition. In fact, in one of the Broadway shows I did in years past (I can't remember which one), for some reason we rehearsed one time in the dusty, unused New Amsterdam rooftop and imagined old ghosts waiting there for their next cue. When the renovation was done, Disney opened *The Lion King* at the New Amsterdam and made even more money.

Confession: on a week's vacation from *Big, The Musical*, I took the so-called "magic" or "sacred" mushroom for the first time. It was an astonishing experience. Life altering. Sometime during the hours of this amazing journey, I began thinking about the theatre district, Broadway, where I was now working and where I had spent the first 15 years of my career. The New Amsterdam Theatre? Ah, yes, N.Y. was originally *Nieuw Amsterdam*, a Dutch settlement, Peter Stuyvesant and all that; I grew up in Brooklyn, *Breuckelen*, Dutch bought Manhattan from the Indians for 24 bucks, we sneer at the dumb savages for giving away some of the world's most valuable real estate for the price of a cab ride, Indians thought it was as dumb to think about owning land as owning air, really gave it to the Dutch, probably out of the goodness of their hearts, exit the Indians, city grows, exit the Dutch, enter the British, exit the British, enter the Americans, New Amsterdam Theatre built, Times Square, time squared, Indians now singing in *Pocahontas,* another Disney cartoon turned into a stage musical, symbol of Disney?, a mouse: Mickey (a drink that knocks you unconscious), most recognized symbol in the world, 42nd St. its theatres all shiny and new filled with popeyed tourists happily ingesting their Pablum making oodles and oodles of money for…a Mouse.

But, can you dig it, the quaint aboriginal lived here once and fished the Hudson (what was it called before Henry, I wonder?) And, man, look at it now. You want to see the real show? Stand at the corner of 42nd St. and Broadway. Just stand and look around. And, as you do, contemplate what it all looked like way back. Consider the "con" and where those poor quaint aboriginal suckers are now and what we did to them in return for their generosity or their naïveté. And, whatever's playing at the New Amsterdam Theatre, don't go. Send the 200 bucks you were gonna spend on tickets to some Indian Relief Mission and walk the kiddies west, down to the foot of 42nd St. to the river and help them to see the hazy ghost of that birch bark canoe.

- *Can "you" see it?*

28

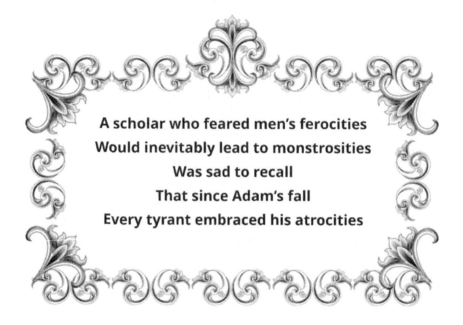

A scholar who feared men's ferocities
Would inevitably lead to monstrosities
Was sad to recall
That since Adam's fall
Every tyrant embraced his atrocities

I wonder if tyrants measure their own brutalities against those of other tyrants? Like, did Saddam Hussein, for example, during his escapades to exterminate defenseless Kurds, compare his exploits to those of the master, Adolph, and find himself wanting? Did der Fuhrer himself look back with pity on the amateurish efforts of Genghis Khan? Was Idi Amin depressed because, lacking the technology, he could never aspire to be a Hitler? Did Franco and Mussolini feel like second class citizens? Or, for that matter, when Daddy Bush assembled a force of half a million to defeat the vastly inferior Iraqi army during the First Gulf War, did he look Saddam in the eyes in the secret sanctuary of his most private heart and say, "Fuck me? Fuck you!" He must have felt pretty perky after we strafed and bombed into non-existence the hoard of men retreating from Kuwait in that famous column. Yeah, I know, I'm not supposed to lump Papa Bush with the aforementioned bad guys, but I just have a hard time getting past slaughter is slaughter is slaughter.—

An additional, related question suggests itself: Do despots know they're despots? Did Hitler know he and his chums were basket cases or did he believe his own BS and think he was one swell dude? Do the people at the Food and Drug Administration know they're slime balls in the pockets of the pharmaceutical industry and the American Medical Association or do they high five each other every time they persecute another physician for using alternative means to actually cure something? (I know you're surprised I've got them in the same category as Hitler, but if you can accept there are known cures for cancer, hep C, and AIDS, etc. proscribed by the AMA and its lackey the FDA, you'll see, at half a million deaths just from cancer every year, it doesn't take long to get past six million.)

I have a great idea. We're all fascinated by numbers and lists: The 10 Best Dressed, The 10 Worst, The 50 Most Beautiful (nobody has the guts to do its opposite), The Longest Underwater Pogostick Jump (I kid you not!) and so on. Wouldn't it work for tyrants, too? World's Most Brutal? World's Neatest Genocide? Or even something like an Oscar for World's Most Evil? And shouldn't the winner get to take something home for the mantelpiece? Maybe a gilded skull or...oh, well, we'll think of something.

- *May I have the envelope please...?*

29

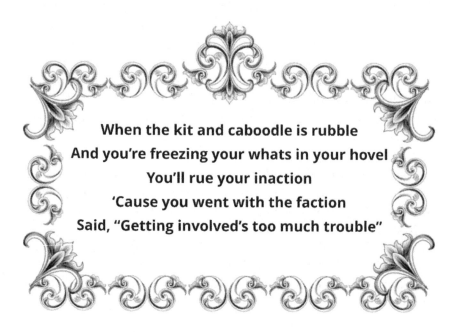

When the kit and caboodle is rubble
And you're freezing your whats in your hovel
You'll rue your inaction
'Cause you went with the faction
Said, "Getting involved's too much trouble"

I had a vision once. Or maybe it was a dream. I imagined myself sitting on the roof of my garage in a deck chair, some booze in hand, wearing my shades and waiting for the Big Bang that was going to obliterate the city in the distance. I don't know how, but somehow I knew it was coming. Maybe it had been announced that a missile had been launched and, since apparently there was no escaping it, I wanted to have a good seat for the Playoffs. So there I was sixth row center waiting for the house lights to dim, smiling at the thought that, in this case, the curtain would go up and come down simultaneously, the shortest run in history. And then it happened. Ten thousand suns exploded; the air boiled. Chaos lunged. "Oh, shit, this is baaad," I thought, "maybe I shoulda done someth..."

We've been Wolfed to the point of inertia. When I was writing this, the N.Y. Times reported that lots of pelicans had died off the northern California coast from - it's believed - eating fish infected with botulism, the Amazon is going up in flames faster than anyone thought, a trillion fish are killed each year in this country by electric power plants (nuclear and conventional), Rwandan women who were raped in the internecine slaughter years ago are struggling to raise the children born to them as a result, ditto the Bosnians, welfare mothers will have a tougher time providing for their children owing to cutbacks in welfare and food stamps, we're broke (aka bankrupt), China's gonna take over as the Big Lolly. interest rates are zero, American industry is kaput, first time ever we've passed 400 parts per million of CO_2, polar bears are losing their fur and their ice and are starving to death and, perhaps most ominous of all, it's no longer a question of *whether* we shall have another humongous terrorist attack, but *when*. Not to mention the fact that, after The Big Con of '08, millions of Americans are still out of work with tens of thousands having quit looking for a job altogether. And, oh, yes, there's the little matter of the exploding national debt.

And the real enemy? If only he were as tangible as our Wolf. But he is frequently invisible. He's a crooked corporation, a government, a president, a huge, self-serving apparatus spewing "disinformation" to mask its perfidy.

We are suffocating in a cocoon of lies. Show of hands, is there anyone who believed tobacco company executives when they rose and swore before God and the U.S. Congress that they were unaware nicotine was addictive? Or that they did not add even more nicotine to their butts? Or who didn't dig that these despicable assholes lusted to hook children as smokers with their cute, hip Joe Camel ads even as they swore to the contrary?

Well, what did you expect, you dick brains on the U.S. Supreme Court? This just in you morons, you assholes: corporations ARE NOT people. Corporations are about one thing: money! They don't breathe, they don't have children, they don't dislike broccoli. And what's terrifying is you idiots on the court knew that.

Or the American Medical Association? Is there one benighted soul who still believes the AMA is the Galahad of health as it portrays itself? This dedicated guardian of the medical fortress has only three arrows in its quiver: the knife, radiation and drugs and woe to the healer who fashions a different arrow for his quiver and actually starts curing patients with it. Say *ciao* to your license, Baby, 'cause it's jail time. It was probably around fifty years ago when chiropractors were trying to get licensed in N.Y. State. I saw the mighty campaign mounted against them by the AMA, a campaign of derision and fear. I've also read the transcripts of the proceedings of the Massachusetts Medical Society in the latter part of the 19th Century. Respected physicians who were curing their patients with homeopathy were professionally burned at the stake. Exit the homeopaths! (Yeah, they're back but it took a long time.)

In fact, the Wolf is staring in the window; the tiny worm of Fear gnaws in your most secret place. He is there. We know he is there. So we rollerblade, spin, doze, check out the porn sites.

- *Yeah, but getting involved is a pain in the ass.*

"More doctors smoke Camels than any other cigarette." Can you believe that was their bullshit commercial when I was a kid?

- *Believe...*

30

As we flirt with the end of our history
Each of us faces the mystery
Of why we do flips
To cash in our chips
While the pace of the game remains blistery?

Since I lived in Los Angeles for 35 years, I've spent a lot of time driving the freeways. Sometimes, when the needle flirted with empty, I kept on going as a challenge to God to see if I could make it home. Pulling off the freeway for a fill up was boring; pressing on, a gamble, an adventure. In the same way, I see in the now universal flirtation with planetary disaster, that we're rolling the dice against the House. If we make it, all well and good. If we lose the gamble, however, and the needle hits Empty, we're gonna be waitin' on the shoulder of the road a real long time 'cause Triple A ain't comin' out for this one.

The yearning for adventure is vastly underrated as a motivation in human affairs. It provides the answer to the age-old question of why men lust to suit up and go to war: it's because war gets the heart a-thumping. "There'll be bluebirds over the white cliffs of Dover..." and all that romantic shit. Some say it's better than sex. Ask yourself why practically every dramatic movie or TV show or video game is about cops and robbers and lawyers and kung fu and violence and war.—

There was an item in Money magazine a while back that grabbed me. They used to have a section in the December or January issue called, "Winners and Losers." It featured all kinds of things that had won or lost big time during the previous year. The one that got me was a story about some guy who walked into a no limit casino in Vegas with a briefcase containing $750,000, converted all the cash to chips, put the entire stash down on the Don't Pass line at a craps table, won on the next roll, took his mountain of chips back to the cashier, converted them back into cash, packed his briefcase and walked out of the casino with a million and a half...*before the on-site IRS agents could wake up and nail him.* And the only thing he said was he had inherited the money and, since it really wasn't enough to live on for the rest of his life, he had decided to go for broke.

I thought about doing it for a while. Selling my house and taking everything I had in cash and packing it all in a briefcase destined for a green felt table at The Golden Whatsis. It "got my attention" as people like to say nowadays; made my heart pound just thinking about it. I imagined how great I'd feel when I was rich. Free. Powerful. Important. I was sailing. Then one day I had the annoying thought that I might lose. That I could walk out of the joint homeless and impoverished. Nevertheless, I was still tempted. What am I, chicken, I thought? Back and forth. The drama of my wealth was exceedingly attractive. The melodrama of my poverty daunting. But, even if I lost, I'd be remembered as somebody who'd risked it all. Somebody who had taken the ultimate rafting trip down a #10-rated river without a lifejacket! Somebody who'd made the big bungee jump off what used to be the World Trade Center without measuring the cord! What a guy! Somebody.

- *Sanity prevailed.—*

So we're standing at the cashier's window in a no limit house with all of human history in a briefcase. Are we going to put all those chips, and there are so many of them, tens of thousands of years of them, civilizations of them, symphonies of them, Vermeers of them, on the table? The heart thuds. Do we play nice or play tough with the planet?

72

Here we stand: hard-eyed, tough-bellied, waiting to see if we'll blink. We're rafting on that great river of testosterone, the wildest white water in the world, no mealy-mouthed nerds on this baby; the roaring ahead is like some ancient mythological monster ravenous for prey and it makes us feel brave, manly, lusting for the triumph of it. You know, that great feeling we men love to have: I lopped off the Gorgon's head and lived to tell the tale. I get to stand on the mountaintop or at the craps table and beat my chest like Tarzan.

- *I beat The House!*

Or are we going to beach the raft before we hit the rapids, ask the croupier for our chips back and wuss out? —Go home, tend the garden, kiss the sleeping kids good night?—

If we do that, and this is the tough one, we'd have to talk to our adversaries as if they were as human as we think we are, we'd have to start treating the Earth like the Queen she is. We'd have to keep our chips in the briefcase and maybe never again get to feel our hearts beat out that ratatattat. Never get to swing through the trees yodeling like Tarzan.

- *We'd have to play it safe.*

- *Drag.*

31

If after we won't know who wins
And there'll be no way of saving our skins
Then why fight the battle
If we're butchered like cattle
With all of our kith and our kins?

One of the great things in the previously- mentioned 1983 film *Testament,* was that, at the beginning, the only thing anyone knows is that something has happened. The people in the small bedroom community where the story takes place have seen a great flash in the sky in the direction of San Francisco and all forms of communication have suddenly ceased. The realization gradually dawns that an atomic explosion has possibly destroyed San Francisco and actress Jane Alexander's husband, played by actor William Devane, may never again return home from his routine trip to the city. Because telephones, radio, and television are all defunct, one old ham radio operator in town becomes the community's only hope of reaching the outside world. But with all his effort, he is never able to raise anyone. Out there, only silence.

- *Then everyone begins to sicken.*

This is, of course, according to experts on the subject, the way it will be. Huge electrical disturbances in the upper atmosphere following any kind of nuclear exchange will make communication impossible, even for the military. Retaliatory commands will be impossible to deliver. No one will know what happened. No one will know who started it or why or what to do next. It'll be like *Testament*. If you think I'm exaggerating, rent the film...if you can take it. You'll understand.—

Right now you're thinking, this guy Cypher is really negative. Cold War is over. The nuclear threat is inconsequential. Can't happen. Cypher responds: Right on! And it's that very complacency that's terrifying. Like a stock market dump, it happens at the exact moment everyone decides it can never happen again. Before The Big Bubble burst and the market tanked in '04, when everyone was rich and we were all stoned out of our gourds on money, and all the Gurus on the money shows were saying, "This time it's different," I remember hearing one lone Cassandra wail, "The most dangerous words in the English language are, 'This time it's different.'"

And remember, if you go, everyone you know goes, too. Those pictures we have in our minds of people in Hiroshima wandering around burned, dazed? Quaint. Those bombs were like firecrackers compared to what we have now. No more wandering around now. Now everyone goes. Everyone.

- *But the thing about war is it's really no fun at all unless you can keep score.*

Just a thought: killing at a distance is kind of like buying packaged meat in the supermarket. It doesn't have much to do with looking your pet pig in the eye while you stick a blade in his throat, the Blue Ribbon he won for you at the fair fluttering on the barn wall in the breeze from his screaming. Easier to buy him under plastic wrap at the Safeway. Easier to see pictures of war, even when they include photographs of inconsolable mothers with black shawls over their bent, grieving Moslem heads.

- *Easier to see them than know them.*

75

I've been worrying that all this nuclear blather I've been huffing and puffing may be kind of obsolete, what with the Cold War being over and our missiles maybe being retargeted. But wouldn't ya know just today, December 28, 2017, some important guy has predicted we'll be at war with North Korea within three weeks. And we're talking nuclear in case you haven't seen the news lately. Even more dangerous than during the nasty old days. The Nuclear Club has many new members and the fiction that missiles have been retargeted to "safe" sites like the ocean are merely sops to our fears. Missiles, *60 Minutes* pointed out in an old show, even after launch, can be retargeted in seconds to old Cold War destinations like London, New York, and Moscow. I remember the show told the story of a Norwegian launch of a scientific mission that the Russians were unable to identify. Two minutes away from a massive retaliatory strike, sanity prevailed. —But it was close.—

- *So why worry?*

32

> We were praying for sevens like saps
> When both of the die came up craps
> Ah, seven, eleven
> Now we're singing in heaven
> A swan song that sounds lots like Taps

On an initial roll, seven and eleven are winning numbers. Two is "craps." You've "crapped out" and you lose your money and the dice. Two is called "snake eyes."—Interesting, huh? That old snake keeps popping up at The Beginning and at The End. —At the risk of taking the gambling analogy too far, the only way to beat ole snake eyes is to stay away from the table.

Princeton professor Immanuel Velikovsky wrote a book called *Mankind in Amnesia*. In it he conjectured that, in ancient times, human beings endured a great cataclysm. A catastrophe that lives on in humanity's collective, subconscious memory and, like individuals who have repressed some intolerable early life scene, humanity itself is from time to time compelled to act out the very circumstances that have been repressed: humanity itself driven to self-destruction. Other scientists have always put Velikovsky down for his unconventional ideas. In his books he presents a lot of evidence that the planet Venus was not a member of our solar system until recently but was, in fact, a comet that had zipped through our neighborhood several times before being captured by gravity and planted in orbit around the sun. These events caused tremendous havoc on earth, even the Great Flood, and it's from these ancient disasters and their repression that we all still suffer today

I read him years ago with great interest but, not being a scientist, I cannot say yea or nay with any kind of authority. It so happens, however, that once - it must have been 1978 or '79 - I happened to be listening to the NPR evening news and I heard Velikovsky himself interviewed. A NASA flyby had just discovered a gas or something on Venus that Velikovsky had predicted would someday be found if we ever got to that planet. The discovery corroborated Velikovsky's thesis that Venus was not an original member of the solar system, that Venus was indeed a newbie. He was asked if he felt satisfaction that his prediction, scoffed at by traditional scientists, had been proven correct all these years later? He said that he did feel satisfaction. The "scientists" were wrong: Immanuel was right.

Evidence? It's well known that mastodons, those extinct Big Guys have been exhumed in the far north with tropical vegetation in their mouths and stomachs, killed and frozen instantly. Try to explain that one without something very large flipping the earth!

I don't know if psychiatrist Velikovsky was right in his assertion that we go on generation after generation repressing awful memories of The Flood and other cataclysms and are thus compelled to perennially reenact humanity's early destruction. But, to me, it's the only psychological explanation that makes any kind of sense out of what makes no sense at all: that we feverishly strive to destroy ourselves and our dear Mama Earth.

- *And, hey Jocko, next time you roll the dice remember...the singular of dice is "die."*

- *Cute, huh?*

33

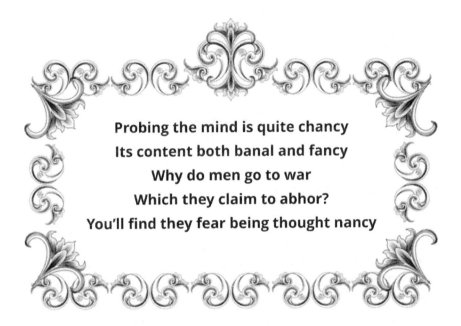

Probing the mind is quite chancy
Its content both banal and fancy
Why do men go to war
Which they claim to abhor?
You'll find they fear being thought nancy

As mentioned previously, I was inducted into the Army in October, 1953. We were first sent to Fort Dix in New Jersey where we remained for two weeks. Then we were flown to Fort Bliss(!), El Paso, Texas to begin Basic Training. While we were at Dix, I was OK. It was mostly raking leaves and talking about how they must be putting something in the food.

EARLY MORNING. THE YOUNG RECRUITS ARE IN THEIR DOUBLE-DECKER BUNKS. A NONCOM HAS JUST PASSED THROUGH THE BARRACKS YELLING FOR EVERYONE TO FALL OUT OF THE SACK

Passman - (tapping his watch) My watch musta stopped. It says 4 AM!

Bush – That's funny, mine's stopped at exactly the same time.

DiPiazza – They're puttin' saltpeter in the food.

Passman – They couldn't do that. That's illegal.

DiPiazza – I know they're puttin' saltpeter in the food 'cause formerly I couldn't live without it for a week!"

Of course, they weren't. They didn't have to. Fear works even better than saltpeter for your peter.

When we shipped out to El Paso, I was in serious emotional trouble. I wanted to be an opera singer and I was struggling with the troublesome thought that two years in the army was possibly not going to further my vocal training. I decided to leave the army and go home. I knew desertion was probably not a sensible plan, so I thought to use my potential histrionic abilities to accomplish my goal. After all, hadn't I won the Drama Medal at my graduation from Erasmus Hall High School? I asked to see the Chaplain. It was arranged and I sat down with this gentleman and cried for an hour. I have no memory of what I said, but he must have been impressed because I was invited back on two further occasions to vent my *angst*. Which I did, copiously, on the theory that my only out was a psychological profile that might make the tough boys not want me around. I think it may have been called a "Section Eight" discharge. You know, guy don't wanna kill people, send the nancy wimp back to his mommy.

Now it so happened, we had a Field First Sergeant named Fowler in charge of the first eight weeks of our Basic Training. He was black, he had been all through the Second World War and had then fought in Korea, and he was and still remains to this day the toughest, kindest SOB I ever knew. I'm 84 years old as I write this and the sarge is certainly snuggled in under a grass blanket in a military cemetery someplace, but writing about him brings tears to my eyes. The Basic Training workday began with a company lineup, a roll call and duty assignments. When Sgt. Fowler came to my name, he read it with a sibilant "s," "Sssypher, to the Chaplain! Again!" His intonation was laden with scorn. I was deeply humiliated. His swishy reading of my name implied I was effeminate. Not a real man! The company laughed at me.

I won. I was informed I'd earned a psychological discharge. I'd be returning home to my opera training in New York with Madame Forrai. But I couldn't go through with it. I couldn't bear the derisive stares, the sarcastic laughter, the thought that I was a pussy, a pansy, a wuss. And I felt guilty. I knew that some of these young men would probably die soon on a frozen battlefield in Korea and I'd have to spend the rest of my life knowing I escaped their fate by putting on an act. Besides, the sergeant called us "Young Warriors" and I kinda liked that. I needed Sergeant Fowler's respect. So I caved and stayed in.

As it turned out, at the end of my second eight weeks of Basic, we were on orders to go to Korea, duffels packed, when an Armistice was declared and the orders changed. I ended up staying at Bliss for the rest of my time and listening to Milton Cross on the Metropolitan Opera broadcast every Saturday morning ("Texaco presents The Metropolitan Opera!") on the classical music station I had found. I even came to love the barren landscape.

But I would have gone to Korea with Sy Passman, Roy Bush, and Joe DiPiazza and that whole funny Jewish Italian crew from Brooklyn. I would have gone and, who knows, I might have died.

- *Anything to avoid that Sssypher.*

34

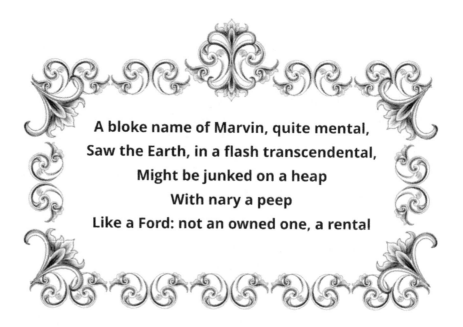

A bloke name of Marvin, quite mental,
Saw the Earth, in a flash transcendental,
Might be junked on a heap
With nary a peep
Like a Ford: not an owned one, a rental

There is the perception that people who rent cars do not treat them as well as cars they own. The same holds true for rental property. Land-lording is supposed to be trying because some tenants trash the apartments or houses entrusted to them. For example, friends of mine, when they moved to California, rented their brownstone in Brooklyn to a very presentable couple. Yet after several months their renters stopped paying rent. After entreaties and threats went unanswered, my friend flew to New York to ascertain the status of his property. He found his tenants had fled, taking with them all the expensive fixtures the house had contained. In addition, a bathtub on the top floor of the building had been stoppered and the water turned on. My friend said, when he opened the front door, water was cascading through the house like one of the Seven Wonders of the ancient world.

That is how we are now living on this planet. Like renters, not owners. *But, hey Melvin, in reality we are owners, not renters.* So how come we don't get this? How come we're ripping out all the beautiful old fixtures and preparing to flee as if we're getting away with something? I believe the answer is contained in a 1992 book entitled *The Great Reckoning* by James Dale Davidson and Lord William Rees-Moog. This enthralling volume enumerates and describes the catastrophes which almost certainly await us given the course we have presently charted for ourselves. For example, the authors spend considerable time discussing the impact terrorism will have on the world in the coming decades. —From the vantage point of 2018, pretty prescient, huh?

The book also contains an important concept which I think bears repeating in this discussion of why we act like renters when we, in fact, own the deed. The concept is called an "Incentive Trap."

The authors ask us to imagine that 500 people have been issued a credit card with the exact same account number, a card that can be used to acquire anything we need at any time and that, when the bill is tabulated at the end of the month, we will all owe an absolutely equal share of the amount due. Now it's perhaps obvious that two kinds of people with two different approaches to this situation will emerge. The first group will see the danger such a temptation poses and will act with restraint, purchasing only those items they truly need. They will be the frugal ones. A second group will perceive this circumstance differently. This group will view the card as an opportunity to acquire everything they would not otherwise have been able to afford, and they will purchase unrestrainedly. They will be the profligate ones.—

At the end of the month, when everyone receives the same bill, those who have been frugal will be required to pay more than they themselves have spent and they will understandably feel put upon and cheated by the spendthrifts. In the forthcoming month, therefore, they will reason that it only makes sense to accelerate their own purchases, since clearly frugality was not previously practiced by all. It doesn't require a vivid imagination to foresee the rapid, upward spending spiral that will ensue as restraint erodes.

In this sense, the Earth can be seen as the universal account. Against this account, we have all been issued magical credit cards. Some will use their cards wisely and live frugally. Others will seek to maximize their withdrawals, with or without the awareness that, at the end of the era, everyone will pick up the tab for their actions. Furthermore, Capitalism, which celebrates acquisitive success, teaches and encourages each of us to run the biggest tab we can. The question which faces us all then is, now that the cards have been distributed and anyone can take as much as they can connive to take, how do we learn to act with restraint when profligacy, in the short run, is so clearly the more profitable choice?

In family counseling there is the concept that sooner or later someone is going to have to "pick up the tab." —For example, if her Dad has run up a tab by being cruel and cold, somewhere down the line some suitor may have to pick up the tab for old Pop's behavior. She might be in a relationship, say, with a really good guy but, no matter, if she hasn't worked it out, she's gonna make the poor slob pick up Daddy's tab. In the same way, we've been running a big tab on this planet for a long time now and, sooner or later, someone is going to have to pick up the check. If not us, our children.—

- *So, the drill is, if we're not going to scrap this baby in the big Planetary Junkyard, we'd better somehow figure out a way to cut up that credit card or, at the very least, run a major credit check on the Big Spenders.*

35

When I'm done to the nines, feeling spiffy,
On top of the world, in a jiffy
I start to reflect
It all may be wrecked
And those mornings at seven? Iffy

PIPPA' SONG

The year's at the spring,
And the day's at the morn;
Morning's at seven;
The hill-side's dew-pearled;
The lark's on the wing;
The snail's on the thorn;
God's in His heaven -
All's right with the world!

-Robert Browning (1812-1889)

- *Honestly now, in your wildest fantasy, can you even begin to imagine anyone writing that beautiful verse today?*

36

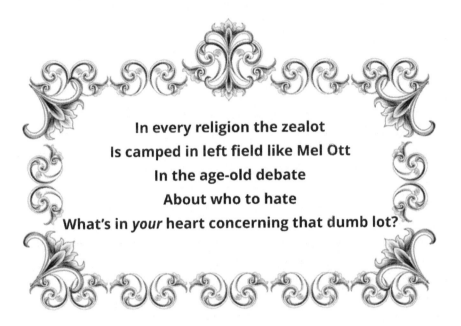

In every religion the zealot
Is camped in left field like Mel Ott
In the age-old debate
About who to hate
What's in *your* heart concerning that dumb lot?

Check out this delightful American idiom: Fundamentalists are "out in left field." I love baseball metaphors because they can't be translated. And, for those unfortunates not privileged to know, Mel Ott was a great Hall of Fame left fielder for the New York Giants before they finked and moved to San Francisco!. (And, let's be honest, what the hell else rimes with "zealot"?) Of all the currents surging in the world today, the sweeping tide of fundamentalism is the most disturbing. The fundamentalist is consumed with passionate zeal, a zealot. He is not himself but literally "beside himself" in a transport of certitude, shouting his *idées fixes* to the uninspired. The uncertain.

He says to all, not, "God, our father" but "God, *my* father. And, because he's my Father, I know His wishes. And, by the way, if you don't happen to agree with me, watch your back."

That God is a jealous, wrathful, vindictive, vengeful old man sitting on a throne someplace up in the sky choosing sides in our endless "human" conflicts has got to be the single wackiest idea we've ever come up with. Much less that Mr. G is some kind of megalomaniacal *Svengali* who requires the "H" to be capitalized when we talk about Him. Or that He cares if we bow down five times a day facing east. Or is it west?

- *Balmy. And I don't mean "pleasantly warm." I mean wacko.*

Back in high school, probably 1947 or '48, when the state of Israel was struggling for its existence, I stood on the corner of Church and Flatbush Avenues holding a little cardboard cylinder with a slot on top to raise money for the United Jewish Appeal.

What did those coins I collected so long ago get me? Palestinians are fed up and enraged at not having a state of their own; Israelis are fearful and insecure behind their long wall that gives them a lot of control over who they have to rub elbows with at teatime. But what can impoverished Palestinians do considering Israel is armed to the teeth? Since 9/11, there's been much talk about so-called "asymmetrical warfare." When little David looked up at Mr. Goliath, that was an asymmetrical face-off. Obviously, Golly had the biceps, but Davey had a small secret weapon. And we know who won...asymmetrical though it was.

Are Israelis zealots behind their wall? Are Palestinians? Well, probably both are. Like Goliath, Israel has the muscle. And the Palestinians? I would think there probably exists a no more perfect way to define zealotry than strapping on a bomb and tootling off to blow yourself and as many others as you can manage to kingdom come. When people feel they have no recourse, when all else has failed...well, so long Charlie, no more Mr. Nice Guy.

- *Bananas.—*

37

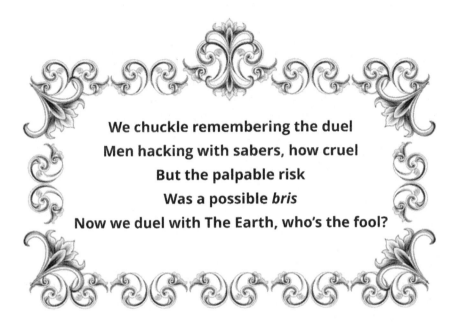

We chuckle remembering the duel
Men hacking with sabers, how cruel
But the palpable risk
Was a possible *bris*
Now we duel with The Earth, who's the fool?

When one of National Public Radio's news programs, *Morning Edition,* reported on the opening session of trials in Tanzania to prosecute those accused of fomenting the paroxysm of genocidal slaughter in Rwanda several years ago in which perhaps a million people were murdered, the first man to be brought before the tribunal was the former mayor of a Rwandan town of fifty thousand. The accused, a member of the Hutu majority, was one of the leaders of the uprising against the Tutsi minority. He had, according to testimony, always been friendly with many of those he later turned against. In that town, Hutus and Tutsis had always lived harmoniously side by side, as had Muslims and Christians in the former Yugoslavia. But when the Rwandan President died, presumably murdered, ten days later a tidal wave of violence was unleashed throughout the country, directed by Hutu leaders in the Rwandan capital.

89

Our mayor, summoned to the task by senior tribal leaders, was instantly at the helm of marauding bands of Hutus attacking and killing many of his former "friends." Before the very soul of affability, he harbored in his heart, according to testimony collected from hundreds of survivors, an inconceivably ravenous appetite for blood.

While the institution of the duel seems to us today to be a ludicrous vestige of an impossibly distant, barbarous past, it undoubtedly served a need in our nature not met by other means. When slighted or discounted, when pride is injured, ego demeaned, justice withheld, we are apt to become violently angry. We see in the drug culture, whose members live outside the law and cannot go to the police or seek redress in the courts, that disputes over shipments of drugs of poor quality, territorial infringement or a host of other transgressions *must* be resolved by violence. But we, too, except for the courts, have no socially-sanctioned recourse for venting our rage.

Desmond Morris, the anthropologist author of the 1967 bestseller, *The Naked Ape*, said it's likely we're descended from a branch of killer apes and we must either acknowledge the genes we carry and create some socially-acceptable means of dealing with this or, in this age of The Bomb, face the devastating consequences. The psychologist George Bach called collecting small, unexpressed angers "gunnysacking." One collects a sack full of slights and outrages from one's spouse or boss, saying nothing, maintaining a friendly facade but, when the sac is full, one unleashes a volcanic rage, dumping the entire sack on the head of the unsuspecting offender. Bach called this practice, "Dropping The Bomb on Luxembourg."

In Rwanda, the Hutus had stuffed numberless Tutsi injustices into their gunnysacks until a point was reached where only "The Bomb" could settle the score. The outside world, having for the most part never heard of Tutsis and Hutus, sat awed by the spectacle of the genocide. How much more sane if each outrage could have been settled by an individual confrontation, a struggle for justice and redress, an institutionalized "duel" of some sort to seek satisfaction. I mean, if it was good enough for Aaron Burr and Alexander Hamilton, how bad could it be? Of course, Hamilton was killed in the exchange. Hmmm—

The fact that we are supposed, in this "modern" age, to be more civilized means nothing when confronted with the realities of the "Naked Ape" sacked out within our seething bosoms. The power of human emotion is greater than, indeed controls, the eruptive force of the split atom. All well and good to pound the pulpit and rail against the Devil and his works. But Mr. D does not slink away in fear. Before such moralistic ravings, he merely grins and waits.

I say (only partly facetiously) let's bring back "The Duel" and (not facetiously at all) let's Stop the Bris! For those who may not know the word, a *bris* (a Jewish word meaning "covenant") is the ceremony of circumcision performed on the eighth day of a boy's life. Much is made these days, and rightly, about the loathsome practice of forcing young women to undergo clitoridectomy. Yet we accept the equally barbaric assault on the penis of a tiny, defenseless boy.—

- *Yeah, like Jehovah needed my foreskin!*

38

When the trumpet is sounding an "ism"
The fanfare we hear is a schism
Like a smelly ole fart
It drives us apart
For its call is not Love, it's Jism

That I should be required to light candles before painted plaster statues or genuflect five times a day before somebody's idea of a deity or place a shawl about my shoulders and a little hat on the crown of my head or perform any of the infinite sops to human conceptions of the magnificent sweep of universal power is humiliating and ridiculous. —Marx was right. Religion *is* the opiate of the masses. It numbs our brains and our feelings. To understand its effect on people, one need only observe its failure around the world in its many manifestations: murderous Ayatollahs, corrupt Popes and pedophile clergy, brutal, bloody wars and assassinations, innumerable women (aka witches) burned at the stake, whole peoples and their cultures exterminated in its several names. And none more destructive and genocidal than the insane reign of terror wreaked upon the world over two millennia in the name of the Prince of Peace. Christianity is a joke; Islam has failed to grasp even the simplest tenets of its founder;

Judaism...ism, ism, ism. Fundamentalism, jism, jerk off, wack off, wacko.

Why not make Earth our "ism"? Instead of mouthing meaningless platitudes in empty rituals, stop cutting and burning forests, clean the oceans, rivers, and lakes, and the air, too, And, while we're at it, leave our brother and sister animals and each other alone.

- *Want a God? Need a God? Make Love your God.—*

(Shit, if I keep talking like this, I'm gonna have to get ahold of Salmon Rushdie to see if he's got an extra bedroom.)

39

Sail in your mind to the stars
The Pleiades, Venus, or Mars
Look back on this prize
With curious eyes:
Are you trapped behind dogma like bars?

The earth and the ocean it swims in is so much vaster and more complex than anything we believe about it, that it seems to me ridiculous, when faced with its majesty, to get hung up on any kind of dogma. Today's certainty is tomorrow's curiosity. Dig your heels in about virtually anything, guaranteed you'll pretty soon get knocked on your butt by new information barreling through. For example, I'm continually astonished by the complexity of the human body. It itself is the vastness of universes. In its amazing functioning, the perfection of its myriad interrelationships, its thousands of enzymes and hormones, its trillions of cells singing their ancient chorales, it's almost impossible not to posit the existence of an omnipotent brain, some God/dess conceiving and executing this stunning creation.

And, if the universe of the body will never be fully known - and I think it will not - what can we say about its Creator (assuming for a moment there is One)? Not much. We can fall back in wonder before its invention, its creation, its beauty, but we will perhaps never fully comprehend it. Are we maybe the proverbial ant crawling on the elephant's toenail? And if we're merely an infinitesimal part of Creation, then how can we know the Creator's will?

Because, Brothers and Sisters, you and I may think we know what the Creator wants but, truth is, neither of us has the faintest idea (yeah, I know you know Chapter and Verse). The only conjecture we might make about Her is that, like any artist, She may enjoy her creation. Which, if true, would suggest She may become slightly peevish whenever we set about destroying it.—

So then, instead of screaming at one another from the ramparts of dogma, perhaps our task is simply to appreciate and protect the creation. Appreciate and protect *all* of the creation. Including ourselves and one another.

Imagine for a moment our brains are prisons. Imagine God/dess has declared a general amnesty for all prisoners. The doors of our cells slide open, the main gates swing wide, out there the sun is shining in a cobalt sky. Over the loudspeakers we hear, "Prisoners you are free! Breathe! See! Love one another!"

- *Whoa! Scary as shit.*

40

The Master said, "All life's perplexity
Will vanish accepting complexity"
When questioned what fate
Condemns us to hate
"By heaven, it's mad, but no hex," said He

We're big on identifying cults. Some group thinks there's a UFO hidden in the tail of a comet and they commit mass suicide to beam up…cult. Waco, Texas, Branch Davidians torched the place (you believe that, don't you? I mean, the FBI wouldn't do something like that, would they? Nahhh! And then lie about it?)…cult. Jim Jones proposes a toast, "Bottoms up with the Kool Aid." No problem…cult.

But what, after all, are religions except cults that made the cut? Cults that are still around. And what are political parties? Let's hear it! And all the other stupid things we belong to with their idiotic, secret handshakes and silly passwords that we don't call "cults." (Good God, presidents of the United States and other big shots belong to the Skull and Bones Society.) But what is so problematic is they all separate us: I'm a this; you're a that. And my this is better than your that!

But each of us embracing a faith, a cult, has chosen its simplistic pov to make ourselves feel especially loved by our own exclusive deity. We choose the altar on which to sacrifice who we are. No one put a spell or a charm on us. No one hexed us. The Kool Aid we're chugalugging, we chose.

Of course, we could just choose to love one another and all the things of the Earth we live on and not call it anything. It could be called the Cult with No Name. I mean, do we really have to be as stupid as our history would indicate we are? That stupid?

- *Hey, think about it. That's pretty stupid.*

When I was playing Thomas Jefferson in the musical *1776* on Broadway, I had to sit in the Continental Congress reading a book for the first fifteen minutes of the show and then fall asleep. During my run in the show, I read three books. One of them was about how human organizations go through an inevitable, predictable process from flexibility to institutionalization. In other words, somebody says, "Let's do unto others as we would have others do unto us." "Great idea," says another, "In fact, let's love our neighbors as ourselves." Others say, "Yeah, even better." Others say, "Let's get together and practice doing that." Then a power player says, "Let's make up some rules about how to do that." Somebody says, "Right, and let's codify the rules and make them compulsory." Others say, "Wow, yeah, and make everybody else follow our rules." Somebody says, "Sure, and let's kill the ignorant, less-than-human vermin who disobey our rules. Oh, yeah, and by the way, from now on let's call our rules the Will of God."

- *From love to murder. Easy.—*

There is a great Zen story recounted in the book *Zen Flesh, Zen Bones* that tells of a university student visiting a certain Zen master, Gasan.

The student asks the roshi if he has read the Christian Bible. "No, read it to me," said Gasan.
The student opened the Bible and read from St. Matthew: "And why take ye thought for raiment? Consider the lilies of the field, how they grow. They toil not, neither do they spin, and yet I say

unto you that even Solomon in all his glory was not arrayed like one of these…Take therefore no thought for the morrow, for the morrow shall take thought for the things of itself."

Gasan said: "Whoever uttered those words I consider an enlightened man."

The student continued reading: "Ask and it shall be given you, seek and ye shall find, knock and it shall be opened unto you. For everyone that asketh receiveth, and he that seeketh findeth, and to him that knocketh, it shall be opened."

Gasan remarked: "That is excellent. Whoever said that is not far from Buddhahood."

I love that one master instantly recognizes another just from the shape of his words. And notice, Gasan is not hung up on any "ism." He just recognizes and honors the truth when he hears it even across the great chasms of time and culture. They even say a master can merely look into the eyes of another person and know exactly the level of their attainment.

- *Sunglasses anyone?*

41

"Forget it," said Solem N. Dismal,
"Our prospects for life are abysmal!"
"Moreover," he raved
"Our souls are enslaved
By enshrining the nuclear gizmo"

A letter to the New York Times of September 29, 1996 from Franklyn Holzman, who was a fellow at the Davis Center for Russian Studies at Harvard University, said this:

...First, it must be noted that the United States, with a military budget in the neighborhood of $260 billion, is spending almost as much as we did at the peak of the cold war, when the Soviet Union was spending as much as we were, if not more. The cold war is over, the Soviet-East European bloc has been dismantled, and the Soviet Union itself has broken up...Is $260 billion enough to meet our current military needs? One way of approaching this issue is to ask how much other nations are spending...the United States is spending almost as much as the combined military budgets of Japan, France, Britain, Germany, Russia, China, Italy, Saudi Arabia, and South Korea...

And in an accompanying letter Michael J. Fonte concludes:

> "...A range of respected analysts, from Lawrence J. Korb, Mr. Rausch's colleague at the Brookings Institution, to William E. Colby, the former Director of Central Intelligence, have spoken clearly - we spend far more than we need to for today's threats. With the cuts in discretionary spending in the 1996 budget, we are balancing the budget on the backs of the working people of this nation, not on the back of the Pentagon."

The word "overspending" seems decorously understated when describing this frantic urge for ever more of the means to wage war. It is, in fact, a bender of mythical dimensions. When they who are intent on squandering vast portions of the public treasury pursue their profligacy despite the impact their wastefulness has on the nation and the world, we can clearly see the power of the addiction consuming them. The word "addiction" means, in one of its definitions, "surrendered" which contains as its root the word "rend" - to tear apart. We have surrendered to our addiction to war and it has torn us apart. We snort the national paycheck up our collective noses like any blowhead. And the euphoria we seem to experience in the satisfaction of our lust for ever more firepower is indeed "slavery." (Well, of course, in 2017, many years after I initially wrote this, and after more war-war-war, the all-consuming maw of the military has taken on truly epic dimensions, making the 1996 figure of $260 billion seem positively frugal by comparison. Trump is asking for 650B for 2018 for the Pentagon. And I ain't gonna Google this to see if I'm right on the money. I mean a few billion here or there, who needs to be accurate?)

While thinking over the nature of addiction, it occurred to me that the object of our addiction assumes a central place in our secret life and becomes, in a very real sense, sacred to us and is enshrined in the *sanctum sanctorum* of our hearts. The addiction becomes the focus of the life, the individual life, the life of society itself. This consuming focus must inevitably become an object of worship, meaning "something of great worth." What we worship becomes our religion. If this is true, if we have focused the innermost urgings of our cultural soul on the willingness and ability to make war, then we have become acolytes of Mars, the God of War, and war is our liturgy, the battlefield our cathedral.——

When we see on television the immense destructive capabilities of the military arsenal we have built (and massively borrowed to pay for), we fall back in veneration before such awesome power. "Veneration" of course derives from the Latin word for love or sexual desire, as in "Venus," "venereal," and even "venom" which means poison and, in its derivation, "magical potion" - presumably to be taken to enhance sexual desire. If war is our religion and weapons the objects of our veneration, then the "nuclear gizmo" has powerful sexual overtones and, like some dark ritual of Black Magic, is enshrined on the highest altar within the Holy of Holies. Kind of a shiny new Ark of Some Other Covenant.

Back when Blair was the PM of Merrie England he fell into the throes of scandal. An arms expert name of Kelley whispered to the BBC that the British government had "sexed up" its assertion that Saddam had weapons of mass destruction ready to be deployed on 45 minutes notice. In retaliation, the Blair government apparently outed Dr. Kelley causing him to commit suicide. (Or maybe they just wacked the poor guy and said it was suicide.)

- *Either way, there's that word...SEX.*

42

Astounding we have this proclivity

For unremitting cupidity

We've forgotten the Dove,

Whose message was Love,

Meant year round, not just His Nativity

Love is not possessive. Love gives. Cupidity, greed, avarice take. Love opens and expands. Cupidity clutches and contracts. Love is communal. Greed isolates. —Capitalism is not love. The bed rock, the fundament of our culture is desire, not love. —Cupid is this cute, chubby little fella with the bow and arrow who zings people to make them fall in love. News flash: the word "cupidity," i.e., greed, the desire to possess something, is the same word as Cupid. So that sweet little archer is about the desire to possess, not about Love. With apologies to Hallmark and St. Valentine.

I was in Barrymore's restaurant after a matinee with my friend George Hearn who was starring in the hit musical *Sunset Boulevard*. Before sitting down for dinner, we stood at the bar for the final three outs that gave the Yankees the Eastern Division title over the Texas Rangers, allowing them to move on to play for the Pennant. In this case, three outs took fifteen minutes and, during that time, the strangers at the bar became a joyous, kibitzing, rollicking community, momentarily bonded by love of the Yanks. Events like citywide power failures, major acts of terrorism and sporting events bring us together and allow us to live for the time being in the way we were meant to live.

Human beings are happiest living in small, cohesive groups. But the life our culture hands us, while it serves the economy (you buy a TV, I buy a TV; you buy a lawnmower, I buy a lawnmower), separates us from one another. It's called a "nuclear family" because what was once part of a community has now been split like the atom. Our lives are mostly fueled by the all-consuming desperation for money. I sometimes wonder how many people seek solace in 12 Step Programs because they get support there from people who recognize their faces, a place where the desire to possess doesn't much enter the equation. I wonder if they'd had the community in the first place, would they have felt the emptiness that drove them into the programs?

I stand at my back window and look across the backyards that separate my brownstone from the ones on the north side of West 70th Street. There's a fellow over there who lives alone with his enormous TV set. He channel surfs at night, lingering for a moment over a sex scene, sometimes on a game in progress or the news: a Bedouin who's pitched his tent where there are no others to share his fire.

- *His community? A remote control.*

43

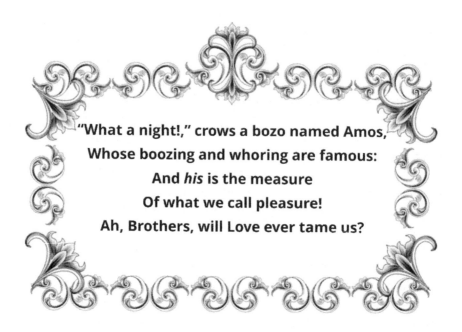

"What a night!," crows a bozo named Amos,
Whose boozing and whoring are famous:
And *his* is the measure
Of what we call pleasure!
Ah, Brothers, will Love ever tame us?

Based on my necessarily limited experience of other men, I believe most of us are in the same boat. We feel desire, lust, attraction, infatuation, but rarely love. Our penises, our eyes fall in love, rarely our hearts. The battering, the brutality, the rage, the disillusionment, the massive divorce (rate) stem from this fact. Klimt got it right. Klimt understood. In one of his most famous paintings, "The Kiss," the man inclines over the woman, his golden robe enfolds her, his lips press her cheek. Her eyes are closed. She is held in an ecstatic embrace... It is sublime for them both. The Ecstasy of Love: what, in the main, we men rarely experience but desperately seek. Furthermore, if we were truly engulfed by Love, it would be impossible to harm any creature. When the heart truly opens, it does not open solely for one particular woman or man, not solely for a dog, God, or the Church. When the heart melts, when, as they say, the heart chakra opens, we experience universal compassion. I think that is the passion some women seek and say they cannot find in us men.

104

Overwhelmingly, it is men who inhabit the world of fantasy relationships through escort services, massage parlors, prostitutes, and the zillion dollar porn industry. —Is it because these relationships offer men maximum control? One may indulge and at the same time remain invulnerable. I think of the old 4F mantra from my college days: "Find 'em, Feel 'em, Fuck 'em, and Forget 'em." I think it was psychiatrist Wilhelm Reich who observed that we are profoundly frightened of falling: falling down, falling asleep, falling in Love. All of these imply a loss of control and thus a loss of power. We men wish to feel we are captains of our ships and reminders to the contrary are not easily embraced. When Love tames us, time stops. A sense of disorientation may threaten us because all the "purposefulness" that drives us, the engine that moves the treadmill on which we spend our lives, may suddenly stop.

In Love, women and men are equal. The film crew member I hear trading tales of conquest with his pals in the hotel restaurant about the massage parlor hand job he'd purchased, within an hour of arriving in the location town and three hours after having left his wife in LA, is crowing about his power. And he *is* powerful and probably tough as nails to boot. Definitely no pink shirts for this guy. The other day, I wore a pink shirt to a friend's house for breakfast. His wife embarrassed him by telling me that he owned six pink shirts but was unable to wear them, especially to his Lions Club meetings, because of the suspect nature of the color. My dearest late friend Charles Nelson Reilly, who was the funniest man in the hemisphere, was openly gay. If I said something to him about his wearing pink he'd say, in a phony bass voice, "Jeez, man, this ain't no goddam fairy pink…this here shirt's Truck Driver Rose!".

Why are we so willing to trade Love for power, money, fame, status at the drop of a hat when that lifelong quest must inevitably harden the questing heart?

- *Ah, Bro, we've misplaced our golden robes.*

44

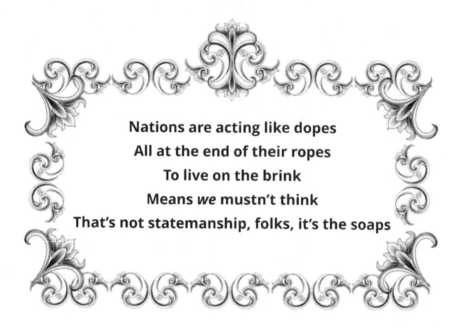

Nations are acting like dopes
All at the end of their ropes
To live on the brink
Means *we* mustn't think
That's not statemanship, folks, it's the soaps

In 1977, halfway through a Masters Degree program in Marriage, Family, and Child Counseling, I left the California Family Study Center in Burbank, California, to return to my hometown, New York, to spend two years on *As The World Turns*, a show that'd been for many years the top-rated afternoon soap opera.

It so happened the Family Study Center's daily staff meeting occurred during the hour when *World Turns* was on the air in Los Angeles and, after I joined the cast, the TV set at the school would be on and the teaching staff would routinely interrupt their meeting to watch my scenes. Chris Varnes, who had been one of my teachers at the school, reported to me later that they were flabbergasted watching the show because it exactly mirrored the therapy sessions they had with her clients' families. In other words, people in therapy with Chris and the staff were functioning in their lives as if they were in a soap opera. And there I was in New York hurling my scripts against the wall, tossing them out the window of my car on the West Side Drive and generally despising the drivel I was required to memorize day in and day out because *I thought it was profoundly false*!

In the course of my career, I've done five soap operas. In the 50s, it was something called *Our Five Daughters*. In that one, I was killed overnight in a car crash because I invited the well-known soap director, Paul Lammers, to engage himself in an unnatural act after he told me my new haircut accentuated the narrowness of my face. Then, in the 60s, it was a show called *Love Is A Many Splendored Thing* on which I played an attorney. I forget why I left, but it was after a long, painful child custody case in which I represented one of the actresses on the show. I did those two years on *As The World Turns* from '77-'79. In the early 80s, I did about a year on *General Hospital* during the famous Luke and Laura madness when it was the highest rated show in the history of afternoon television. I was part of the gang planning to destroy the world. And in the late 80s, I worked about a year and a half on the Emmy-winning *Santa Barbara* before begging the producer to allow me to get out of my contract. I just couldn't take it anymore.—

I spent enough time on these shows to have learned a very important fact about them: the difference between art and soap opera is that art attempts to lead us out of ignorance towards the light of self-awareness. Soaps are written to keep us mired in ignorance and turmoil. If Bill and Marsha's storyline calls for them to fall in love and eventually marry, it's absolutely guaranteed their romance will be long and stormy and, at the moment of consummation, The Marriage (always a big deal on soaps), the head writers are already salivating over the couple's inevitable Divorce. And we gotta believe the head writers in Washington, in every world capitol, are busy creating storylines for us, not to lead us towards understanding and self-awareness but to embroil us in war and calamity. Keep 'em stupid and scared gets top ratings on TV and gets us reelected! Very soapy shit!

Actors who work in soaps frequently find their viewers have difficulty distinguishing reality from soap opera. In a memorable series of encounters in Bloomingdale's department store, for example, no less than nine women - some of them expensively dressed in furs - asked me for my medical opinion about their health challenge because they saw me two or three times a week as the tough but brilliant Dr. Alex Keith, Chief of Surgery on *World Turns*!

- *To some of these nine "patients," I divulged the disappointing truth that I was not a real doctor...others got a "diagnosis."*

But let's face it, we're all contract players in carefully scripted storylines as sudsy as they come. Of course, the soap in question is generally called "politics" or "international relations" or the Six O'clock News. Just as the producers of a soap hate to divulge more of the forward story to the actors than they absolutely must, we dopes are also kept in the dark by the "head writers." Actors at least *know* they're acting and rarely confuse their roles with their real lives. How could they when I've had to, on *World Turns*, look the wonderful actress Marie Masters in the eye and actually say to her, "Are you telling me that the woman I love is being faithful to a man who's being unfaithful to her with you?!" Immortal words etched in my memory for eternity. While actors are aware they are actors acting, "civilians" - one of the names actors call non-actors - frequently forget they've been cast in a ludicrous but deadly long-running soap written by writers they've never met.

Every day, we tune in the radio, turn on the TV, or mosey down to the corner newsstand to pick up our "pages" (our scripts) for today's show. And we think, feel, act as if this script is real when, in fact, it's just another old storyline plunked out by writers who ran out of new plots eons ago.—

- *Hey, Pal, you probably don't realize it, but you've been cast in Search for Tomorrow.*

- *Better keep an eye on your storyline.*

45

Peacocks are pretty and proud
They're also stupid and loud
Macho means male
Not spreading your tail
Sing alone, don't squawk with the crowd

It occurred to me the other day that the most powerful emotion men experience is not the fierce loyalty to flag, the passion for a woman, love of family and children, not the lust for power. None of these. The most powerful emotion men feel is the fierce desire for acceptance by other men. This is the secret driver that causes us to act as we do.

During the millions of years preceding the home office, if I happened to be stuck out there on the veldt by myself, alone, separated from my tribe, I was pretty much nothing but a tasty snack for a hungry lion. Survival, chancy at best, was, without my tribe around me, impossible; living alone, inconceivable. My tribe *was* survival.

When we hear stories from around the world of the powerful hold tribal life still exerts on the lives of its members, we chortle patronizingly in disbelief that such a thing could still exist. But the primal identity of millions *is* the tribe. But we in the "civilized," industrialized nations who imagine we have long flown such ancient nests huddle there still, simply calling them by another name. Our tribe is a religion, a corporation, a team, a town, a club, a cocktail lounge, just like that association that claimed my loyalty and conformity long ago on that distant veldt. The concept of the "hero" proves the point. The sports hero doesn't win for himself; s/he wins for the team. The military hero saves the patrol. The corporate hero plucks the company from the jaws of bankruptcy or hostile takeover.

The power of the tribe derives from the absolute necessity of its members to belong. I've read that the ultimate punishment administered in the Amish tribe is a "shunning," whereby the individual is no longer recognized by his or her fellow tribal members, no longer looked at or spoken to. To be shunned is to "disappear" from the tribe.— Excommunication is the Catholic Church's ultimate punishment. In the military the non-conforming soldier is court-martialed and cast out or "busted" if found guilty of breaking the tribe's rules. The fate of the whistleblower who squeals on his tribe is well known. And, at an English soccer match, even death may befall the unlucky fan cheering for the wrong tribe.

And women? Some have, I believe, a mandate superseding that of men. Men seek to preserve their status in the tribe (don't rock the boat, don't be a loose cannon, be a team player, go along to get along); while women seek to preserve life itself. Men feel the tribe is fundamental. Women know the child is. This is the reason women are frequently more fiercely outspoken and independent on peace and environmental issues than men holding similar views. The Maternal Order transcends the Fraternal Order.

Perhaps peacocks aspiring to independence of thought *and action* will consider Kipling's famous advice in

IF

If you can keep your head when all about you
Are losing theirs and blaming it on you;
If you can trust yourself when all men doubt you,
But make allowance for their doubting too;
If you can wait and not be tired by waiting,
Or, being lied about, don't deal in lies,
Or, being hated, don't give way to hating,
And yet don't look too good, nor talk too wise;

If you can dream – and not make dreams your master;
If you can think – and not make thoughts your aim;
If you can meet with triumph and disaster
And treat those two imposters just the same;
If you can bear to hear the truth you've spoken
Twisted by knaves to make a trap for fools,
Or watch the things you gave your life to broken
And stoop and build 'em up with worn out tools;

If you can make one heap of all your winnings
And risk it on one turn of pitch-and-toss,
And lose, and start again at your beginnings
And never breathe a word about your loss;
If you can force your heart and nerve and sinew
To serve your turn long after they are gone,
And so hold on when there is nothing in you
Except the Will which says to them: Hold on";

If you can talk with crowds and keep your virtue,
Or walk with kings – nor lose the common touch;
If neither foes nor losing friends can hurt you;
If all men count with you, but none too much;
If you can fill the unforgiving minute
With sixty seconds' worth of distance run –
Yours is the Earth and everything that's in it,
And – which is more – you'll be a Man my son!

- *Corny, huh?*

111

46

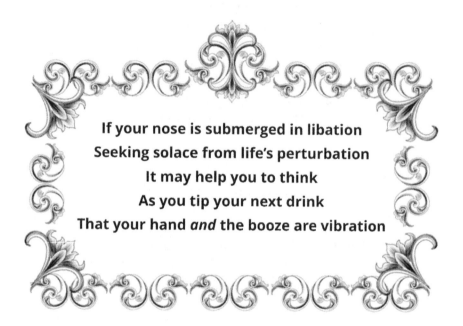

If your nose is submerged in libation
Seeking solace from life's perturbation
It may help you to think
As you tip your next drink
That your hand *and* the booze are vibration

Late in October of '96, the New York Yankees won the World Series in six games, coming back from a two-game deficit to win three straight in Atlanta and the wrap-up game in "The House That Ruth Built" against the defending world champion Atlanta Braves. The Yanks poured onto the field afterwards, wept with joy and relief and fell on top of one another in a great mound of writhing bodies. The Braves and their owner, Ted Turner and his then wife, movie star Jane Fonda, left the field of battle quietly, dejected. Since I was rooting for the Yanks and they were, after their pileup on the field, now consuming rather significant quantities of champagne in the locker room, I felt justified in creating a small celebration of my own and, therefore, turned my attentions to a dusty bottle of *Moet et Chandon* for me and my wife. She, unfortunately, does not drink, forcing me to care for the entire magnum myself. At bedtime, alert to the fact I had possibly committed a grave error, I swallowed two aspirin.

And my joy? My need for celebration? Certainly not from any connection I have with the Yankees. I'm a Brooklynite. A Dodger fan. So why the elation? The shameful answer is that, because of a deep aversion to Jane Fonda, I did not so much want the Yankees to win as I wanted the Braves to lose. And why the aversion to Fonda? — Because once I read for a part on a sitcom she was producing and, instead of allowing me to read the scene I had been sent and had prepared, they gave me a new scene *at the reading*. Stupid and disrespectful (besides being infuriating). And instead of telling the truth about how I felt about this bad business and walking out, I did what I usually did: I walked in, smiled and read anyway...badly. And when I entered the room, Fonda had the temerity to say, not, "Sorry we changed the scene," but, "Nice jacket!" I betrayed myself and, instead of learning, I took the easier course of despising Miss Fonda ever since.—

- *Popularly known as Bad Vibes!*

For me, life is a carom shot. I'm bouncing from one cushion to the next and, Godlike, some omnipotent Minnesota Fats is providing the English. The team has won...joy. The team has lost...devastation. I got the job I lost the job. Up down. Elation dejection. The sun is out rain is falling. The play runs the play closes. She loves me she hates me. I'm healthy I'm sick. YoYo time. The Prince of Polarities.

Just around the time of the Yankee win, Timothy Leary's cremated remains, aboard a Pegasus rocket strapped to an L-1011, took off from Vandenburg Air Force Base bound for Spain, there to be launched into space by a company called Celestis. Along with Leary on this first "Founder's Flight" were the remains of 23 others, including Gene Roddenberry, the creator of *Star Trek*, the famous space scientist Kraft Erike, Gerard O'Neill, the head of the Space Science Institute, Todd Hawley, the co-founder of International Space University, and other distinguished souls.

Leary's message, engraved on the tiny vial of his ashes, reads: "PEACE LOVE LIGHT YOUMEONE"—

- *Not bad, huh?*

Boy, if I could only get that, I could say, as I do now, "Hey, Jane, sorry I harbored those nasty vibes all these years."

- *And for nothing.*

47

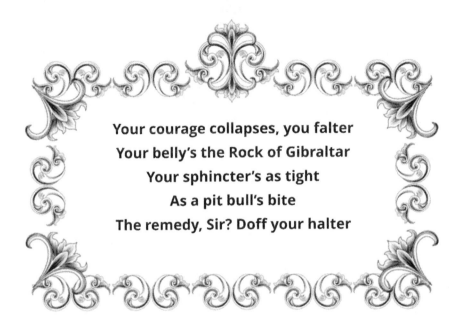

Your courage collapses, you falter
Your belly's the Rock of Gibraltar
Your sphincter's as tight
As a pit bull's bite
The remedy, Sir? Doff your halter

A halter is a rope around the head to lead or restrain a horse. It is also a hangman's noose. (Don't believe "hangman's noose"? —Check it out in the dictionary.) The horse cannot remove the halter. The condemned man, his hands bound, cannot remove the noose. However, *we can reach up and throw off the restraint*. But for the most part we don't. We remain on the scaffold, blindfolded, waiting for the trapdoor. Afraid.

But, in reality, the audience has departed, the hangman has long since returned to hearth and home. We wait alone in the empty courtyard, daylight failing, a night fog barreling in from the sea, barely breathing, frightened, beside ourselves.

Relax the belly. Lower the shoulders. Spread the feet into the ground. Breathe.

- *Listen. —Listen. —It's quiet.—*

Your hands are not tied.

Reach up, remove the halter, the blindfold…

- *Walk away.*

- *You're free.*

48

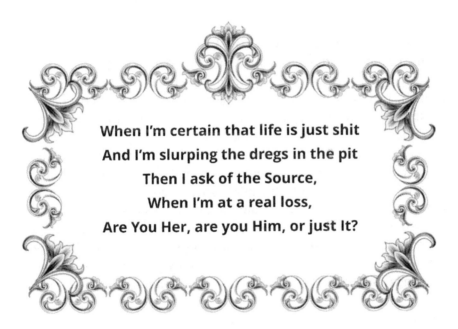

When I'm certain that life is just shit
And I'm slurping the dregs in the pit
Then I ask of the Source,
When I'm at a real loss,
Are You Her, are you Him, or just It?

As I've suggested, men get weirdly bent out of shape over the issue of gender. When the Russians wisely decided to finally pull the plug in Afghanistan after a long, losing struggle, Moslem fundamentalists swept into the capital, Kabul. As we know, these boys were the Taliban who immediately forbade women to work or even leave their homes unless cocooned in the now familiar ridiculous blue tent accompanied by a male relative. Female doctors and nurses, government employees, shopkeepers, teachers, etc., were henceforth to be immured in their homes. Great move by the Taliban for now, along with the depredations of perpetual war to which the nation had been subjected, there would be a work force and cultural crisis of staggering proportions.—

As the Moslems were bearing down on Kabul and it was becoming increasingly evident the Russians would have to withdraw, I happened to hear a young, Afghan woman interviewed about how she felt about this development. I think she was a government employee. —She said she had been able for so long to dress in modern clothing that, realizing she would immediately be forced to disappear inside the blue tent, she was resolved to commit suicide. Well, tough. Woman's an obvious whiner.

Read Riane Eisler's powerful book *The Chalice and the Blade*: "And for the crime of believing in a faith that encourages equality between women and men, and for organizing women, in 1983 ten Baha'i women, including Iran's first woman physicist, a concert pianist, a nurse, and three teen-age college students were killed at a public execution." —Well, who did those three bitches think they were anyway!! And the insanity of marriage in India? The wife's family is expected to cough up a huge dowry for the groom's parents. Later, if the groom wishes to start a business, wife's dad coughs up again. One Indian women's rights advocate called the system "extortion" and pointed out that between seven and 15 thousand women are murdered every year by the husband or the husband's family for not kicking in the bucks. They even have a Mother-in-Law Jail, exclusively for the husbands' mothers who've murdered their daughters-in-law!

Of course, lest we think such attitudes towards women are only exhibited by The Others, it goes without saying one need only read any newspaper on a regular basis to discover megatons of barely concealed bigotry and sexism within our own "Christian" bastions of enlightenment. For example, misogynists froth at the mouth to keep women out of Virginia Military Institute, The Citadel. These patriots also diligently strive to keep the ladies from flying combat missions in the Air Force while, if they do become Top Guns, it's apparently Ok for our red-blooded American boys to rape and fondle them *ad libitum* with even the occasional general looking on. And just recently, not to be outdone by the Air Force, we learn virile young wannabes at West Point have performed the same service for female Plebes in that sacred institution. And, in the first two decades of the 20th Century, the problem of rape in the various branches of the military is so great that a struggle in Washington has developed about how to deal with these execrable acts.

When a woman aspires to tread these hallowed paths, her failure to cut the mustard for whatever reason is widely reported with much scoffing and chest thumping among the Neanderthals rooting for her failure. She couldn't cut the obstacle course, she's overweight, she crashed her plane, she wept at the board meeting, empathized with the competition for God's sake! They can't play chess, can't think logically, don't have the killer instinct. And if they do? Horrendous bitches! Dykes doncha know? It hasn't changed much since I was in college and some young stud at Delt Psi would crow, to the enormous cheers of the assembled "brothers," "Keep 'em Fat, Fucked, bareFoot and Fertile," a sensitive variant of the more classic previously mentioned 4Fs.

(For those too young to remember: 4F during World War Two meant that one was physically unable to serve in the military.)

Speaking of fertile, a Nigerian court just freed a young mother who gave birth nine months after she was no longer living with her husband that quickly saddled her with an automatic charge of adultery or, to cite the technical name of this monumental transgression: Fucking Without Permission. The punishment for this high crime in Nigeria is being buried in a hole with only your head sticking out and then being stoned to death. I'm uncertain whether they have an Official Stoner or Stoners in Nigeria or whether just anyone can show up and take a turn. Kind of like a live Hit The Bottle carnival attraction. "Get your stones right here! Five stones for a dollar! See the little lady! Hit the little lady! Win a prize!" It would be nice to know the Nigerian court overturned this barbaric judgment for some enlightened reason. Perish the thought. It was overturned because, when the knowledge of the stoning became an international *cause celebre*, the outcry it provoked shamed the Nigerian government into caving to world opinion.

The fact is men spend a lot of time worrying about all this petty stuff because we can't deal with the Big One, which is so big it isn't even discussed. The really Big One is what is the gender of God/dess? It wouldn't be so bad if the Deity turned out to be merely a Supreme Intelligence, an It (again, capitalizing here just to be safe). —Men could maybe deal with That. Iffy but possible. But if She were of the female persuasion, that would be tough to swallow. The CEO of the whole universe, maybe the actual Creator of the entire Creation is a Woman? Cue the laugh track.

119

Because, let's face It, that would mean someone had goofed and really there shouldn't be a Glass Ceiling. Nasty, because if God is a woman, men might then have to accept that women are as good, as smart, as powerful as they are. Or, since the Great Goddess Herself was a Woman, could it mean (big drum roll here) women are even better, smarter, wiser than men? Better than men in every way!

- *Talk about bad news. —Hey, Joey, take a nice deep breath now.*

PS: I meant it when I said read *The Chalice and the Blade*. It is a vitally important work examining the insane worldwide power of the "Dominator Model" in relations between the sexes. I suppose it goes without saying that, unless we become aware of the overarching reach of male domination and find our way to an alternative Cooperative Model, events on the planet are going to continue unfolding in a decidedly thorny direction.

PPS: But things are lookin' up: it's October, 2016 and Trump is in the building and the Donald's gonna make it all ok!

- *Harvey Weinstein? Oh, shit*

49

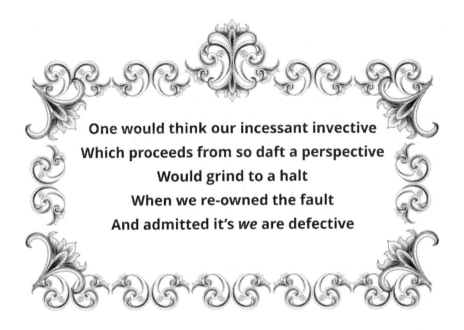

One would think our incessant invective
Which proceeds from so daft a perspective
Would grind to a halt
When we re-owned the fault
And admitted it's *we* are defective

Kikes, Polocks, Micks, N-words, Jigaboos, A-rabs, Towelheads, Jews, Immigrants, Foreigners, Commies, Liberals, Radicals, Anarchists, Right-wingers, Spics, Greaseballs, Wetbacks, Hebes, Rednecks, Southerners, Northerners, Beatniks, Yuppies, Weirdos, Chinks, Japs, Slopes, Slanteyes, Christkillers, Extremists, Eggheads, Fatties, Liberals, Wops, Porkers…hey, jump in...

- *Vital for superior us is to have inferior them to peer down on.*

And, as far as telling the truth is concerned and admitting who and what we are, I'm watching *60 Minutes* one night a while back when Ed Bradley's doing a story on child prostitution in South East Asia: Cambodia, Thailand, those parts. One of the male producers of the show books a popular sex tour through a company providing information, guidebooks (*How To Avoid The Thai Police*), tour guides, and the entire travel/lodging package to men who want to have intercourse with ten year olds. *60 Minutes* films the tour with a hidden camera and does what they do best - they get the guy who owns the company on camera, get him to lie, and then show him the film they have and watch him squirm.

Except this guy doesn't squirm. He's fine with what he does. He won't admit he's setting up tours for American men who want to have sex with little girls from impoverished families who've sold their daughters into sexual slavery for 200 bucks to support Dad's opium or booze habit. Guy looks at Bradley like they're talking about growing roses. Won't admit the truth. Guy's a pimp. Everybody watching knows he's a pimp. Bradley calls him a pimp. Guy won't admit he's a pimp.—

Calling somebody the "n" word or a kike, easy. Sure, you already know you're hateful. But admitting to yourself you're a sick, child-abusing loser,

- *yeah, that's the real toughie!*

122

50

Some love it and say, "Never ban it!"

Others fear it and pray we can can it

And me? I'm with the latter

For he's mad as a hatter

Who thinks we can live *sans* a planet

The March 4th, 1996 issue of TIME magazine featured a cover story: Blowing The Whistle On Nuclear Safety. How A Shutdown At A Power Plant Exposed The Federal Government's Failure To Enforce Its Own Rules and showed a picture of an embattled whistleblower, George Galatis, against the Millstone Unit 1 nuclear power plant in Waterford, Connecticut.—

The story tells of two gutsy nuclear engineers who put their careers on the line by first attempting to get the company they work for to come into compliance with the safety regulations of the Nuclear Regulatory Commission (NRC) and then, failing that, prodding and threatening the NRC itself to enforce its own regulations.

"Every 18 months the reactor is shut down so the fuel rods that make up its core can be replaced; the old rods, radioactive and 250°F hot, are moved into a 40-ft.-deep body of water called the spent-fuel pool, where they are placed in racks alongside thousands of other, older rods. Because the Federal Government has never created a storage site for high-level radioactive waste, fuel pools in nuclear plants across the country have become de facto nuclear dumps - with many filled nearly to capacity. The pools weren't designed for this purpose, and risk is involved: the rods must be submerged at all times. A cooling system must dissipate the intense heat they give off. If the system failed, the pool could boil, turning the plant into a lethal sauna filled with clouds of radioactive steam. And if earthquake, human error or mechanical failure drained the pool, the result could be catastrophic: a meltdown of multiple cores taking place outside the reactor containment, releasing massive amounts of radiation and rendering hundreds of square miles uninhabitable."

The story tells tales of the kind of collusion the public has come to expect between government agencies and the industries they are supposed to oversee. Where one hopes to find ethics, one finds greed; where one looks for common sense, one finds self-interest. Galatis discovers that these spent fuel rods are warehoused around the country because no state will permit the construction of a permanent storage facility for the thousands of tons of nuclear waste resulting from our atomic bomb production and power generation from the 110 nuclear plants around the U.S. People are terrified of nuclear waste and want it stored anyplace else.

The bureaucrats who are supposed to be overseeing this stalemate are saying to themselves, like everyone else in government service including members of Congress, "Well, gee, after I retire, if the revolving door can revolve me into a better-paying, more-prestigious job in the very industry I'm supposed to be regulating, I just might consider turning a blind eye to those infractions which, if pointed out, will inconvenience the company I one day aspire to work for."—

Andre Gide, the great French novelist and playwright, said he wished he could write plays for marionettes because those annoying, live actors always came along and plopped their own interpretation on his words. This is what will and must happen when self-interest collides with regulation. It is the element we fail to address with all our rules and legislation: they are administered by actors who will change the play to suit their own interests. An example from another field is instructive in this regard. Mike Wallace once reported, again on *60 Minutes,* that not-for-profit hospitals are being sold by their boards of directors to large hospital chains for enormous profits for, guess who: members of the boards! And these are transactions that are in direct conflict with the interests of the communities the hospitals serve. One sleazy deal he reported on was pulled off by an order of nuns! Nobody talks. And we're shocked once again at the cupidity, the sheer gall, the consuming greed of our fellow humans. But sorry fellow suckers that *is* the way it works. As my friend Alan used to say, when apprised of some governmental or corporate chicanery, "So what's new?"—

The Nuclear Game gives The Killer Ape, us, the opportunity to kill on an unprecedented scale. And this opportunity is afforded us not only by the possibility of nuclear war perennially hovering over all our heads but by *all* nuclear activity, the executioner's axe forever raised. Wherever there is a nuclear facility of any kind anywhere in the world there are, on one side, human beings administering and running it and, on the other, human beings who are supposedly regulating it. The reason this setup so often fails is that the slap on the back, the wink, the handshake are more powerful than any regulation. The wink (sometimes known as "turning a blind eye") must somehow be factored into human transactions.

- *And, Bozo, this ain't just Pandora's Box! This is her whole trunk.*

- *And now it's 2019. Anybody remember Fukushima Daiichi?*

51

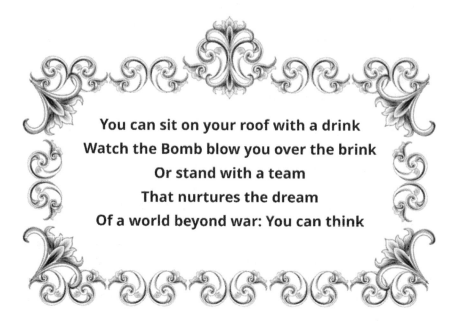

You can sit on your roof with a drink
Watch the Bomb blow you over the brink
Or stand with a team
That nurtures the dream
Of a world beyond war: You can think

I owned a book once called *Scenes de la Vie de Boheme* (*Scenes from The Bohemian Life*). The author, Henri Murger, was a poet and novelist who serialized his experiences of the left bank Bohemian life of mid-19th Century Paris in a series of separate episodes. (The great Giacomo Puccini opera, *La Boehme,* is based on Murger's sketches.) As I recall, there's a scene in the book in which the painter Marcel tips his concierge to bring him coffee every morning and keep him informed when the government changes. When I read this as a young man, I was very taken with Marcel's contemptuous attitude towards politics. I thought that since, from any objective point of view, the behavior of our politicians would be considered normal in a mental institution for the criminally insane, it was proper for me to remain aloof from the petty, corrupt games played in Washington. I fashioned a pose of sneering mockery for myself that I carried around for decades. I was an artist and what went on in the loony bin of government was beneath me.

Then one day, already in my early 50s, when the possibility of nuclear war between the Soviet Union and the United States seemed to loom ever larger, I saw an image of myself sitting in a deck chair on the roof of my garage guzzling a rum and Coke while watching the mushroom cloud in the distance mount the sky and, just before the noxious blast melted me, thinking, "Gee, maybe I really shoulda done something!"

- *Maybe Marcel was wrong.*

It was at that point I joined an organization called *Beyond War* which was dedicated, among other things, to educating people about the realities of nuclear conflict. What was problematical for me was, when I stopped tipping the concierge, when I emerged from my mental garret in other words and took a look around, what I saw was so horrendous, so unbelievable in the most literal sense of the word, that I could not bear how I felt looking at it. To think at all about the precarious situation of our world in the clutches of the rapacious, greedy, mindless thugs that control it can be a tad unsettling. Indeed, awareness of the peril, rather than summoning us to action, may cause us to become paralyzed when faced with the facts. On the other hand, of course, there can be no action or change without awakening to the peril.—

Some who can still think cannot perceive the peril because they cannot *feel* what they think. Their souls are dead. I think of Nikolai Gogol's satirical novel *Dead Souls*. I understand now, these many years after reading it, what Gogol was talking about. People move, they act, they make fortunes perhaps. They are seemingly alive. But they are dead souls, zombies. "Rich and famous" they may be, but they are already dead: vampires draining a dying planet. Sacrificing even their own children. These are the living dead, serene because their souls are fled. If I am right, there are an awful lot of dead souls in our midst. And I say "our" because, if you're still with me, you're not dead. Living souls can't strip forests, shoot elephants, prostitute, even rape children, wreak havoc on whole populations of innocent people. Live souls can't exploit the planet or its creatures.—

The American dentist who recently paid fifty thousand bucks to go to Zimbabwe to murder a beautiful lion named Cecil is, by definition, a

127

dead soul. And why? Because he planned to mount that gorgeous animal's head on his wall to show his pals how big his dick is. And let's not forget the photo of President Trump's son celebrating his murder of an elephant.

- *And I know it's hard to believe but this shit is called "sport."*

Many so-called conservatives see virtually all mandates to protect the environment as depredations by government on our freedoms and the great institution of private property. (I say "so-called conservatives" because it seems only logical to me that conservatives ought to be interested in conserving.) Right-wing theorists tend to believe reports of the destruction of the ozone layer, vanishing forests and the species that inhabit them, global warming, melting glaciers, etc. are either anti-Big Business or bogeyman stories to frighten us into the arms of an authoritarian government.

Don't believe it? Hey, check out President DT's beliefs about global warming! Always remembering DTs are the initials of Delirium Tremens, i.e., when you get off the booze you collapse rapidly into confusion and shake like hell.

A few weeks ago (October, 2015) one of our own professional schmucks…Rep. Steve King, an Iowa republican, at an event sponsored by the climate change-denying Koch-funded Americans for Prosperity told the audience that climate change, "…is not proven, it's not science. It's more of a religion than a science." That, despite the fact that 97 percent of scientists agree that climate change is devastatingly real.

Of course, there are still many who don't accept the reality of the Holocaust either: witness the doofus who was lately president of Iran. I sometimes imagine these people won't believe in global warming till they're paddling their elegant canoes down Broadway for the opening of the Met season at Lincoln Center.

- *So…fuck 'em.*

If you think and, thinking, perceive and *feel* Mother Earth's peril but your fear trumps action, do not despair. Begin slowly. Join something where there are others huddled together for warmth and strength. Send money to people who are trying to repair some corner of the world. For example, FACT in Chicago educates consumers and farmers about the horrors of factory farming.—

The Dolphin Project, whose director Ric O'Barry (the original dolphin trainer on the famed *Flipper* series) is spending his life retraining imprisoned dolphins to return to the wild, is worthy of your best. See Ric's documentary, *The Cove*. If that doesn't move you to action to protect these amazing creatures then, dear Brothers and Sisters, check your pulse.

Give your bucks to People for the Ethical Treatment of Animals (PETA) and all animal sanctuaries. The Sierra Club. The Institute for Security and Cooperation in Outer Space (ISCOS) has struggled valiantly to stop the insane weaponization of space.

There are a million heroes out there shouting to us. They need money. 25 bucks is OK, but you can probably afford a hundred or a thousand. Your nest egg won't be worth a helluvalot if there ain't no more nests.

Then, when you feel a part of something positive that's happening, offer your services in some way. Climb outside the box and create something new, something innovative. Get to work in a garden; find the people and communities who are working to produce free energy and pure water. Visit and actually talk with decision makers or, better yet, become one. Write letters. The Dead Souls pay attention to letters because their eyes are fixed on the bottom line: reelection, wealth. If enough people write on an issue they sometimes back down since most of them are mechanical people who, beyond reelection and money, have no real positions of their own. Or, perhaps more accurately, they *had* a position, but it's been auctioned to the highest bidder.

Hey, don't yell at me. It was no less than the great American humorist Will Rogers who said, "America has the best politicians money can buy." And he said that in 1924!

- *Be a spiritual 911: give soul-to-soul resuscitation.*

And check out a number of recent TV shows. Got lotsa zombies slurping blood in *The Walking Dead*. I mean, what's the deal with all the vampire movies and TV shows? Zombies and Vampires?

- *Hey, we talkin' reality TV?*

52

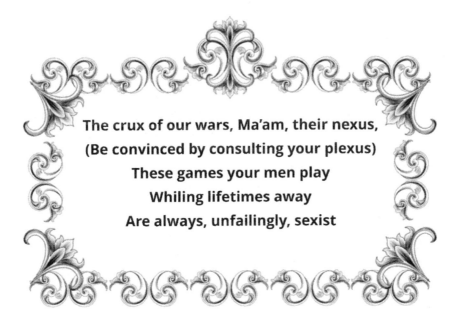

The crux of our wars, Ma'am, their nexus,
(Be convinced by consulting your plexus)
These games your men play
Whiling lifetimes away
Are always, unfailingly, sexist

- *Since women create life and war destroys it, war can be seen as the ultimate sexist enterprise.*

After the genocidal conflict in Rwanda, a half million Rwandan refugees fled from camps in Zaire where they had sought refuge. Yeah, some refuge. Now Zaire is the so-called Democratic Republic of Congo where levels of rape and murder are reportedly at catastrophic levels. The refugees fled to escape a war between the army of Zaire and Zairian rebels that was moving towards them. The U.N. High Commissioner for Refugees said at the time that this movement of people from the camps constituted one of the greatest potential human disasters in history. In history! Did the leaders of the two armies care that such a tragedy was unfolding before their very eyes? Did Mbutu, the former American-supported, sybaritic dictator of Zaire, who lived in luxury in the south of France, care? Yeah, right.

And today, 2017, with millions fleeing the insane conflicts in the Middle East, dying to reach Greece, then Germany, trudging with their families and miniscule possessions along European railroad tracks, do so-called decision makers care? Really care? Care? Stupid question. Of course they care. They want to keep them out.

The purpose of war is supposed to lie in the attainment of some palpable objective. —This aggression is repelled, that border protected, this threatening government is destroyed, that empire is preserved and so on. But suppose these "objectives" are just cover stories. Suppose the purpose of war is the consequence of war itself, not the cover story. In other words, suppose the real purpose of war is its result...destruction and death, domination and control and, oh yeah, moneymoneymoney. There's a great George Carlin line that goes something like, Have you ever noticed how everyone driving slower than you are is an asshole and everyone driving faster is a maniac?

- *"Man One:*
- *'Who the fuck are you to sit in my chair?'*

- *Man Two:*
- *'Who the fuck knew it was your chair?'*

- *Man One:*
- *'Stand up motherfucker, I'm gonna kick the shit outta you.'*

- *Man Two:*
- *'You just say I fucked my mother? I'm gonna kill you, you sonofabitch.'*

- *Man One:*
- *'Did you just call my mother a bitch, you scumbag? You're a dead man'."*

The above confrontation is an almost word for word exchange I once overheard in Greenwich Village between two young men of Italian extraction who were apparently rehearsing for their Mafia auditions. It preceded a brutal street fight that took place below my window.

War is a street fight between men so profoundly sick they ache to create outside themselves the havoc they feel within. The assassination of the Archduke Ferdinand, the invasion of Kuwait, communism in Vietnam, my god can beat up your god: these are merely cover stories for carnage.—

That men feel rage towards women is only too well documented. Mayhem fills our airwaves and the pages of our journals with infinite tales of rape and beatings and murder. War is simply spousal and child abuse on an operatic scale, wife beating gone international. In the war in Bosnia, there was actually a government-sanctioned, organized policy of rape of Muslim women by the "Christian" Slavs. When this policy was revealed to the world by the testimony of its victims, I was appalled and fascinated. What kind of purpose could be served by such an outrage? What pleasure can be had raping women or having sex with a child sex slave? The answer is easy: the purpose is destruction. The pleasure, destruction. The payoff? Power, baby, power! War has always included rape and pillage, but in the Bosnian disaster it may be that sex was used for the first time as a formal instrument of war: the penis a weapon as savage as a bullet or a missile. In fact, less abstract than the latter: a bayonet of flesh!

Until the Bosnian conflict, one could have written off rape, as I believe has always been done, as a byproduct of the "real" war—

- The-boys-are-uptight-and-horny-and-away-from-home-so-naturally-they'll-impale-a-few-babies-and-rape-their-moms, the "boys will be boys" scenario. Until Bosnia, when one can legitimately ask if the real purpose of war, the real war, is not destruction itself, destruction of creation?

And why should men harbor such rage towards women? Is it that we were cast out of the original Eden, the womb, violently, in fear, with pain, forceps, light, suffocation, struggle, another Eden, the breast, warm soft engulfing paradisiacal, another casting out, weaning too early, ("primitive" people kept the child at the breast for years), deprivation, rage, rage, another casting out, a sibling comes, make do, swallow it, smile, good boy, but harbor it and wait? Or is it simply that when the drums are beating and the torches flicker, when the oily faces around the fire are chanting "War!" the heart races, boils, and the old lust surges urging us to destroy the Creator and Her creation. I once was watching TV with my wife. She was sick in bed. We were watching a talk show that I think was called *The Randy Show*. There were guests on the show who had filmed Unidentified Flying Objects. One was an ordinary citizen, one a news photographer, and one a computer expert who analyzes and authenticates such footage. They also showed a NASA film of UFOs that was shot on a shuttle mission. The computer expert's analysis of the piece of film taken by the ordinary citizen was that it was authentic and showed a very large round object between a quarter and a half mile in diameter at approximately 75,000 feet moving at speeds, depending on the estimated distance from the camera, which were in the vicinity of Mach 10, a very great speed.—

After viewing the various pieces of film and deciding that extraterrestrial spaceships are real and are here, the discussion turned to why our visitors have not made themselves known to us in a more public, more formal way; why have our visitors been so reticent to make themselves known? "Reticent?" I thought, "Nah, they're not reticent, we terrify them."

- *I mean, if you'd been hovering over this planet for ten thousand years checking out what goes on here, would you want to land on the White House lawn?*

- *Suicide.*

53

O, Goddess, Jehovah not Satan
Saps joy from our lives, aggravatin'
Our senseless rejection
Of Love and affection:
God's soldiers may kill but no matin'

I heard someone on the radio one day who'd recently seen movies and TV in Europe say that, in the U.S., it's all violence and death, in Europe it's nudity and sex. Ya know, sex, that yummy stuff from Satan that Christians love to get all frothy about. Let's face it, the God of the Christian Bible is an enraged, truculent, unpredictable, judgmental, joyless, humorless, punishing old misanthrope. Then, probably feeling bad He'd been so nasty all those millennia, He sent his Son Jesus as His emissary to teach us about Love. Still not strong on humor, but nevertheless a serious improvement over His Old Man. Unfortunately, the religion established in His name is crackers. The Inquisition (five million women rounded up and burned), the Crusades, genocide, the great priestly Shtupping of the Choir Boys: August, 2018, 300 more priests outed by the church! I mean, compared to Jehovah and Christianity, I'll take Satan any day of the week.

There's a book by Josephine Tey, the well-known English mystery writer, called *The Daughter of Time*. The title is from the saying, "Truth is the daughter of time." It's a book in which Tey, using her powers of detection, investigates the origins of the reputation of King Richard the Third. (By the way, did you pick up on the fact that they recently discovered his bones under a church parking lot. Yeah, King Dick's bones!) As the title character in Shakespeare's play, we know him to be an evil, Machiavellian, ruthless hunchback. According to Tey, however, the play itself is based on earlier writings depicting Richard as a bad apple. And her investigation of these earlier sources leads her to the conclusion that Richard's reputation was destroyed after his death by those with a vested interest in trashing him. And, since his enemies were in power and Richard was dead, there wasn't a helluvalot he could do to defend himself. Thus, when Shakespeare came along and wrote his great play based on what Richard's detractors had said about him, the poor king's reputation was sealed.

I have a feeling the boys who wrote the Bible laid the same kind of rap on Satan who was, you may remember, an angel and the beloved of God and who, when he didn't play the game the way the Old Man wanted, got booted out of heaven. It always seemed to me God was peeved with Satan because he was beautiful and free and having too much fun. Pleasure to this day not being a strong point with Christians like the late Jerry Falwell and the boys. Really. If you were in solitary confinement for a decade with nothing but your imagination for company, could you, by any stretch of your creative faculties imagine Jerry Falwell with a member of the opposite sex?

- *See it:*

- The lights are low, only a single candle flickers, you're feeling that deep slow burn down there, you lie back waiting, waiting, the blood is hot, you're ready, the air warm and vibrant, everything is still save the tom-tom of your heart when, finally, out of the bathroom he emerges, moving slowly towards the bed, he looks teasingly into your eyes with that smoldering sensuality while playfully opening his silk robe. Then, with the slightest shrug of his powerful shoulders, the crimson silk drops to the floor.

136

- "Oh, Jerry, Jerry," you cry, "Jerry Falwell, take me!"

Nudity, sex, mambo, martinis, pornography, masturbation, ease, joy, fun, pleasure, homosexuality, love, sodomy, whoopee!

- *Answer quick: God or Satan?*

54

Some say it's our fate: Armageddon

That we might as well meet it full head on

But I say such pains

We'll avoid with our brains

If our target is peace and we're dead on

When Reagan was president, it came out that he and a bunch of his boys, good Christian gentlemen, Born Agains, fundamentalists, the Bible-as-literal-truth posse weren't really worried about the Big Gunfight at the A Bomb Corral because it's supposed to happen, it's in the Bible and we're obviously in the Last Days and so we might as well march cheerily forward arm in arm to embrace our fate. If you read the Christian literature - *The Late Great Planet Earth* and that stuff - you will see it's true: there are an awful lot of people out there who think it's a wrap, the question not *if* but *when*. I, of course, use the word "wrap" as it's yelled on a film set when the day's filming is over…hmmm, that's pretty much the same thing only instead of the day's wrap, it's the forever wrap.—

To realize that a person in a position of great power may be acting on the supposition that, since it's gonna happen anyway, we may as well get it over with sooner rather than later, is a bit like waking up from a nap in the back seat of the Buick only to realize you're hurtling down the 101 with your bipolar doped-up five year old at the wheel and realizing you forgot to stir his Ritalin in the OJ this morning. Of course, if you feel a certain responsibility to make what it says in Revelations come true, feel obliged to prove the Rapture is nigh, you're gonna *need* tens of thousands of bombs to pull it off. It's a big job. But then, fulfilling those dippy Prophesies has never been easy. This hypothesis may finally address the question of why we continued (and continue) to manufacture and stockpile thousands of Mr. Universe-sized nuclear muscles to "contain" the USSR, now Russia, when really 20 would have been just peachy.

- *Well, I'll be damned! It wasn't just the Russkies we were after, it was the Planet. We needed 30,000 bombs!*

The thing that always bothers me is, there's a West Point to train elite officers and a slew of ROTC programs to train regular officers for the army, an air school to train Airpeople, an Annapolis to train Seapeople, a War College to study war, infinite numbers of military schools to turn young kids into the right kinds of robots, Departments and Ministries of Defense, but (is it possible?) there's only one measly Peace University on the planet and that's in Costa Rica?

Am I wrong, or does that not seem somewhat overbalanced in the direction of check out? It's like that famous observation that the Greeks have thirty words for blue while the Eskimos have only one, but the Eskimos have thirty words for snow and the Greeks a measly one. We've got thirty ways to prepare for and wage war. But to prepare for and wage peace...?

When I originally wrote those last sentences, I thought the University for Peace in Costa Rica was it. Reworking this now, I figured it might be a good idea to jump on the web and see if that's true. It's not. UPeace is still there for sure. But I found a website that lists 200 schools in the U.S. and around the world offering studies in Peace and Conflict Resolution and I assume there are others that may have slipped through the cracks. In addition, former Ohio Congressman Dennis Kucinich, who was one of nine candidates seeking the Democratic nomination for president in '04 and '08, did introduce a bill to establish a U.S. cabinet level Department of Peace (poor guy, talk about naïve) and even introduced a bill and companion treaty to ban all space-based weapons. And Kucinich now? Gerrymandered out of congress. Of course!

So this new information forces me to entertain a different question: not how come there is so little focus on teaching and studying peace, but how come these schools have churned out perhaps thousands of graduates and we never hear about their interventions or their attempts at intervention? When Bush was selling the Iraq War II (don't laugh, it was called "Enduring Freedom"), was there a team trained in conflict resolution, their whistles slung round their necks, shuttling to and fro throwing yellow flags on the field to halt the game and call the foul?

Frankly, I don't think there was such a team. Of course, Bush pretended he wanted peace. They all do. Before Iraq War I ("Desert Storm") when Pappy Bush needed some quick chaos to dispel the "Wimp Factor," I happened to hear the head of the Harvard Negotiation Team (I think it was called) being interviewed on NPR. It was the day before the ultimatum to former U.S. buddy Saddam Hussein was to run out, which would have made it, I think, January, 16th. This professor was asked what he would have done differently to avoid a war? He said essentially that the *first* thing he would have done was to ring up Mr. Saddam after his invasion of Kuwait and, *duh*, ask him what he wanted? In fact, no one had done that. On the contrary, our ambassador at the time, in a recorded meeting basically said, "Hey, Sadd baby, you wanna go into Kuwait? No problemo. But, shhhh!"

Wait a minute. You mean the Harvard Team was all packed and ready to go and no one called? I'm shocked! Shocked!

Enduring Freedom? Desert Storm?

- *Cast, shot, and in the can!*

55

As I piddle around with these rhymes,

Confronted by wars, changing climes,

An old Chinese curse

Intrudes on my verse:

"May you live in interesting times"

And getting interestinger and interestinger. The so-called "globalization of the economy," a bloc of Asian nations adopting capitalism with its competition for scarce natural resources, the World Wide Web offering instantaneous communication across the planet, the ramifications of a post-industrial age for Western powers with the loss of millions of factory jobs to low-wage countries or little fake people called "robots," the building of a permanent underclass of unemployed and unemployable minorities who cannot find a place in society, sluggish bureaucracies incapable of accommodating the accelerating changes we face, whole nations run by powerful, corrupt oligarchies of drug lords, oil barons, mobsters, catastrophic climate woes, nuclear games, Afghanistan, Iraq, Syria, Yemen, Lebanon, Libya, terrorist attacks...interesting times take on a totally new meaning.

And if we *are* cursed to be living now, who uttered the curse? A curse is "a heartfelt invoking or violent or angry calling down of evil on another." So who invoked, who's angry, who's calling down evil on our heads?—

I read a true story once about an African village long ago whose life was organized around a bucket brigade, the purpose of which was to move water up the line from the river to the town above. To this end, the whole village lined up on the hill every day chanting and singing and muscling water up the slope. When the British took over, some well-intentioned official came along one day and, observing the bucket brigade, declared that, obviously, what the village needed was a generator and a pump. These items were forthwith ordered and installed. But the lives of the villagers, far from being improved, became purposeless.

Take heart, the story ends happily. Noticing their circumstances had changed for the worse, the villagers trashed the pump and went back to singing and hoisting water.—

By contrast, the industrial world embraced the generator and the pump. Indeed, invented better generators and more efficient pumps. And, told this "progress" was inevitable, we believed and went on down that road. Easier? Sure. Interesting? More and more. A curse...?

- *We'll know soon.*

56

The news on the tube starts at ten
You await the Earth's sobs in your den
If you focus on gender,
Most women are tender
And most of the miscreants...men

Republicans are always complaining that Liberals control the media. They don't. *Men* control the media: Jeffrey Dahmer, O.J., Hillside Strangler, Stacey Koons, Bush I and 2, Son of Sam, Richard Nixon, LBJ... schoolpolicegangwarshootshootshoot...check it out. Watch the news from the point of view of gender. Middle East going up in flames? Who's on the news? Serial killers? Floods, hurricanes, earthquakes, twisters, volcanoes, mudslides, droughts? No problem: some police or fire chief or FEMA bloke is being interviewed to reassure the nation that we guys are on top of the problem. Oil wells burning? Offshore well discharging millions of gallons of crude into the ocean? 400 tons of radioactive water from Fukushima pouring into the Pacific every day? Drug lords? Gangland killings? Relax! The boys are on the job.

The heroes and the villains are all men. And women? Ok, I know, Condoleezza was big and Hillary's licking her wounds again and now there's the first female Fed Head in a 100 years, Janet Yellin, and a few others but, come on, let's be serious. Ladies in black with shawls over their heads are grieving over loved ones murdered, "Shucks, ma'am, we thought ISIS was in that house. So sorry we droned your family. And, hey, the U.S. Congress just appropriated five million bucks to pay you off for your loss, so what's your problem, lady?"

A young Australian woman swims the Florida Straits, an astonishing feat of endurance and guts that's eluded every other swimmer who's ever tried it. But did the media pay any attention to this accomplishment? Hell no, cuz former rape suspect Kobe and the other boys just reported to the Laker's training camp. Lately, the occasional female suicide bomber has made the news. But that's a "man bites dog" story. And, no matter how you cut it, that's one helluva way to have to get on the air.

"Miscreant" is a good word, huh? A miscreant is a vicious person, a villain. The etymology derives from an old French word that meant "unbelieving." Maybe then, a miscreant, in the original sense, was an unbelieving or misbelieving person. If many men who reside on our TV screens are miscreants where many women are portrayed as victims, what is it men misbelieve and why are women so frequently presented as "sacrificial beasts"?

- *Wait a minute! Before you spout off, check out the original meaning of the word: a "victim" was a "sacrificial beast." And why?*

Simple. Men "misbelieve" women are their equals. And they misbelieve it with a passion and fervor that undergirds our entire planetary culture. Works good: women get paid less than men. Women walk behind Mr. Macho. Muslim ladies cover their everything. Muslim guy says to his wife three times, "I divorce you" and the little lady is history. Keeps it nice and simple.

Years ago, I heard interviews with a female archeologist who'd been excavating gravesites in central Asia from way back. These were gravesites in which she'd found weapons buried exclusively with female skeletons. Zip weapons were found in male gravesites. Nowhere else had this ever been discovered. According to archeologists, this clearly indicated a culture in which women were the warriors.

The famed Amazon archers of mythology? Could they have been real after all? I hope so 'cause bows and arrows and Amazons are a definite for the News at 10.

- *Go Amazons!*

57

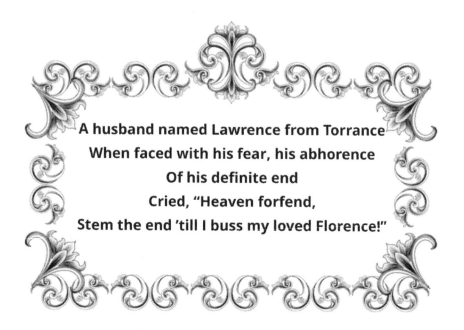

A husband named Lawrence from Torrance
When faced with his fear, his abhorence
Of his definite end
Cried, "Heaven forfend,
Stem the end 'till I buss my loved Florence!"

There's a crackup on the freeway. It's around 9:30 A.M. Anyplace else in LA this morning would be bumper to bumper but it's the Glendale Freeway north of the 134 on the way to Montrose and there's practically no traffic this Monday. Cars zoom by the body laid out under a blanket on the shoulder of the road. As I pass by, I wonder who he was. I think he was a "he" because the big black Mercedes all smacked up looks to me like a "he" car. I think, Wow, the poor slob woke up this morning, showered and shaved, picked out one of his $2,000 hand-tailored suits, gave himself the thumbs up in the mirror, kissed Florence and the kids goodbye and rode off in search of oblivion. He was almost dead when he was eating his Grape-Nuts and he didn't even know it. All those small Monday morning rituals were moving him inexorably forward on a Fate Full journey towards his mysterious destination.

If you knew with certainty you were going to die, if it had been reported, for example, that an incoming ICBM would drop on your head in ten minutes or an angelic voice had whispered in your ear that, unbeknownst to you, it was curtains, what would you do with your remaining moments on earth? I say, "*If* you knew..." but of course you *do* know. The only thing you don't know is when the angel will whisper and where, on the long freeway of your life, they'll cover you with a blanket.

So your choices are: a shave, a bowl of Grape-Nuts, CNN or one last chance to buss the sweeties.—

- *Quick, decide.*

58

Mornings while searching for meaning
Attempting to hammer my gleaning
Into five lines of verse
That are teasingly terse
My heart leaps when I capture its leaning

One time an actress working with the great film star James Cagney was having so much trouble doing a scene the director called Jimmy aside and told him that, as much as he hated to, he had to fire her. Cagney said, "Lemme talk to her first." Then the great actor took the young woman aside and said, "Look, it's simple: you walk through the door, you plant your feet, you look me in the eye, and you tell me the truth. Ok, let's try it again." The girl entered, she planted her feet, she looked Jimmy in the eye and told him the truth. She stayed on the picture. Cagney's words are still the best short course in acting ever. And probably in life as well.

But the trouble with acting for me was, after forty-four years of doing it, the words I was supposed to plant my feet and say were always someone else's words, and only rarely anyone's truth.

I did a couple of seasons on *Dynasty* as a recurring character. The first season I played the attorney of another character, Peter de Vilbis, played by the once well-known German actor, Helmut Berger, who'd been hired as a regular on the show. Berger had three problems: he didn't speak English well enough to learn his lines as quickly as the medium demanded, he was a homosexual, and the young leading lady on the show, Pamela Sue Martin, with whom he was supposed to be having a torrid affair, couldn't stand him and would have nothing to do with him. These problems caused the poor fellow extreme discomfort, making him sweat profusely and provoking in him yet another problem, the frequent need of a cigarette, which habit further disgusted Martin in the extreme.—

So, they hired me to speak for him. He would say to me, "Go to them, you know what I want, tell them!" and I would go to John Forsythe or Pamela Sue Martin and say, "Mr. de Vilbis has sent me and wants me to tell you...blah, blah, blah..." and I would babble all the things Helmut couldn't remember. And since I didn't smoke, was heterosexual and learned lines rapidly, I filled the bill. But the "blah, blah, blah" I was hired to say to the other actors was such consummate garbage I found myself, as I had frequently in my career, embarrassed to say the words.

One morning, I was sitting in a makeup chair at Goldwyn Studios committing the day's drivel to memory. The head makeup honcho, who'd been with producer Aaron Spelling for years, was working on me when, suddenly, I couldn't take it a moment longer. I looked at him (I think his name was Bill), and said, "Bill, how come Spelling accepts shit like this from his writers? I mean, I'm also doing *Hill Street* regularly and there *are* great writers out there!" And I'm babbling on in this vein when the old makeup man interrupts me, "But you don't understand, Mr. Spelling thinks this *is* great writing."

- *I was struck dumb.*

There ya go: because Spelling's taste, his emotional limitations coincided perfectly with what a large audience thought was classy stuff, actors, to make a living, had to play footsy with the soul of truth. And, of course, it didn't end with *Dynasty*. Spelling later had other very successful shows like *Melrose Place* and *Beverly Hills 90210*.

- *Shows you what I know.*

I had only been an actor for about four years when I traveled to Europe in 1960. I was twenty-eight. It was spring in Paris and I found myself in a cafe on the *Rive Gauche* among a group of artists caught up in a hot discussion about art. I spoke French fairly well in those days because it had been my major in college. One older painter asked me what credentials I possessed that had emboldened me to participate in the discussion. He said, *"Et vous? —Qu'est-ce que vous faites, alors?"* What do you do, Pal, he wanted to know?

I said, *"Je suis acteur,"* knowing I wasn't too confident about it, but thinking that at least it qualified me to sit at the table.

Hearing what kind of "artist" I was, the older painter took a contemptuous drag on his *Gauloise,* blew smoke in my face and said, *"Mais vous n'etes pas createur! Vous êtes recreateur!"* You're not a creator! You're a re-creator!" (With profound apologies for my French some fifty odd years later.)

It wasn't the smoke from the butt that pissed me off. It was the fact that he was right

Somebody once asked Alfred North Whitehead, the great Harvard philosopher and mathematician, why people busted their humps writing poetry, a painfully difficult craft offering absolutely no financial remuneration. He said they did it because when it worked, when they got it, they could exclaim, "That's it!"

- *Nobody ever said it better!*

59

We've a planet to live on, let's better it
Make a poster, LOVE EARTH, and we'll letter it
In two words so big
That every bigwig
Gets we nurture Her now or She's preterit

Maybe I'm wrong. Maybe George Carlin had the right idea. In one of his standup routines, he scoffed at the idea that something as insignificant as human beings could destroy something as magnificent as this planet: "And we're arrogant enough to think we can destroy Her with PLASTIC!!!" Not an exact quote, but close

Probably Carlin was right. Even after the most brutal nuclear war, our Earth will still be spinning, the sun rising and setting. Over the billions of years of Her existence, Old Mama been through it a lotta times. Whole species swept away in seconds. Evidence our poles may have reversed themselves several times. The Biblical Flood is confirmed in the stories of other cultures worldwide. Ice has triumphed. Deserts have thrived where forests have died. And this old "Spaceship Earth" (oh, do read Buckminster Fuller...he coined the phrase) has shrugged and kept on humming.

So perhaps when I speak about the destruction of the planet, I'm really just bewailing the end of human civilization as we know it, the "farewell to Brahms and polenta" feeling I've already spoken about, not the literal end of the third planet from the sun. And what the hell, right? If we're willing to trade Rachmaninoff and zabaglione for roaches and weeds, let's keep on chuggin' along spending vast sums on new generations of weapons.

And let's get some weapons up into space, for God's sake! You know the old war game adage, "Take the high ground" and you control everything below. Well, the high ground's not hills and mountains anymore, it's SPACE. You know, we gotta have space-based weapons (otherwise known as Big Brother's wet dream) so Big Bro can look down at anything on earth, dominate or destroy it at will with consummate precision whenever he decides to. For some really big bucks, let's continue to burn fossil fuels like they're going outta style and suppress the development of all forms of free, non-polluting energies; let's foul the oceans and waterways with our radiation, our chemicals, our garbage; let's continue to accelerate the reproduction of our own species in such numbers there will be no room whatsoever for any other creature; in fact, let's work at turning the whole planet into a zoo where billions of us surround tiny enclaves of them where we can peer at odd vestiges, tattered remnants of another time. Let's slash and burn and bulldoze all the forests for more pastureland, for more cattle, for more steak for more of us. Yeah, just yesterday morning I learn that the "lungs of the planet" the Brazilian rain forest is going up in smoke despite laws to prevent it. Gotta get rid of all those pesky trees to plant more soybeans to feed more animals that we can kill for those nice big inch-thick juicy steaks for bigger and better heart attacks.

- *I mean, fuck the rain forest. Fuck all those illiterate, unproductive tribal folk who are so backward they don't even own guns yet. Much less a decent suit.*

These are good things. It is well known that whales and dolphins and other sea mammals actually fornicate and defecate right there *in the ocean*! While bears and other lower order creatures do their business *in the woods*! Right there on the ground. These habits are horribly polluting and unsanitary. And, let's be honest, better our shit than

152

their shit. And, come to think of it, why should I care? I never swim in the ocean anyway; I've never seen a gorilla or a bear in the wild; I live in a nice house so screw the starving masses. All of us important people live in gated, patrolled, armed communities around lovely golf courses and, in the future, we'll just never leave; we'll simply use the Internet to talk amongst ourselves and use armored cars for those rare trips beyond the perimeter.—

- *And on the off chance you might wanna see what animals used to look like, hey, you got the Animal Channel. What more do you need?*

On the other hand, very occasionally, I do harbor the tiniest flicker of fear that sometimes in my dreams I may remember what it was like for so long before and how it took us only a little while to take it all apart. At fleeting moments like those, I'm just a little scared I might dream tales of a verdant land, of air so pure it burned the nostrils, of rivers and lakes abounding with fish and forests so lush, so immense, they say a squirrel could jump from one chestnut tree to another from Maine to North Carolina and never set foot on the ground.

- *But perhaps in the middle of the night I'll awaken.*

I'll get up and go to the window of my palatial home; I'll look out past the armored cars in the driveway and sigh in relief then seeing the neatly manicured putting green of the third hole safely slumbering under the moon.

- *A Stranger in a Strange Land!*

PS: It's 2018 and a dead whale was just cut open to determine why it had died. Hmmm, I wonder, maybe it was the 23 kilos of plastic in its stomach?

- *Now that's a lotta plastic!*

As we face an old epoch that's crumbling,
The madness of men, the Gods grumbling,
Why not sign a new lease
On our home and in peace
Kneel with reverence to still Gaia's rumbling

When I was studying to be a Marriage and Family counselor, I loved an assigned book called *Change*. In it, Paul Watzlawick, the author, applies General Systems Theory to human transactions. He points out that, when we attempt to change our lives, we generally make what in General Systems Theory is referred to as "First Order Change," more commonly known as "more of the same." So, for example, if laws preventing the sale and use of certain drugs have proved ineffective, the solution is seen to be more laws or the same laws with harsher penalties. This is similar to a driver deciding the way to go faster in first gear is to floor the pedal, failing to realize the way to go faster is to shift into a higher gear, namely, "Second Order Change."

We live on this planet like a fly trapped on the wrong side of a screen door. Poor little bugger hurls himself against the devilish barrier again and again, occasionally pausing to rest and contemplate his seemingly insoluble predicament. He sees outside, gets a whiff of the flowers as he struggles, but all his efforts are in vain. Sooner or later, exhausted, he collapses and dies on the kitchen floor, never realizing, had he strolled calmly to the edge of the doorframe, he might have easily squeezed through the crack to freedom. Solutions to our plight, of course, are as close as the flowers, even as we frantically buzz until we drop from exhaustion.

Watzlawick tells a wonderful true story: In the Middle Ages a castle is under endless siege. The defenders are in despair, at the end of their resources. With only one animal and one bag of grain remaining, they realize surrender is near. "We must ration our last reserves of food," they exclaim to their commander. But that worthy instead orders his troops to slaughter the animal and stuff it with the remaining bag of grain. This is done and the carcass is thrown to the besieging army camped below. The beneficiaries of this largesse, weary of the long siege, themselves hungry and out of patience, and having presumed the defenders were at the point of starvation logically conclude their adversaries are seemingly prepared to hold out indefinitely. Thus, they fold their tents and, disheartened, begin to trudge the long way home.

- *First Order Change: ration the remaining food. Second Order Change: give it to the enemy.—*

The medical establishment in the United States is under siege. According to the Journal of the American Medical Association, more and more people are visiting "alternative" healers, indicating a growing loss of faith in the poison, slash, burn approach of authorized medicine. Trillions of research dollars have been spent to "study" heart disease and cancer, the major killers. We've been assured *ad nauseum* that this or that new wonder drug would finally lead us to the Promised Land only to learn later of yet another dismal failure, a failure that may have actually killed those trusting patients who took it. Let's hear it for Vioxx and those fifty thousand deaths it caused.

Wrap your head around this: the third leading cause of death in the United States is "iatrogenic disease," a fancy way of saying "doctor induced disease." *The third leading cause of death!* You die on the operating table or your immune system goes bonkers from the side effects of "legal" drugs wrongly prescribed or prescribed in improper

155

dosages or combinations with the other 20 drugs you're swallowing. You're diagnosed with cancer and instead of asking what you eat or what deadly chemicals may have already set up housekeeping in your body, they drip poison in your veins and/or bombard your immune system with deadly radiation. Hey, that's a nifty way to cure people: knock out their immune systems! Clever, huh?

- *Kiddo, if cancer patients knew the actual success rate of chemo "therapy," they'd seek refuge in the Witness Protection Program.*

The solution of the embattled oncologists? Circle the wagons. Better chemo or radiation or the next pill with a snazzy name. In other words, First Order Change. I can't wait for the drug ads because they're the best comedy on TV: the voiceover actor reading the side effects of the advertised drug with that little smiley lilt to his voice: "...and possible death. So ask your doctor if the pretty pink pill is right for you."

Or the lawyer ads that end with, "...so if you or a loved one has died or committed suicide while on Whizzo, please call Fartworthy and Sleazall for a free consultation. You pay nothing unless we win!!!"

- *Whadya mean I pay nothing? I'm already dead.*

Second Order Change for doctors? Take the terrified dogs you're currently using for your horrific experiments home to the kids. Return the monkeys and baboons to the jungle. Find a fellow physician who's actually curing something and go study with him or her. Numbers of the latter are to be found in prison or in court or in Mexico.

- *And Second Order Change for the rest of us?*

- *Shift into drive, Baby, and get outta Nutsville.*

61

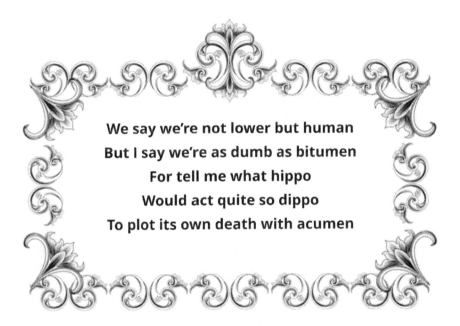

We say we're not lower but human
But I say we're as dumb as bitumen
For tell me what hippo
Would act quite so dippo
To plot its own death with acumen

Back in March of '97, presidents Yeltsin and Clinton held a joint press conference to report the results of their summit. Among other things, they proudly announced to the world that each country had agreed to gradually reduce its stockpile of nuclear weapons to 2,500. The remaining weapons would then be only eight per cent of the maximum Cold War level of around 30,000. This sounds like a triumph of statesmanship and a move towards sanity and is supposed to make us all heave a profound sigh of relief.

- *Bullshit.—*

Even assuming we both achieved the combined reduction level of 5,000 warheads, that number is already ten times more than we ever needed in the first place to toast the planet. The other 25,000 had just been a pissing contest by hawks in both countries.

(By the way, let's stop for a moment to remember and posthumously thank the great newscaster Daniel Shore who, in his analysis of that announcement from Helsinki, actually pointed out this phony "success," going so far as to refer to nuclear weapons as "useless." He also had the honor to be on Nixon's Enemies List and got fired from CBS over the Pentagon Papers flap. You died at 93 Daniel and, wherever you now may be, I hope you know how exceptional you were. Thank you and Bravo!)

They're useless. Daniel Shore knew it. I know it. You know it. The question now is...and it's a big one...do terrorists know it? It's one thing to sit down with the president of another nation and rap out a deal. You don't hit me; I won't hit you. But there is no sitting down with terrorists. If a city gets smoked, no one will ever know who did it. No retaliation on ghosts, folks.

Soldiers ordered into a withering fire are referred to as "fodder" (feed) for the cannon, i.e., "cannon fodder." The phrase is beautifully defined in the Random House Dictionary under "fodder" as, "people considered as readily available and of little value." One wonders how men have always charged or rode straight ahead into murderous fusillades to almost certain death. Comrades fall beside them, bombs and shells hurl fragments of their fellows' bodies at their feet as they race ahead. And yet they come.

(Speaking of the idiocy of constant warfare, it so happens today's my birthday and I heard on the radio this morning that it's also the 100th anniversary of the start of the First World War! Never knew that! Cool, huh? Born on the same day as The Great War.)

Face it! For a very long time now, we've all been racing blindly across Flanders Field, as thousands did in that First Great War, towards a destructive fire that, if unleashed today, would make the 1917 blood-muddied fields of France seem like an English garden. And yet we come. We're as dumb as a chunk of bitumen. We live in the dark awaiting the moment when we'll be dug up and immolated on the blazing pyre of our national passions.

- *Cannon fodder.*

"In Flanders's Field the poppies grow
Beneath the crosses row on row."

-Rupert Brooke-

- *Great poem. Brooke died in 1915. Wherever you are, Bless you/*

- *And, by the way, don't we just tsk tsk when we learn the Aztecs offered human sacrifices to their strange Gods!?*

- *Yeah, nutty. But at least they called it like it was.*

62

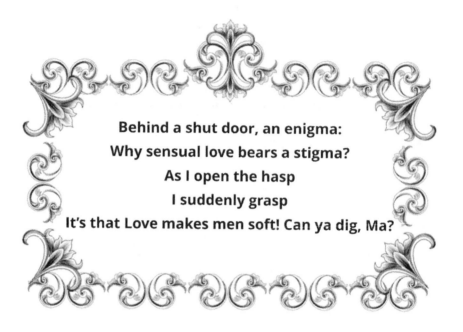

Behind a shut door, an enigma:

Why sensual love bears a stigma?

As I open the hasp

I suddenly grasp

It's that Love makes men soft! Can ya dig, Ma?

At the Battle of Agincourt, ole Harry doesn't advise his yeomen to relax, kick back, nap or chow down. He tells them to stiffen their sinews and screw their courage to the sticking place. And it wasn't just King Harry. Men are exhorted to be tough from Day One: Big Boys Don't Cry, Take It Like A Man, Work Hard Play Hard, No Pain No Gain, Play To Win, No Quarter Asked No Quarter Given, and Winning Is Everything, Be Competitive. Muscles hard as a rock, hard body, six pack. Unlike the Misses, the Misters America, Universe, and Olympia don't have to sing a cute song or recite a poem or do a little dance or even answer a boring question to prove to the judges they're not brain dead. All the boys have to do is oil up and pop some major muscle. And with steroids, we're talkin' major. Even way before 'roids, I knew a former Mr. Universe whose goal was to sculpt his body to the exact dimensions of the famed *Farnese Hercules*: 52 inch chest, 32 inch waist. Talk about hard body. Many a time, I've touched a man's shoulder and felt him tense his delts in reaction to my touch to show me he was ripped. Hard. Well, good God, you wouldn't want another man to know your shoulder was soft, would you? And some men don't have to tense for the touch. They've arrived; they're hard all the time. Perpetually tense. True hard bodies. Serious bodybuilders have always got a picture in mind they're working towards, which is why they're always looking at themselves in the mirror...to check out how the statue is coming along. And make no mistake, the computer geek down the hall who's never so much as sniffed the inside of a locker room, much less hefted a chunk of iron, is secretly in awe of those lumbering behemoths he sneers at over coffee in the lunchroom. Guaranteed.—

But muscles that are always hard are sick muscles. At rest, animals don't have hard muscles. Can you imagine Kitty Kitty stalking by all buffed and pumped and rock hard? I've spent a lot of time in gyms around bodybuilders because I was one and, I can tell you, there is no more obsessive pursuit than the quest to get big and strong and hard. But, let's face it, the obsession of the bodybuilder is self-obsession, which is about as sexy as a mirror.

Like the *Farnese Hercules*, whose dimensions my Mr. Universe friend Bruce Randall once attained, the great Western, masculine ideal is exemplified by an extremely muscular torso, emphasizing an enormous chest and a narrow waist with highly defined abdominal muscles. This is in sharp contrast to the Eastern ideal where the body is soft and rotund. In the ideal Western body, the center of gravity is high, making it possible to topple its possessor with a slight push of a finger in the middle of the chest. By contrast, when the chest is relaxed and the belly is soft, the center of gravity is in what the Japanese call the "*hara* place," two inches below the navel. It is impossible to push someone over who is centered in the *hara*. The first ideal - high chest, sculpted waist - is the poster boy for Hitler's ideal of the so-called Aryan Race. The second - soft round low belly, relaxed chest - is Buddha. The first man, no matter how big, how muscular, is a "pushover." The second, your local Aikido master. Or check out the sword play of the Japanese actor, Toshiro Mifune, in his great samurai roles: *Yojimbo, Sanjuro, The Seven Samurai.* Mifune was a Kendo player, a swordsman. Get one of his marvelous movies and check out his center of gravity!

161

A slogan started appearing on women's T shirts a few years ago: "A Hard Man Is Good To Find." No man wants to be thought of as a wimp (rhymes with limp!) or a bleeding heart, a sissy, a softie, a wuss, a pansy or a pussy. But, ladies, a question may arise when you find that "hard man." Will there be a lot more that's hard about him than his dallywacker?

Like maybe his eyes? —His heart?

- *Caveat emptor!*

63

Our infamous leaders are famous
For falsehoods designed to inflame us
To horrors so desperate
That sadly we're less for it
Yet given their lies, who can blame us?

George Two lands on an aircraft carrier in a U.S. Air Force flight suit and declares victory in "Enduring Freedom." (At least he didn't say "We kicked Iraqi butt" like his father did after "Desert Storm.") I heard a fellow on the radio once who had just written an article for Harper's magazine called something like, The Militarization of American Politics. He pointed out that the aforementioned gave many of his speeches on military bases surrounded by gung-ho, oo-rahing youngsters. The author also said that, although a number of American generals have gone on to become president, Bush is the only president to have actually donned a military uniform while in office since G. Washington took his old duds out of mothballs to put down the Whiskey Rebellion.

We attacked Iraq "preemptively." What that means is, since we're worried you might be planning to harm us in the future, we're entitled to whack you today. This is, of course, old Cold War Arms Race thinking: because we're worried that someday you might have such and such weaponry, we'll lie and tell the nation that you already *do* have it, allowing us to escalate our weaponry to enable us to counteract what we already know you do NOT possess. (Were you able to figure that out? Our government, our military is hoping you won't be able to! So please go back and dwell on the previous sentence a moment longer.)

Look at what we just went through. Before we attacked Iraq, the Bush II administration had the nation standing on a dirty New York street corner betting on a shell game. And if you ever stood on a New York sidewalk and tried following the shell or the cards, you learned the hard way that the hustler's hands could move a lot faster than your eye. So, we were force-fed lies and exaggerations and make believe like some poor, sad French goose hanging on a wall being fed with a hose down its throat waiting for its liver to get fat enough for the slaughter. Yummy, huh?

Watch the shell: Saddam has amassed great arsenals of weapons of mass destruction. —Heavens to Betsy, he gassed his own people (Yeah, while we were providing the poison and he was Our Boy); he's importing aluminum tubes that will give him the capacity to make nuclear weapons; he's attempting to import "yellowcake" uranium from Niger which will give him the capacity to make more nuclear weapons; British intelligence informs us that Hussein is capable of launching a nuclear strike within 45 minutes; Ooo, look at those photos Colin Powell is using to illustrate his testimony before the UN Security Council showing Iraqi chemical plants in the desert; Ooo, mobile labs; Ooo, Iraqis meeting with terrorists; Ooo, Saddam supports Al Qaeda.

- *Feel it yet? You were nailed on a wall like that French goose while they poured lies down a hose in your throat.*

At least Hitler said it flat out in *Mein Kampf:* "The broad mass of a nation...will more easily fall victim to a big lie than to a small one."

In this age of mass communication, one would think the artifice and contrivances of these frauds would be their undoing. Good lord, unless you've been searching for grubs under a large rock, you've gotta know governments engage in what is so delightfully labeled "disinformation." And it goes without saying that government lies are not peculiar to our time. Questions about Churchill's prior knowledge of the sinking of the Lusitania or FDR's of the Japanese plan to attack Pearl Harbor, cover-ups by LBJ and Nixon of the level of our involvement in Vietnam (not to mention the Gulf of Tonkin invention), the secret bombing of Cambodia (certainly not secret to the Cambodians) and lately the revelations of Edward Snowden about which high-level assholes at the National Security Agency have flat out lied to Congress: all these are history.

- *Cue the laugh track.*

Maybe naïveté dies hard because we need something to hold on to, to believe in, as the tsunami of mendacity overwhelms us. If priests bugger children while the Church winks, the president of the United States *shtups* an Arkansas beauty for twelve years who then writes a book describing his personal sexual predilections and the actual appearance of his wee wee (while he staunchly denies what the whole world knows to be undeniable), maybe naïveté is a sort of flotation device to keep us from sinking in the cesspool of perfidy in which we are all desperately attempting to keep our noses above the swill. I mean, we keep doggy paddling when the Old Boys are promoting another "conflict," another "police action," another "mop up," another "engagement," even when the lives of our children, the very fate of our planet is up for grabs.

There might be a rule of thumb: if a government says it's true, it's false. (In fact, I've heard there's a saying in D.C. that goes, "Nothing is true until it's officially denied.") But what astonishes is not that we are lied to, that's a given. It's that, knowing we are lied to, knowing we've got a hose down our throats, we still swallow. We send our children to war to murder innocent people (a million in Iraq and Afghanistan?) based on the horseshit concocted in our capitols that's pumped into our livers by the media. A bit like sauntering into the same restaurant after you got food poisoning from the fishy fish the night before.

That we swallow the offal yet again, that is what astonishes. Talk about naïve! Nah, tell it like it is, it's not naïve, it's stupid.—

165

Naïve is when you don't know. Stupid is when you know but you swallow, anyway.

- *Poor, sad goose has no way to pull the hose out of its throat.*

- *But we have hands.*

64

When issues domestic are irksome
There's a time-tested ploy that's their perk, Son,
They launch a quick war
To splatter your gore,
Add lies to your death: that's a jerk's sum

When Teddy Roosevelt said about the Spanish-American War, "It wasn't much of a war, but it was the only war we could get," at least he was calling a spade a spade. He wanted a war, he needed a war, and he said as much. Of course, he also thought "superior" nations had a duty to dominate "inferior" ones in the interest of civilization and said once, "No triumph of peace is quite so great as the supreme triumph of war." So, he was wacko, too. —But at least he was who he was. Neither "Desert Storm" nor "Enduring Freedom" were much of a war and the presidents who led us into them were certainly incapable of ever calling a spade a spade. But the sad, dull, insipid, uninspiring George Bushes (no Teddy Roosevelt there) also desperately needed an opportunity to bury, on the one hand The Wimp Factor and, on the other, the fact that the economy was tanking, and he had not been elected by a majority of the people. (Let's hear it for the U.S. Supreme Court...ugh!)

As I rewrite this section of the book, I'm reminded of the daily revelations we endured in the Clinton/Lewinsky affair. Back then, miraculously, a film entitled *Wag the Dog* with Dustin Hoffman and Robert De Niro popped up in movie theaters at the same time. The plot of the movie was almost identical to Clinton's sexual imbroglio: a president, suspected of sexual indiscretion in the oval office, manufactures a bogus war with Albania (!) to divert the attention of the public until the forthcoming election. As amazed as I was by the film, I was even more amazed by its failure to attract a large audience. Every talk show on the air was mentioning the obvious similarity between Slippery Bill's escapade and the movie, but the theatre was empty the night I attended, and the grosses were unimpressive. And why? The answer is that we already *know* all this stuff. We *know* everyone is lying. We *know* a president will go to war to distract us. We *know* presidents will say and do all the things we didn't used to believe they would. We've become jaded. Or maybe the better word is numb. Or...could it be...smarter? Either way the film was not a revelation, simply corroboration.

All wars are mad. They're fomented by leaders who vie for power or covet territory or need to distract the citizenry in order to entrench their positions at home; wars are disastrous conflagrations, not epochal dramas as we are wont to depict them. They may alleviate boredom and temporarily lift us from the unreality of spiritless lives, but they are not romantic or epic. As Desiderius Erasmus once said, "For the ultimate aim of that vice [war] is to involve ever-increasing numbers of people in its game until all mankind is consumed. This is the basic aim of war as it is of fire."—

When fires flare, trucks roll, houses are evacuated, backfires are lit, trenches dug, everything and anything to staunch the blaze before it completes its destructive task. Firefighters are trained to do this. But firefighters also spend a great deal of time inspecting potential hazards in order to prevent fires before they begin. By contrast, millions of soldiers around the world stand poised, weapons at the ready. But no feasible program of prevention exists that I have ever heard of. No Smokey The Bear reminds us to protect the defenseless creatures of the forest by our careful use of fire, no weed reduction program before the hot winds blow in August, no building inspection for fire hazards, no mandatory smoke alarms, no experts at the ready, their gleaming trucks all shiny and ready to roll at the first claxons of war.

- *How come?*

All those programs exist to train potential warriors to do battle for the state. But where can a young person trained in the Art of Sweet Talk earn a living? When the bell clangs and the flames of war summon them, where are the brass poles for the peace warriors to slide down? Where are the troubleshooters, the Peace Inspectors overseeing the Hate Abatement Program? Why no spiffy red trucks with friendly mustachioed heroes aboard out and about in the world, their trained eyes peeled for the faintest, telltale puffs of smoke?

Yeah, war is crazy. War is hell. But so is fire. However, facing fire, we give hoses and ladders to heroes.

- *In politics, we give matches and gasoline to arsonists.—*

65

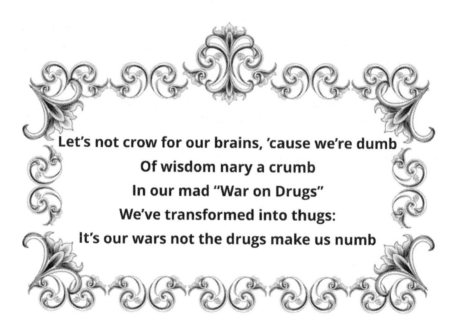

Let's not crow for our brains, 'cause we're dumb
Of wisdom nary a crumb
In our mad "War on Drugs"
We've transformed into thugs:
It's our wars not the drugs make us numb

A fiercely fought Proposition was on the ballot in California in the November '96 election that would allow people whose doctors considered them to be terminally ill and in great pain to raise and consume Marijuana. A majority of Californians saw the reasonableness of the proposition and, with reason and compassion, passed it. However, before the election, President Clinton vowed, should the measure pass, to use the power of Federal laws to override it. Not surprising. No politician can be seen to support the use of mind-altering drugs for any reason whatsoever. Except, of course, those infinitely more dangerous mind-altering drugs pumped out by the pharmaceutical cartel. Although too late now, this impasse could have been easily resolved before the election had the supporters of the California Proposition only realized a small donation to Clinton's reelection campaign, something in the neighborhood of perhaps a quarter of a million dollars, would have garnered the president's immediate, vociferous support. Including possibly a sleepover with

170

the Pres. Pity. The man was up for grabs by anyone, any nation, any cause, and they blew it. Integrity is a terrible drag.

Back when I originally wrote this, John Ashcroft was the Attorney General. This worthy was a Born Again Christian who reportedly held prayer meetings daily for his staff and vowed to fight any relaxation of the drug laws anywhere in the U.S. Never mind citizens of the sovereign states of Oregon, California, Washington, and now Colorado (and even Vermont just signed on!) have certified the humanity of allowing desperately ill people to find solace in a plant that Ashcroft's God presumably placed on earth for the purpose of alleviating pain and suffering. But, nah, this Onward Christian Soldier was resolved to smite the wicked with his sword of certainty. And who can fault a man who spent $7,000 bucks to cover the breasts of the Statue of Justice in the rotunda at the Department of Justice? Can't let an image of a God-created bosom hang out there exposed to the passing lascivious eye. No way. Pisses God off.—

The president can appoint a different Drug Czar every month to lead the entire U.S. military into the Drug War and it will not bring the War on Drugs to a "successful" conclusion. Our anti-drug forces regularly mass and charge on yet another offensive while the "enemy" disappears like fog on a hot day.

- *The real problem with the kind of drugs I'm talking about is they heal, they work.*

We are thus doomed to remain the muscle-bound giant that we are: slow, stupid, and totally ineffectual, stumbling forth into the same old bog flailing at phantoms, unaware we're being sucked down deeper and deeper as we sink into the muddy quagmire.

- *Does anyone in Washington ever ask the question why millions around the world, many of them young, are willing to risk everything for the experience that certain drugs offer them?*

If the question why so many billions are spent on heart- and mind-expanding drugs were ever asked and answered, might one not be forced to conclude that life as we're living it has become increasingly unendurable? Or that millions of us now know there are dimensions of existence they cannot yet contact without the aid of native substances that indigenous peoples have always used to visit such distant galaxies of the soul? Or that these millions want to flee from the omnipresent war mentality that's now considered normal? Flee into the soft, welcoming arms of forgetfulness where they are able to find momentary peace, love, and solace? Or simply that most of us are unaware of the sacred center of our lives?

Why drugs? Perhaps their use conjures a prettier world, a living world suffused with color and exotic form and dimension infinitely more variegated and vivid than the execrable mess we see around us. Maybe the relief the drug affords is so profound, so palpable, the soaring, majestic journey of the drug so inviting, the voyager is willing to face imprisonment or even death to travel that powerful inner jet stream to some personal infinity. Perhaps, from this point of view, the next Czar might consider the defiant use of drugs as heroic, not criminal. And those wishing to embark might be guided by experienced travelers to those forbidden, enticing, gorgeous, inner Shangri-las. Scary stuff for the legions of left-brained Drug Warriors who officially tolerate and encourage only those drugs which keep us earthbound: the Prozacs, the Marlboros, and Dewars ("While you're up, get me a Dewars" so I can stay down!); the Xantacs, the Joe Camels, the Johnny Walkers (Johnny! Cute, huh?) And let's not forget that touch of chemo and radiation. Another bowl of Frosted Flakes anyone?

- *It's all swell as long as we remain lashed to the planet.*

Attention Please! Attention! All flights on Leary Intergalactic Space Transport are and will remain officially grounded.

- *But, pssst, there are special charter flights leaving daily.*

172

Number of American deaths per year that result directly or primarily from the following selected causes nationwide, according to World Almanacs, Life Insurance Actuarial (death) Rates, and the last 20 years of U.S. Surgeon Generals' reports:

TOBACCO...40,000 to 450,000

ALCOHOL (Not including 50% of all highway deaths and 65% of all murders)..150,000+

ASPIRIN (Including deliberate overdose)...............180 to 1,000+

CAFFEINE (From stress, ulcers, and triggering irregular heartbeats, etc...1,000 to 10,000

"LEGAL" DRUG OVERDOSE (Deliberate or accidental) from legal, prescribed or patent medicines and/or mixing with alcohol - e.g. Valium/alcohol...................................14,000 to 27,000

ILLICIT DRUG OVERDOSE (Deliberate or accidental) from all illegal drugs..3,800 to 5,200

MARIJUANA..0

66

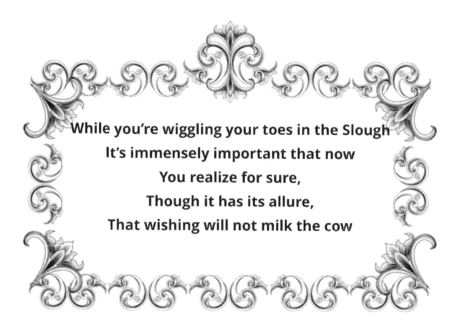

While you're wiggling your toes in the Slough
It's immensely important that now
You realize for sure,
Though it has its allure,
That wishing will not milk the cow

Drugs give us a tool to alter our reality, to make the intolerable tolerable, to journey to dimensions not readily perceived within the confines of the general agreement. But traveling the Silk Road again and again in order to make the intolerable tolerable permits us to forever evade the soul's summons to get up and go after the bastards and actually *do* something about what can no longer be tolerated.

To wish the world was in a better place is dandy, but when last night's buzz wears off this morning, no matter how many sticks of incense we've burned, how many insights we've had, how many visions we've ah-hahed, it's vital to cock an ear to the swelling chorus marching by, to fall in shoulder to shoulder with the thousands of courageous men and women who daily "sally forth into the world to right all wrongs." (A Dale Wasserman line written for the character of Don Quixote from the great, hit musical *Man of La Mancha*.) To grab a banner and rush to the barricades.

Feel the fervor of the song as they sweep by...

You who have dreams,
If you act they will come true.
To turn your dreams
To a fact it's up to you.
If you have the soul and the spirit
Never fear it you'll see it through.
Hearts can inspire other hearts with their fire...

That's the verse from the song Stouthearted Men from the operetta *New Moon* which we shall change this instant to Stouthearted Men *and* Women.

- *Learn the lyrics. Your stouthearted brothers and sisters will help you remember the tune.*

67

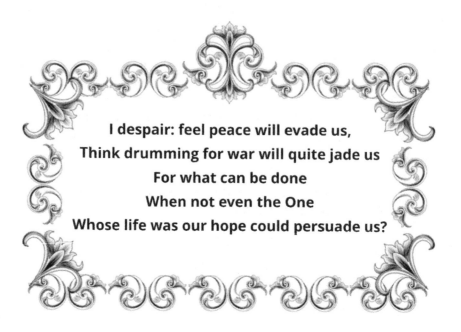

I despair: feel peace will evade us,

Think drumming for war will quite jade us

For what can be done

When not even the One

Whose life was our hope could persuade us?

I'm standing in a pew in the old Dutch Reformed Church at the corner of Church and Flatbush Avenues in Brooklyn, N.Y. singing "Onward Christian soldiers marching as to war, with the cross of Jesus going on before..." and thinking this song is nuts. How can Christians march like soldiers or go to war of any kind? World War Two is blazing and it seems wacko to this kid that chaplains are performing services for Christian soldiers, followers of the Prince of Peace, who then march out to seek to kill other Christians whose chaplains just held services for them. What Jesus said about turning the other cheek seems pretty clear to me and I'm only thirteen years old!—

I knew enough from Sunday school to figure out that killing people for any reason was certainly not what the Man had taught. Could I be right? Could all these people call themselves Christians and be participating in the greatest slaughter in the history of the planet? There had to be something I was not getting, some codicil somewhere

I hadn't been shown. Because it was one thing for the dumb grunts who bowed their heads not to understand the implications of what they were doing, but it was another thing entirely, I thought, for that chaplain to stand there in his uniform (a priest in a military uniform?) with his little white scarf over his shoulders conducting a service in the name of the Prince of Peace, the Lamb of God, blessing the actions of the penitents who worshipped before him. Something fishy here, I thought.

Cut to a month before "Desert Storm" is launched. —Could that be the President of the United States emerging from that church in Washington, hand-in-hand with Babs? Could that be the Christian gentleman who's amassing the largest army in fifty years? And, yes, it was and there I sat thinking the same thoughts I'd thought when I was 13.

Fortunately, fifty years later, I knew for certain that I wasn't alone. Listen to Erasmus in 1525 exhorting Emperor Charles V to hesitate and ponder before sending his troops against a neighboring state:

ERASMUS IS IN THE EMPEROR'S GREAT HALL. IT IS FILLED WITH ALL THE COURTIERS, NOBLES, AND LEARNED MEN AND WOMEN OF THE HOLY ROMAN EMPIRE

"I am greatly honored and humbled to accept the title Councilor to Emperor Charles V, who may be young in years but excels many of his elders in wisdom and a love of concord and whose reputation is spotless.

"On this occasion, I would like to take the time allowed me to introduce myself to all those gathered here to speak on a subject that is so widespread and pregnant with every kind of calamity that it is considered a way of life...an inevitable part of the human condition.

- *War.*

"I am not unaware that those who warmly...dissuade mankind from war are suspect: accused of weakness, effeminacy, a lack of patriotism or even heresy; while those with artful salvos and quibbles contrive to dilute the strength of the Gospels and find out plausible pretexts by which certain Princes may justify their lust for war and plunder without appearing to act openly against the law or Gospel principles. They are deemed teachers of true Evangelical Christianity, whereas a true minister or teacher of Christ can never give his approbation to war.

"But we must meet force with force and defend life and liberty and money, too," they say. These arguments are as old as man's thirst for more. But according to the testimony of Tatian, Justinian, and Tertullian, the first Christians held the profession of soldiering to be incompatible with the teachings of their Founder. Men were forced to choose...am I to be a Christian or a soldier? But when the Christians revolted against Diocletian in the Third Century they were allowed to commune after committing murder!

"St. Augustine developed the theory that a war to resist evil or aggression or to enforce justice was not only permissible but a Christian duty. Thus, did war and honor get mixed together. This was at the time that the true spirit of Christianity began to languish.

"St. Thomas Aquinas, in his lucubrations, determined what was "just" and what was "unjust." Like everything else he wrote, the church took this as law. Pacifism was considered cowardice at best, heresy at worst. The rest is a bloody history."—

- *"Why are people so ready to listen to injunctions from men and to disobey the teachings of the Prince of Peace who says, 'Resist not evil'?"*

Couldn't have said it better myself. And probably only a heavyweight like Erasmus could have stood before the Emperor of the Holy Roman Empire and told him he was butt naked. And I'm grateful to Timothy Helgeson who made Erasmus's speech available to me. It's from his book about that great philosopher *The Last Man to Know Everything: The Renaissance of Erasmus* (which can be found at www.fractalspirit.com).

Of course, when I was just a kid watching that chaplain leading the troops in prayer on the Movie Tone News on a Saturday afternoon at

178

the Patio Theatre on Flatbush Avenue, I had never even heard of the concept of "rationalization."

- *Now I have.*

I can't say I never heard of Desiderius Erasmus because I attended Erasmus Hall High School in Brooklyn! Famed alumna? Barbra Streisand. Alumnus? Maybe the greatest chess player ever, Bobby Fischer.

Trivia question: In what famous movie does a character tell the star that she attends Erasmus Hall?

Now that I know something about what he stood for, I'm really proud of Desi and kinda proud, too, that I attended a school named after him.

- *Answer: All About Eve. Towards the very end of the film.*

68

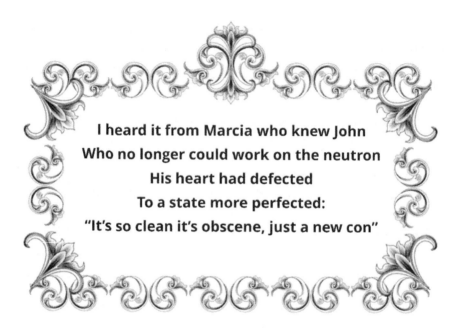

I heard it from Marcia who knew John
Who no longer could work on the neutron
His heart had defected
To a state more perfected:
"It's so clean it's obscene, just a new con"

"Neutron Bomb, a nuclear bomb releasing a shower of neutrons fatal to life with a relatively small amount of blast and small amount of contamination, so that the target area may be occupied and used in a normal manner shortly after the detonation of the bomb." — *Unabridged Random House Dictionary of the English Language—*

- *What else is there to say other than it's always fun to look up new words?*

And I like that part where it says the real estate "may be occupied and used in a normal manner shortly after the detonation of the bomb." I mean, that's good, right? All you'd have to do would be to remove and bury the decaying bodies of every single living thing within probably a twenty-mile radius...normal cleanup. But the real estate would be ok, and that would be good for business. Right?

Jeepers, think about it. A team of really great guys, really smart guys, probably all family guys invented it. And, when it worked, they probably all felt swell about it, right? And then people actually started building them in a factory in someplace like Texas or New Mexico or Nebraska, the kinda people who regularly got their kids to soccer and ballet after school, snuck their own popcorn into the movies Saturday nights with the little lady and felt really good they had a good-paying job. Because everyone knows that without a really good-paying job and all the swell benefits that go with it, it's really hard to feel really good about yourself or really anything else. Really.

- *No matter what it is you really make. Right?*

- *Yeah! Really!*

69

Those I believe say a New Game
Is afoot in the world, not the same,
For we saw we must change
Or our Home on the Range
Would be dust and thus Trust is its name

Edward Snowden's revelations proved the United States is spying on everyone. Even slurping up the private cell phone conversations of the leader of a friendly nation, Germany's Chancellor Angela Merkel. The National Security Agency collects and stores millions of phone calls and text messages. And if it isn't every nation spying on every other nation, then corporations are stealing from... In other words, everybody distrusts everybody and here we are.

- *Ain't it grand?*

I sit here wondering if there's a way out of this endless maze of distrust? Is it at all possible to contemplate a New Game in which nations and corporations play all their cards face up? I wish I could imagine such a Game. But, whoa, somebody brought down three (count 'em 3) buildings at the World Trade Center, not only dropping them in their own footprint but, once again, instantly shattering our sense of invulnerability. And what if it had been a nuclear attack? So, all this spying and secrecy and plotting and planning is necessary, huh?

- *I dunno. Is it? Is a New Game possible?*

Well, it *is* naive. Here's the origin of the word from an etymological site: "1650s, 'natural, simple, artless,' from French *naïve*, fem. of *naïf*, from Old French *naif* 'naive, natural, genuine; just born; foolish, innocent; unspoiled, unworked' (13c.), from Latin *nativus* 'not artificial,' also 'native, rustic,' literally 'born, innate, natural'."

But think about it: what did the Main Man mean when he said, "Unless ye be as little children, ye shall not enter the Kingdom of Heaven"? I think He meant what he said right there in the Good Book! Go with naïve, trust your Nature which is kind and good, help the poor, the weak, the needy, turn the other cheek, reach out even to those who've harmed you, who've betrayed you. Be like a child.

Try trust for a change? It can't be worse. Or haven't you noticed the Old Game never worked? Bill Tilden, the great American tennis player once said, "Never change a winning game; always change a losing one." One war after another? Sounds like a losing game to me.

And if you can't trust, can't change, can't turn the other cheek, at least stop telling yourself you're a Christian. And here's the latest breaking news from The Man: you ain't gonna be setting up housekeeping any time soon in The Kingdom of Heaven!

> "O give me a home where the buffalo roam.
> Where the deer and the antelope play.
> Where seldom is heard a discouraging word.
> And the skies are not cloudy all day."

Nice, huh? Oh, wait a minute, Native Americans had their home on the range from the get-go. And they trusted us.

- *Yeah, they trusted us white guys? You know, the Christians.*

70

A carpenter came, name of Jesus
With a message of Love he said frees us
Those pounding their Bibles
With slanderous libels
Don't they know that His words were to ease us?

You'd think I was a Christian the way I rant on sometimes about Jesus. I'm not. But He *is* the philosophical, spiritual, cultural guide of our entire Western culture and people profess to be Christians and follow His teachings and look up to Him as the Son of God. And that's pretty high up. I mean, it doesn't really get much higher up than Son of God. So I always wonder why everybody who professes doesn't act like He acted.—

I read a book once called *The Imitation of Christ* by Thomas á Kempis. It's about emulating Christ, actually living His words. It seems to me, if you call yourself a Christian, that ought to be something you'd want to do, i.e., live his words. To say, "Well, yeah, it would be good to be like Him, but I can't do that because it's too hard," doesn't really cut it because it's also hard to become a physicist or a brain surgeon or a trapeze artist but lots of people do it. I think the reason many Christians don't act like Jesus is not because it's hard but because they don't want to. Kicking hatred, violence, and competition is like tossing the Marlboros. You know you ought to but dragging on that butt feels so good. —You know, War, Marlboros...it's called *adickshun*.

During one of the Republican debates that preceded the 2,000 U.S. presidential election, all the candidates for the nomination were asked by the moderator, "Who is your favorite political philosopher?" Some of the candidates gave thoughtful, interesting answers. Bush II answered, "Jesus Christ." And I would guess that a whole lot of Americans flushed with great pride at his response. But now, looking back on the eight years of the Bush dominion, I wonder, could it have been a mere slip of the tongue, could he have meant, "Machiavelli"?

I went into a church once in New York just to look inside. It was down in the Village. I think it was on Hudson Street by the old White Horse Tavern (where the great poet Dylan Thomas used to drink). It was an old, small church and above the two or three steps that led up to the altar there was a kind of proscenium arch and along the top of the arch was lettered, "I have come that ye may have life, that ye may have it more abundantly." It was the first time I had ever seen those words and they blew me away. "More abundantly" had a very powerful ring, as did the whole utterance, but "more abundantly" was like a drum roll on a tympani, or two or three tympanis. And I felt I understood what He was saying.

I suppose His words could be used to justify anything - from killing a doctor outside an abortion clinic to waging war so we can have what we consider a more abundant life. But what He was saying to me was "Remember me and take it easy, smell the roses, love all creatures, tickle the baby." It might be interesting, as an exercise, to wonder how Jesus would handle whatever it is we're confronting daily in 2018.—

President Jesus? Head honcho at the UN?

- *I wish.*

71

Fiddling, Piddling, and Twiddling
World leaders perpetually diddling
Each other and us
With their ludicrous fuss
Deadly fools with results less than middling

Whenever a President of the United States or a candidate for the job mentions the country, he always refers to it as "this great nation," or "the greatest nation on earth," or "the most powerful nation on earth." Of course, that kind of talk makes Americans feel strong and potent. And exceptional. Oh, yeah, that's right, it's called "American Exceptionalism." Of course, other leaders are saying the same thing to their suckers. Oh, sorry, I mean, citizens. Although it's hard to imagine the president of Paraguay calling his country "the greatest nation on earth." But there it is; I'm doing it, too. Political bigotry.

Of course, I don't live there, so I don't really know what other presidents and kings say to their peoples. But I do think I know why the President of the United States is always calling this country, "The most powerful nation on the face of the earth," or, for variety, "The most powerful nation in all of history." I think it's because he wants to feel powerful, thinks he should feel powerful, but doesn't so he has to keep reminding himself that he is.

For example, every time there's an act of terrorism: a plane is blown up, a barracks is demolished by a suicide bomber, even when the WTC pancakes, the Pres will stand before the nation and promise the perpetrators swift and terrible retribution. He hopes he sounds tough and forceful saying he's going to commit "the full resources of the Federal Government of the United States" to back up his promise. But really, in his heart, he's got to know he's flailing at phantoms. And even if he could catch the people behind the crime, he knows there are twenty or a thousand more preparing to replace them. There are people who hate this country for reasons they consider valid and as long as we go on giving them reasons to hate us and their hatred is nurtured, they will strike and probably do so with impunity. To their own peoples they may be heroes, possibly the Patrick Henrys of their cause. And perhaps nothing any president could do would ameliorate the situation or assuage their hatred. But it might be interesting to listen to them for a change instead of posturing and posing and pretending we're strong, unafraid, and impregnable.

The reason the words of our leaders sound so empty is that they are almost always inauthentic. When Nixon resigned, all the media ran to Gerald Ford's house because, as vice president, he had just been bumped up. I remember watching the event live. Ford came out of his house in shirtsleeves to talk to the nation. He had nothing prepared so he spoke off the cuff. Although I don't remember what he said, I will never forget how he said it. He spoke like a man, like a citizen, a regular guy. I was thrilled and I remember thinking, Wow, this guy is gonna be great, he talks from his heart. But that was the last time. Next speech was scripted, and I watched him sink into the great Bog of Platitude.

But their rhetoric may not be entirely the fault of our leaders. We, after all, don't want them to speak from their hearts (assuming they still have hearts to speak from after a lifetime in politics). I mean, how would it have been for a president to stand up after two hundred Marines were killed in a terrorist attack and say something like, "Gee, folks, I'm really sad because I realize that, even if we learn who's behind this, there's not much I can do about it? Suppose we learn it's

187

Iran who was behind this terrible deed? What can I do? We can't bomb Tehran, murder innocent people. Sanctions already in place are clearly ineffective, so I feel powerless and afraid and unsure of how to proceed. Maybe I should call the top guy in Iran and ask him how we can improve our relationship with an eye to possibly becoming friends so things like this won't happen in the future."

- *Ain't never gonna happen, Pal.*

At Thanksgiving we expect one kind of speech from the White House, Veteran's Day a different one, Tomb of the Unknown Soldier soapier yet, Mother's Day (My Mom was the greatest), Labor Day (Love them unions). At this age, I know them all by heart. "The Chest Thumper," "The Human Values," "The Greatest Nation," "We'll Get the Bad Guys." After all, presidents, prime ministers, kings are on the payroll. And if you're paying a prostitute, what you want are "oohs" and "ahs," certainly never Truth.—

Back when then Russian President Boris Yeltsin fired his whole cabinet, I asked a Russian friend of mine what he thought about it. My late friend, Grigori Khozin, was very bright, a prolific author, a professor in Moscow. He answered my question in his inimitable Russian accent, "Well, if you're running a whorehouse, isn't it good for business to change the prostitutes occasionally?"

Good line but I don't agree Grigori. Our Congress? Hey, we change our hookers every once in a while, but it doesn't help.

- *I mean, look around.*

72

Look in their eyes, cold and beady
These are not statesmen, they're greedy
War-waging brokers
Shoveling skulls like mad stokers
The lineage of Adolph and Idi

Erich Maria Remarque had it right in his great anti-war novel *All Quiet On the Western Front* – round up all the world leaders and dump them in an arena and let *them* fight it out.

It's easy to put the finger on guys like Hitler and Idi Amin as I've done in my jingle, but the rest of them are in there playing the war game in their sometimes flagrant, sometimes subtle ways. We in the U.S. always cast ourselves as Keepers of The World's Moral Flame, Boy Scouts, apple pie, mummy and all that. LBJ mouthed off about the heavy moral burden of sending American boys to their deaths but he lied through his dentures about the Gulf of Tonkin so he could send *more* American troops off to their deaths. Kennedy had his Bay of Pigs. The Bushes got their wars and stood tall for a while breathing hard over their poll numbers. And Reagan? Well, he had a war. But it was a crummy little war south of the border in formidable Grenada,

189

no less. Sure, they all dribble on their tuxedos about peace but, like most men, they love war.—

It's dangerous to assume our leaders mean it when they say they're striving for peace. They don't mean it. And they're not striving, except to get reelected. Of course, they're all constrained to pay lip service to the platitude. If men meant it when they say they want peace, they wouldn't be paying scalpers and bookies huge money for football tickets, they wouldn't be screaming themselves hoarse at the cage fights when one of the fighters starts to bleed and it looks like a knockout may be imminent, and they wouldn't be slapping the wife and kids around. Nah, very few men mean it when they say they want peace.

- *But, very occasionally, one really does*

It was '95 or '96 and I had the privilege of suggesting to the Academy of Motion Picture Arts and Sciences, of which I'm a member, that they give a special Academy Award, a Lifetime Achievement Award, to actor Lew Ayers because he was old and ailing and because he had the balls to put his life and a major career on the line as a Conscientious Objector in the Second World War when that was most emphatically not a popular thing to do. Ayers, of course, had starred in the aforementioned *All Quiet on the Western Front* and in a lot of other movies including the enormously successful *Dr. Kildare* film series. He was a fine actor and a huge box office name when he declared himself a non-combatant. Although he did serve in the army as a medic, he refused to bear arms and kill. What's more, he stood up and said so in the face of withering scorn. And, of course, he suffered the big hit on his career.

And my suggestion for a special Academy Award for Lew? Well, how unexpected...the Academy didn't go for it. No Oscar for Lew.

He died in 1996. Most people under the age of fifty have probably never even heard of him or his courage. But I can tell you for a fact that Goddess and all Her Angels were awaiting that great man, actor Lew Ayers, who lived his conscience despite withering scorn. They were there en masse with wings spread wide when that brave soul strode through the gates.

- *He stood up. Bless you, Lew.—*

The headline review of *Western Front* on rottentomatoes:

- "Director Lewis Milestone's brilliant anti-war polemic, headlined by an unforgettable performance from Lew Ayers, lays bare the tragic foolishness at the heart of war."

73

Consider the last lonely whale
Her wail in the void makes me quail
In that vast empty space
The last of her race
Ah, your woes next to hers I say pale

I read a book once called *Ishi.* —It was about the last Native American living in the wild, i.e. not on a reservation. He lived in California. His tribe had been wiped out by U.S. forces when he was a child and he had escaped to live off the land in the way of his people, alone for his entire life. He was like one of those old Japanese soldiers who used to occasionally emerge from the jungle after fifty years who didn't know the Second World War was over. —Ishi walked out of the underbrush in the 1920s and gave himself up. Anthropologists smacked their lips and jumped all over him as a way to study a real live "wild Indian," something they had never had the opportunity to do before and so Ishi lived in some university for the remainder of his life and was studied.

The above paragraph was written from memory. While rewriting, I decided to check the facts, so I went to the library and took out *Ishi In Two Worlds, A Biography of the Last Wild Indian in North America* by Theodora Kroeber. It was published by University of California Press. Theodora was the wife of Alfred Kroeber who was the head anthropologist at UC Berkeley in charge of caring for and learning from his charge. It was not the 1920s but on August 29th, 1911 that Ishi appeared. He was discovered in the corral of a slaughterhouse:

> "The wild man was emaciated to starvation, his hair was burned off close to his head, he was naked except for a ragged scrap of ancient covered-wagon canvas which he wore around his shoulders like a poncho."

The remnant of his tribe had numbered fewer than a dozen. This number had gradually diminished over fifty years until at the end Ishi had been alone for four years. He was a Yahi, the last of a tribe which had probably numbered around three thousand individuals. At the end, exhausted, starving, alone, he had walked out of the Stone Age into another world, a world he then lived in for four years and seven months before he died.

When I first read the book, I thought he must have been the saddest and loneliest man in the world. Now many years later, I cannot reread it. I try to imagine what it would have felt like to have been born into his world and to have, fifty years later, walked into ours. To have been the last one.

Here is the dedication from the book, it's worth reproducing here:

"To Alfred Kroeber
- through whom we principally know Ishi and

To the First Californians:

Indians who knew their land
Its bounteousness
Its varied beauty
Its fragility.
Who used it well
Benefiting man
Leaving unraped

Its animals, plants, trees
Earth, streams, beaches, ocean.

Whose Way
Was one of reason
Contentment
Self-knowledge."

But many individuals of many species have wandered alone, the last of their kind, sounding their mating call or their warning cry into an endless void, and have heard in return only silence.

Cut to: the following is an article from the New York Times of October 8, 1996:

1,096 Mammal and 1,108 Bird Species

By LES LINE

"Since 1960, when it started a card file on 34 rare animals, the Species Survival Commission of the World Conservation Union has kept a rapidly growing list of threatened wildlife on every continent. The Red List, as it became known to conservationists, was updated last week using revised criteria for determining the risk of extinction, and the news is grim: 1,096 mammals, nearly one-fourth of all known species, are considered threatened, as are 1,108 birds, more than 11 percent of the world's bird species.

"The number of mammals listed as critically endangered (169), endangered (315) or vulnerable (612) is startling, since this is the first time that the organization, formerly known as the International Union for the Conservation of Nature, has fully assessed the status of each of the 4,630 or so species in the world's 26 orders of mammals. In the past only birds, which number 9,670 species, have been evaluated on a comprehensive global scale.

"The three risk categories are based in large part on the rate of a species' population decline over the last 10 years.

"For example, animals whose numbers have dropped by 80 percent are considered critically endangered. Habitat loss, fragmentation and degradation, reflecting human population growth and economic development, were cited as the most significant threats to Red List animals. But the Species Survival Commission said the introduction of non-native species threatened entire ecological communities, especially in aquatic systems and in isolated environments like oceanic islands.

"In a statement, Interior Secretary Bruce Babbitt described the new Red List as "probably the most thorough scientific assessment of the state of the world's wildlife ever undertaken." Dr. Russell Mittermier, a primate expert who is president of Conservation International in Washington, called the report "indisputable proof that warnings about global biological loss haven't been exaggerated."

"And Dr. William Conway, director of the Wildlife Conservation Society at the Bronx Zoo, said, "Few animals that lie in the path of human development and have limited ranges can be expected to survive without special efforts to protect them."

- *More than 500 scientists contributed to the evaluations, which identify 5,025 animals of all kinds as threatened.—*

"The document lists 253 reptile, 124 amphibian and 734 fish species as being at risk of extinction, but it emphasizes that thousands of species in those taxonomic groups have not been assessed.

"It is impossible to make definitive statements about their overall conservation status," the report states. And 1,891 species of invertebrates, mainly crustaceans, insects and mollusks, are threatened, but very few of the so-called lower animals have been examined relative to their immense numbers.

"Among the different orders of mammals, 330 species of rodents, 231 bats, 152 shrews and moles, 65 carnivores (cats, bears, raccoons, wild dogs and weasels), 96 primates and 70 even-toed ungulates (hippopotamuses, pigs, deer, antelope, goats and sheep) are listed as threatened. In the case of primates, nearly half the world's monkeys and apes are on the Red List, along with 11 of 8 species of hoofed mammals, a high-profile group that includes rhinoceroses, zebras, wild horses and tapirs.

"Among little-known mammals listed as critically endangered, the Gulf of California porpoise or vaquita (Spanish for "little cow") has been reduced to around 100 individuals because of pollution, water diversion and entanglements in fishing nets. The pygmy hog, the world's smallest pig species, survives in two wildlife sanctuaries in India. And only 200 Tonkin snub-nosed monkeys exist in isolated forest fragments in northern Vietnam.

"The countries with the largest number of threatened mammals are Indonesia (128 species). China, and India (75 each). The report notes that these countries are species-rich but also account for 43 percent of the world's human population, which puts tremendous pressure on critical habitats. Indonesia, Brazil, and China have the highest number of threatened species of birds: 104, 103 and 90 respectively."

- *And that was on Page 4 of Section C!*

I recently read again one of those immense utterances by the great Native American, Chief Seattle, in which he tells us that the fate of the creatures of the earth is our fate. Of course, he was just an Indian. Probably never even went to college! Besides, to really hear what he was saying would lead to terrible inconvenience.

And what can you say? He may have lived in and understood the Web of Creation but guaranteed he didn't have Hagen Daz. I mean, who gives a shit about a world without monkeys? But a world without Hagen Daz? Unimaginable. I tremble.

- *Nevertheless, one is occasionally visited by that last sick whale haunting a rotting sea singing her grief into an eternity of empty, dead water.*

74

The Majority thinks itself Moral
Their pulpits ringed round with wreaths floral
They've pulled off a heist
They've robbed us of Christ
Which ignites in my cheeks shades of coral

It's kind of embarrassing to be a man. I mean, all the women with half a brain know what we are inside and what we've done to the planet. They know we're arrogant and self-important, competitive, greedy, brutal, stupid; they know we like football, for heaven's sake, know we're desperately trying to quash our softer, feminine side, they know we're really killers in our hearts and haven't got the foggiest notion of what love is all about, that we admire big muscles and big tits (not necessarily on the same gender), that we've perpetrated untold atrocities on members of their sex and their children over eons and they know, to top it off, that we're proud of ourselves and think we're God's gift to women and the world.—

Smart women know all this and more, so it's pretty embarrassing to look them in the eye. And there's no pretending at all we're something else because all the smart women *know* who and what we are.

- *And the reason it's embarrassing is because they're right. We are what they know we are.*

I addressed the U.S. Space Foundation in Colorado Springs a few years ago. I suggested perhaps we should pay a little more respect to the planet we live on. I was gentle, not rancorous in my presentation because I knew I was talking to, as my wife calls them, "the 600 greatest hawks in America," the Military/Industrial Complex itself. The next day, in *his* speech, a super high-ranking, four-star Air Force general, the head of the North American Space Command no less, calls me, in his most demeaning, contemptuous voice, a "tree hugger" even though I'd made zero reference to trees in my address. And I just sat there and smiled up at him. Now I'm embarrassed. Embarrassed because I didn't have the balls to leap to my feet and yell back at him, "I'd rather be a tree hugger than a missile hugger anytime. At least what you think I'm hugging is alive, you fat jerk."

You know how, if you were ever in a foreign country when Americans were talking loudly about how you can't even get a good hamburger in this dinky jerkwater country, you feel like hiding behind your newspaper? Well, that's how I feel about almost every man I can think of. Certainly all the big names. Bill Clinton, you embarrass the hell out of me. You nominated Lani Guenier and others of your friends to high office and when the Republicans jumped all over them, you wussed out and bailed. And you wussed out on gays in the military. And you supported welfare cuts for Mothers with Dependent Children instead of taking on the vested interests behind the ridiculously bloated military budget. Sissy.

George H.W. Bush, shame on you for lying about Iran-Contra to save your butt. Reagan: likewise. Little Bush, you're a joke. Every man in the Chinese government for fifty years, shame on you for what you did and continue to do to the Tibetan people. All you men in the military junta ruling Burma, shame on you all for what you've been doing to that beautiful, courageous, powerful woman freely elected by the people of your country. You imprisoned her, a Nobel Peace Prize winner, you cowardly assholes. All you dictators, suppressors and destroyers of your peoples and your countries, shame on you. You greedy bankers. You laughable politicians, you doctors who will not stand up to the drug companies, all of you, you're pathetic. You men

198

who are illegally cutting down and burning the world's sacred forests for your profit, all you sad, grubby, greedy, heartless pillagers of this Garden of Eden, go fuck yourselves and then drop dead.

Ah, but then, my rancor exhausted, I think of Sitting Bull. The marauding Top Hats (i.e. white men from Washington) told him he must sign a certain treaty but instead he simply stood up and opened his robe to show his manhood. He didn't have to sign; his manhood was his oath. And I think of Chief Seattle and the great leader of the Nez Perce, Chief Joseph ("From where the sun now stands, I will fight no more forever"), who attempted, against overwhelming odds, to lead his people out of the white man's clutches in what historians have called one of the most brilliant retreats in military history. And I think of Geronimo and Audubon. John Muir, and Robert Frost. And Jesus. And Lao Tzu. And so many others now thronging to my heart. The courageous ones: Dr. Martin Luther King, Jr. and the Buddhist monks who immolated themselves protesting the horrors in Vietnam. The truth tellers. The artists, the poets, the filmmakers who have spoken truly. The heroes.

- *Those were men.*

- *So my brothers, whadya say? Do we have the courage to link arms and march together to join these Magnificent Few?*

75

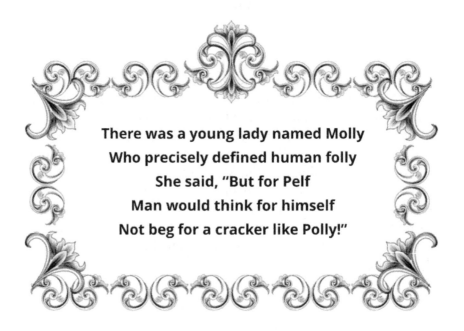

There was a young lady named Molly
Who precisely defined human folly
She said, "But for Pelf
Man would think for himself
Not beg for a cracker like Polly!"

For forty-four years I earned my living as an actor. Occasionally, I came close to having to get another job, but something always came along. It's unusual. Since, according to the Screen Actors Guild, only three percent of actors make a living solely at acting, someplace along the line most actors have to fill in the gaps. Joke:

—Two guys meet waiting for a bus. After a while, they start to chat.

1st guy: "Whaddya do?"—
2nd guy: "Matter of fact, I'm an actor."
1st guy: "No way! Me too! What restaurant you work at?"

But in pulling down a living as an actor all my life, I learned a lot about smiling at people I didn't necessarily want to smile at, saying things I didn't mean, speaking lines I knew were badly written and pretending they were good and keeping my hat in my hands. Begging for my next cracker.

Thousands of actors creep painfully up the steps on their knees and knock at huge temple doors. Occasionally, a High Priest opens the door a crack and beckons one in. The rest remain on their knees, waiting. The High Priests are, of course, the producers, directors, and casting people who open and close the doors of the temple. The mass of supplicants milling about on the steps outside, like some starving throng beseeching food at a Bombay train station, are the tens of thousands of actors clamoring for their moment inside the Holy of Holies.

Because of a lifetime of experience in and out of the temple, I've always envied those who, by chance or design, were able to get an independent living. The cobbler, the subsistence farmer, the small book publisher. I read once the only thing early American farmers required to survive was iron. With iron they could forge their own tools and farm implements. Then they raised flax to spin linen cloth and they were free. It was undoubtedly a difficult life, but they were also very strong people.—

I once quit the acting business for two years from 1960 to 1962 and lived in Vermont. For a while, I worked for 85 cents an hour "pickin' stone" for a French Canadian farmer named Lucien Leroux. My job was to drive a tractor that pulled a "stone boat" behind it. I drove up and down Farmer Leroux's fields loading stones onto this long, flat "stone boat," then hauled them to the edges of the field and dumped them to be eventually built into walls. These were stones that had been heaved out of the ground by the winter freeze. Sometimes there was a huge boulder that had to be removed. I would dig all around it to be able to get a chain around it so I could rip it out of the ground with the tractor. Even so, sometimes it wouldn't come. Then Mr. Leroux would get down in the hole and heave that thing up by himself in an incredible display of strength. And at 6'2" and 210 pounds back then, I thought I knew something about strength myself because I'd been a body builder. I fancied myself pretty strong. But I was nowheresville compared to little farmer Leroux.

There I was killing myself for eighty-five cents an hour, working harder than I ever thought possible, and Mr. Leroux canned me for goofing off.

I can only imagine how strong our forebears were, hammering their ingots of iron into plowshares. I saw remnants of that independent strength and spirit in the Vermont dairy farmers I knew in those two years. But it was dying. It was being killed in them as I watched. Their independence was being assassinated by the local supermarket. They were immured by insurance policies, forced by the local dairy to go deeply into debt to install newly mandated bulk milking systems, the whole swamp into which we've all been herded by our inattention or sloth or desire for the easy life.

- *Then their church-centered social life was slaughtered by a couch and a TV set.*

Who will park his tractor and take up the rusty scythe? Who will lay down his chainsaw for the old crosscut saw hanging in the barn? In the old days, I was told in Vermont, a good man could cut eight cords of wood in a day *by hand* and then spend the hours before sleep sharpening his saw blades for the next day's cutting. Who will shun the hardware store for his old anvil and forge? And even if we could rediscover our lost independence, could we, would we trade our social security, medical insurance, and three TV sets just to stand free and independent?

If you can't live free of the company store, you're doomed to smile at the man who signs your check. If your livelihood depends on the good will of another, you are in fact already on your knees on the temple steps, hat in hand, waiting for the doors to crack open.

Or, even worse, you're already inside and desperate to remain. You're memorizing badly written garbage and mouthing it on cue with a "thank you" on your lips.

- *Been there...*

76

From issues complex, problematical
We urgently need a sabbatical
We need to repair
away from the glare
Of the zealous, the jealous, the fanatical

The book *How I Found Freedom in An Unfree World*, published in the 70s, was written by the late Harry Browne who used to publish a financial newsletter and was author of several books about money. He also ran for U.S. president on the Libertarian ticket in the '96 election.

I mention him because there's a chapter in the book called "The Burning-Issue Trap." The chapter begins with a list of the current burning issues, all of them clamoring for our attention, our money, and our participation. Here's Browne's list in '72-'73: "...pollution, civil rights, overpopulation, drugs, conservation, communism, consumerism, women's liberation, poverty, organized crime, law and order, disappearance of animal species, the sexual revolution, government solvency, pornography, educational problems, mental illness, privacy, high taxes, the Vietnam war, campus riots, the military-industrial complex, police brutality, and disarmament." Today there would be more: homelessness, the ozone layer, accelerating extinction of species and their habitats, fracking, climate change, poverty, terrorism, and so on and on.

Browne points out that, since there is really nothing that any individual can do about any of them, one might just as well live one's life in "freedom"! It's interesting to read Browne's list today. A few issues are gone, most of the others still burning out of control. And there are a few newbies as well.

Because I wanted to be free - which is why I read the book - I decided to adopt Browne's philosophy and not get involved. And, short of sending money occasionally to people like Greenpeace and The Sierra Club, organizations which obviously hadn't read the book, I did nothing.

Until I met my wife, who *had* read the book but was nevertheless dedicating her life to a Burning Issue. She had fallen hook, line, and sinker into the Trap of attempting to prevent the basing of weapons in space. When we married, I fell into her Trap: contributing money to her non-profit institute as well as supporting her in every way so that she could completely devote herself to her Trap. In addition, I educated myself about her Burning Issue and gave several speeches around the country on what a bad idea space-based weapons would be. And through her, during the course of the last 33 years now, I've met a number of people who carry the torch for other Traps.—

Based on this long experience in the trenches (or at least close to the front lines), I think now Harry Browne was wrong. Burning Issues are not fads as he suggests, and, if left unattended by people of good will, such Burning Issues can and often do become conflagrations.

Without Jacques Cousteau to awaken us to the plight of the oceans, we would have remained ignorant. Without Greenpeace to beat us over the head with the worldwide decimation of whale populations, we would have remained unaware of their continued disappearance. Without Ric O'Barry of The Dolphin Project, the original trainer of the dolphins in the hit TV series *Flipper* (who has atoned a thousand-fold for figuring out how to train them), we might never have recognized these magnificent creatures for the highly intelligent, magical beings they are. If you have the courage, see the Academy

204

Award-winning documentary *The Cove* that O'Barry produced. Without The Club of Rome or Astronaut Dr. Edgar Mitchell's Institute of Noetic Sciences, and many others who have lured us into their traps, we might have remained forever the slack-jawed mouth breathers we were before they summoned us to their good fight. People who face the wall of flames of a Burning Issue are as brave as they come, sounding the alarm whilst the rest of us snuggle dreaming in our beds. They are, like firefighters, champions of the future. Heroes.

The trick, for people standing before the roaring conflagration of a Burning Issue, is how do you keep a sense of humor when your lungs are seared, you're feeling the blast on your cheeks, and you're busting your chops digging a trench to contain the flames? When you passionately believe in something, unflinchingly advocate it, put your life on the line to espouse it (O'Barry has been run down by ships while protesting the deadly, insane use of dolphins by the U.S. Navy), lived, breathed your Burning Issue, it's not easy to smile about it, especially when no one around you seems to particularly give a damn. If a corporation is going to cut down 60,000 acres of virgin redwoods and it happens to be the last ancient stand in the world and it's your very own sacred temple and you want to murder the Philistine bastards who are about to perpetrate the sacrilege, it's easy to become a nutcase yourself. A zealot, a fanatic.

Maybe firefighters have the answer. When they hear the bell, they rush to the rescue. But they must live with the fact that sometimes they will save very little or nothing at all. And, as with the 19 members of the Granite Mountain Hotshots lost in the 2013 Arizona blaze that took them all, sometimes heroes don't come home. But when one of their trucks goes by - even though sirens are blaring - their faces are serene. They seem to be in good spirits, even jocular in pursuit of their mission. They're not fanatics, they're firefighters.

Ah, but the question is, when it's a million-alarm fire and the Burning Issue is Mother Earth Herself, can *our* faces remain serene as we tear through the intersection of Past and Future?

- *Listen! Hear the sirens?*

77

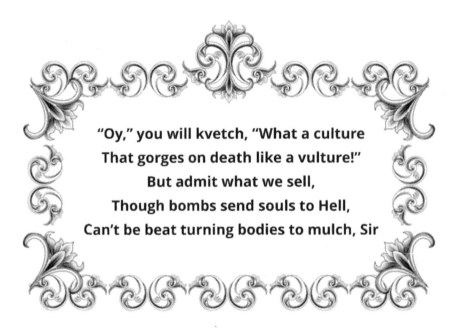

"Oy," you will kvetch, "What a culture
That gorges on death like a vulture!"
But admit what we sell,
Though bombs send souls to Hell,
Can't be beat turning bodies to mulch, Sir

Consider how weird it is that the central symbol of Western civilization is a cross with a dead Guy nailed to it. Spooky.

I walk into a church in Spain in 1960. Maybe it was Seville. A big church. It's dark and mysterious. The pungent smell of incense bathes my nostrils. Candles flicker. A few women in black are scattered in the pews. No men. Above the altar, Jesus hangs dying or maybe he's already dead. Suffering hangs in the air like that poor 33-year-old man splayed out on his crossbeam. I stand in the back feeling the place for a while. Then I flee.

- *Christianity scares the shit out of me.*

A while ago, a resolution was taken at the annual convention of the Baptist Church to proselytize and convert the Jews. When the news was released, Jews seemed peeved by this unwanted, unwonted attention. Strangely, they prefer to remain Jewish. But in their familiar missionary zeal, the good Baptists are apparently arming themselves once again to bring the Good News about Jesus Christ to those unfortunates unlucky enough not to have heard it.

Of course, this touching concern for the world's less-privileged peoples has positively impacted the lives of so many fortunate millions over the last centuries. As an example of the Church's beneficence, the lives of native peoples of North and South America were obviously vastly improved after the arrival of the emissaries of the Prince of Peace. In fact, the lives of all aboriginal peoples around the globe have been similarly enhanced by His teachings. Consider, the people of Polynesia: once a lazy bunch with nothing better to do than fish, lie about on the beach, and make love are now well-clothed, tax-paying citizens of islands that are now, whoops, sinking beneath the waves. And, of course, we mustn't forget how, in the 16th and 17th centuries, former Christian gentlemen pitched right in and helped so many African families trade their little grass huts and subsistence lives for a one-way ticket across the ocean with free room, board, and clothing awaiting them!

And, lest we appear to be sexist, let us not forget the immolation of five million witches, err, I mean, women by those guardians of Christ's words of Love, the Holy Roman Church. Good News of Lord JC lit the torch for all those poor lost souls. It must warm the heart to glance around the world and see the illumination our culture has spread - with Jesus riding point - to every dark corner of the planet, to every unenlightened soul lucky enough to be smitten with His joyous tidings of peace and resurrection.

Ok, I'm slinging it. This culture *is* a vulture that feeds on the bodies it destroys in its wars, its factories, its mines, its cities, its hospitals, its genocides. The Killing Fields were not just in Cambodia; the Killing Fields are everywhere we've hung our symbol of Love.

So sorry, JC, I know you had nothing to do with the carnage. Nevertheless, there you hang above altars around the world. Love murdered.

- *Talk about sad!*

And, get this, those bumptious Baptists are having trouble understanding the reluctance of Jews to embrace The Good News. I must be kidding, right?

- *I'm not kidding.*

PS: And, get this: August 21, 2018, on the news this morning, I hear that, in addition to the 300 priests that've been cited in, I think, Pennsylvania for hitting on young people in their care, the Attorney General called upon anyone in the state in the past who had experienced sexual abuse should call a hotline. Did they get any calls? Yeah, they got so many calls they couldn't handle them.

- *Priests?*

78

Call me nuts, call me crazy, a sap, sure!
My belief is our hearts can recapture -
Though words from above
Speak rarely of Love -
THE DREAM OF WORLD PEACE: that's in caps, sure!

I wrote this at the time of the Big Summits in the eighties when the peoples of the entire globe were regularly treated to the spectacle of two men, representing the most militarily powerful nations in history, circling each other like roosters posturing for constituencies clustered around flickering screens watching their bird-brained leaders slash and flutter.

My faith is strong that the majority of ordinary people are sane and wish only to be left alone to live their lives. The question is - perhaps has always been - how to get the wacko roosters back into their cages where they belong.

The thing I know is, peace-loving people love peace. And, because they love peace, they abhor bloodshed and struggle. But to get the roosters back in their cages may require just that: bloody hands and a real tussle. Because those birds'll do anything to keep on fighting.

And, ponder this, if we could ever somehow get a lock on the cage, are we going to be bored out of our skulls when those nasty cocks are no longer strutting their stuff?

- *Bored with world peace? Hmmm...*

- *PS: It occurs to me that calling world leaders "bird-brained" requires an apology.*

- *Sorry birds.*

79

Carol, who chucked her chinchilla
When she learned of the desperate gorilla,
Then devoted her soul
To repairing the whole:
She supported the Earth like a pillar

There was a time not too long ago when actress Cybill Shepherd was the television shill for the fur industry. I mean, really. What can you say about somebody like Ms. Shepherd? To my way of thinking, her insensitivity to the suffering of animals makes her the most pointy-headed dunce to sail down the pike in a long, long time. To wear a fur coat is one thing. Bad enough. But, come on, to use your celebrity to promote the idea that wearing dead animals is sexy is pretty stinky. But there she was in my living room, looking just delighted with herself, wrapped up in the skins of poor creatures who were raised and slaughtered for the very purpose of adorning people like her. Barf city.—

Life = profit. Capitalism is our religion and *laissez faire* is its liturgy. There's an old joke that goes like this:

- He: Wanna party, Baby?
- She: How much can ya spend?
- He: How about ten bucks!
- She: Ten bucks? Hey, man, you take me for a whore?
- He: That's already determined. We're just workin' out the price.

To put it nicely, people like Shepherd have sold their humanity. By comparison, your average call girl is an ascended master.

I wonder how many women (and men) would wear fur if they had to slaughter and skin the poor creatures themselves or even witness their slaughter? The economies of some Asian countries are exploding and, as the standard of living of their citizens "improves," they are importing huge additional quantities of pigs and cattle. If these new heart attack candidates had to listen to the screams of their marbled steak as it moved on its conveyor belt towards the man with the ice pick or had to look into the terrified eyes of that slab of roast beef swimming in blood, I wonder how many of them would go with the tofu?

Given this trend, one may only assume ladies in the east will soon be sporting dead animals as well. Now *that's* a lotta fur. Ah, Cybill.

And here's a PS from January, 2014: "Dallas, Texas (CNN) -- The Dallas Safari Club auctioned off a black rhino hunting permit in Namibia for $350,000, according to the club's public relations firm. Wealthy hunters gathered Saturday evening inside the Dallas Convention Center to bid on the rare chance to hunt one of the world's most endangered animals."

- *Wait, wait, I have an idea. How about an auction for a permit to hunt and kill the psycho who won the permit?*

- *Or is that just too, too obvious?*

80

If you let slip the dogs of war
To feast on the spatter and gore
You're faced with a puzzle:
When you've buckled the muzzle
Can you lure them with Peace they abhor?

Of course, I stole the phrase "the dogs of war" from Mark Antony's famous speech over Caesar's corpse in Act III, Scene I of Shakespeare's *Julius Caesar*. It's one of the Bard's greatest moments. Caesar has just been murdered by conspirators led by Brutus and Cassius who permit Mark Antony, Caesar's friend, a moment alone with Caesar's corpse while the two conspirators go before the people to present their reasons for having murdered Caesar. Antony, who has shaken the conspirators' hands, pretending to condone their deed, begins with his famous apology to his dead friend:

O, pardon me, thou bleeding piece of earth,
That I am meek and gentle with these butchers!
Thou art the ruins of the noblest man
That ever lived in the tide of times.
Woe to the hand that shed this costly blood!
Over these wounds now do I prophesy,-
Which like dumb mouths do ope their ruby lips,
To beg the voice and utterance of my tongue,
A curse shall light upon the limbs of men;
Domestic fury and fierce civil strife
Shall cumber all the parts of Italy;
Blood and destruction shall be so in use
And dreadful objects so familiar,
That mothers shall but smile when they behold
Their infants quarter'd with the hands of war;
All pity chok'd with custom of fell deeds:
And Caesar's spirit, ranging for revenge,
With Ate by his side come hot from hell,
Shall in these confines with a monarch's voice
Cry *Havoc*, and let slip the dogs of war;
That this foul deed shall smell above the earth
With carrion men, groaning for burial.

There are many descriptions of war and its consequences in Shakespeare's plays but none more terse and powerful than this. Here is the perfect declaration of a man's determination to submit an entire nation to all the consequences of war to satisfy his thirst for revenge. —And what Brutus speaks to the people immediately afterwards in Scene II as explanation for the murder is the equivalent of a policy statement from Washington. Antony's famous funeral oration, "Friends, Romans, countrymen, lend me your ears; I come to bury Caesar, not to praise him," in which he pretends to condone Caesar's murder, is also the kind of masterpiece of sly manipulation we get from politicians. But in the above "O, pardon me" speech, Shakespeare invites us to peer into the hearts of men who entice us into wars where "all pity [is] choked with custom of fell deeds," men who, with our indulgence, "let slip the dogs of war."

Cataclysmic events are triggered by private decisions made by men for personal reasons. If you think otherwise, you've bought the policy statement.

And perhaps Antony should have apologized, not to Caesar, who, in any case, could no longer hear him, but to the common people who would suffer and die satisfying his lust for revenge.—

81

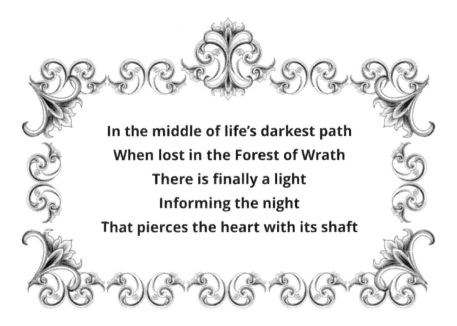

In the middle of life's darkest path
When lost in the Forest of Wrath
There is finally a light
Informing the night
That pierces the heart with its shaft

I love Dante's great lines that begin *The Inferno*:

Nel mezzo del camin di nostra vita
Me ritrovai per una selva oscura
Che la diritta via era smarrita

In the middle of the road of our life
I found myself in a dark woods
That the direct way was mistaken

At the very moment when you think you're home free, you suddenly wake up one day and you're in a dark forest. Who knows why? Maybe you've been lied to all your life. Maybe you've been lying to yourself. Maybe you suddenly question everything you hold dear or sacred because of an illness or an accident or the breakup of your marriage or the death of your child. But, suddenly, night has fallen, the air is cold, the battery dead. It's the dark of the moon and you realize you have no idea in the world where you are. Dread grips the heart. Panic looms. You followed the well-worn path, but somehow you are lost.

Now you're faced with a question. Do you sit down and wait for dawn or stumble through the underbrush flailing at the branches tearing at your face? If you sit down, you're conserving energy and there's a possibility that, if you survive the night, you may find the lost path. But you may also die of exposure. If you charge into the darkness, the exertion will keep you warm and there's the possibility you will find a new path or the salvation of a friendly light, but you may become more and more disoriented and, even with the coming of day, you run the risk of never again finding the original road.

I actually think we are all pretty much lost in the Forest of Wrath as we speak. We've played out the Judeo-Christian and the Muslim dramas and we've run out of storyline. The path has disappeared. We're armed, we're frightened, we're lost, and very scared of the dark. The millennium's turn augured strangely for us: mass suicides, comets, sightings of off-planet visitors, abductions, the murder of children, a tidal wave of pornography, acceleration of technical wizardry. 9/11. Loud voices demand a return to tradition. TV commercials seduce with images of bygone days. But we cannot sit down. There is no place to rest. We must hurtle on towards our unknown destiny.

Is there a light towards which we all stumble? We cannot know. But if there is, I think it's the internet that now embraces us all in its vast hologram of the world's brain. Perhaps there is a faint light we can yet barely perceive in the deep of the impenetrable night, that is the realization we are not alone, that, on the contrary, we are logging on in a mighty electronic chorale with millions of others who also discovered the direct path was mistaken and who even now grope towards us in that "*selva oscura.*" The dark forest.

Perhaps important to remember also that, when Virgil has escorted Dante to the deepest level of hell, they discover a hidden road:

"The Guide and I into that hidden road, now entered, to return to the bright world; And without care of having any rest, we mounted

217

up, he first and I the second, till I beheld through a round aperture, some of the beauteous things that Heaven doth bear; Thence we came forth to rebehold the stars."

O, wouldn't all the saints, the Gods and Goddesses, the weeping children of the world, the legions of our brother and sister fishes and animals, the whole born, living world, all the dreamed of spirits that have ever swum the vast oceans of the cosmos, **would they not all rejoice if we could only now refrain from infecting the heavens with our weapons**, if we would keep the space above all our heads clean and sacred, so that a new era of peace might be aborning in that great black womb in which we live and breathe?

- *O, yes, they all would sing hosannas in our praise if only we "...came forth to rebehold the stars."*

82

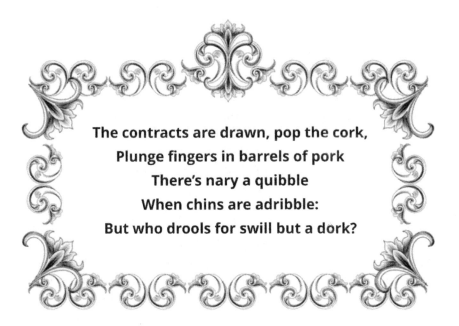

The contracts are drawn, pop the cork,
Plunge fingers in barrels of pork
There's nary a quibble
When chins are adribble:
But who drools for swill but a dork?

Perhaps the most disgusting image in politics is the pork barrel. One thinks of a feeding trough at which each grunting senator and congressperson is elbowing aside their fellow swine to better swill down the slops. Keep the useless military base open (a base that even the Pentagon says is worthless) because it provides jobs for the Folks at Home; put in the road to nowhere because it provides jobs for the Folks at Home; keep the factory open to churn out more unneeded tanks or planes because it provides jobs for the Folks at Home. Pork. Legislation to curry favor with the Folks at Home. Anything to buy our hungry Porkers another turn on the carousel.

What's more, everybody in the country knows the Pork Trough is how business is done. —Surveys measuring the confidence people have in members of various professions consistently place our public servants below used car salespeople for trustworthiness. And it's not even a secret. Everybody knows! Imagine embracing a profession where *you* know *everyone* knows you're a slobbering pig. Even your kids know you're a crook. And then, of course, you yourself know you've got dried muck on your tie. Or do you? To live with yourself, do you have to rationalize how you do business? Do you say to yourself, "If I don't slop in the trough, I won't get reelected to do all the wonderful things I do do?" Or do you finally just look in the mirror and see, "*Do-do?*"

When the line item veto was passed by a Republican congress and handed to a reelected Democrat, a bill allowing presidents to henceforth eliminate specific items they consider wasteful from proposed budgets, did these lawmakers tremble at the implications this act might have for the Pork Barrel? Or will presidents - practiced Porkers themselves - use their hard-won power to raise the feeding game to new levels of gluttony? My money is on the latter…on the theory that Hogs will be Hogs.—

The Campaign Fundraising Scandals we wallowed in during Clinton's presidency are another form of you tickle me here I'll scratch you there business as usual. Big contributors bought access to the president, even got to sleep in the Lincoln Bedroom of the White House, followed presumably by little breakfast tête-à-têtes with Bill and Hill? One wonders if the eggs and scones were provided at the public's expense? Even foreign nations like China, with questionable affection for the United States, funneled monies to the Democratic National Committee. Troughing on a global scale. And Weeny Bush, not to be outdone, raised a war chest for his run in '04 that was larger than that of any president in history, even with a year still to go! And Bush didn't even need to worry about clean sheets in the Lincoln Bedroom. That's small potatoes. He gave whole nations away. Like no competitive bid contracts in Iraq to Halliburton and Bechtel.

- *Sleepovers?! —Penny ante.*

Heady stuff. Sexy. Power as an aphrodisiac. Many of those who've worked there say Washington is the Land of the Lusty Libido. But then, so was Little Rock. But, hey, just necessary legions of high-priced ladies soothing the frayed nerves of stressed public servants.
When Dick Morris was fawning over President Clinton, a man who was a trusted campaign strategist and policy advisor, Bill's feared and revered right hand man, he was outed in a national tabloid by his

hooker. Morris had boasted to her about his access to the president and one day, to impress her, he invited her to listen in on a policy conversation with Clinton. But the hooker, seeing dork Morris as the answer to her prayers, kept a diary and took pictures and peddled her story for big bucks. Morris, of course, like his pal Clinton, is a married man.

- *Oh, sexy place Washington. That is, if you think eating with pigs is exciting.*
- *Uh-oh, clearly an apology is necessary here.*
- *Sorry, piggies.*

I can't refrain from quoting Churchill here: "I like pigs. Cats look down on us. Dogs look up to us. Pigs treat us as equals." Of course, Churchill had never "served" in the U.S. Congress.

83

In the dead of the cold, in December,
The fires of Hope are an ember
Then it's haul out the bellows
Take courage my fellows,
We're kindling the future, remember?

(For the rhyme of this limerick an obvious bow to Tom Jones and Harvey Schmidt and their beautiful song "Try to Remember" from the great musical, *The Fantasticks.*)

I've been involved a thousand times in negotiations for some acting job. The way it used to work, before the Internet, was the agent submitted you for a role by sending your picture and resume to the casting director or the producer. The casting director of the show thinks you may be right for the role, calls your agent and sets up an appointment for you to read for the producer and director. They send you the whole script or maybe just a few scenes so you can prepare an audition. You work on the material, go in and try to knock them out. If you do, they call and make an offer. Peanuts. You try to figure out how much they want you and counter with something more. Say peanuts plus five percent. They counter with peanuts plus one, take it or leave it. Ping pong. —If you need it bad, you take it. If you've got the guts, you go back for more. Bottom line is you have no power in the negotiation unless you're willing to lose the job. But to potentially blow it when you need it (and jobs for actors can be few and far between) takes real courage. None of the above applies to stars!

In the negotiations over the fate of the planet, the "producers" continually offer us peanuts. To hold out for more takes guts. Because we need it so bad (and producers always make it their business to know how bad we need it) the tendency will always be to say, "Thank you for this little piece of ancient forest" or "Of course, let that endangered mouse become extinct, if only you'll save this beautiful bird." For you, it's a question of the art, the beauty, the sanctity of the world. For the "producers," it's always a question of money. To a greater and greater extent, the "producers" and "directors" are corporations. Yes, the Supreme Court of the United States has ruled that corporations are "people." Of course, it goes without saying that corporations are *not* people, they're Golems. They live but they have no soul. They are single-minded, implacable, and exist for one purpose and one purpose only: to make money. And, in order to maximize their take, they seek absolute power. Most of the time we give them all the power they want. We knuckle under. Yes, sometimes we read about a feisty old lady who refuses to kowtow to corporate skullduggery or some town that dares to haul the local company into court, but it's rare because it requires time, immense courage, and a lot of money to do it.

Cut to: Marshall McLuhan once famously said, "The medium is the message." He meant it's not the content of the book or the program on TV that changes us - it's the medium itself. Print changed everything. When we all started to read, we began to think linearly: subject, verb, object. Major change in how we perceived the world. Movies different. TV different. Now it's the Internet, different again.—

I bring up McLuhan, because I think that it may take greater courage to be alive today and not lose hope than ever before. The instant communication of television has indeed turned us into McLuhan's "global village" as he predicted. But McLuhan is wrong about the content. The content of the medium, what it has dumped in our living rooms over the past half century, has certainly confronted us with

223

images no other people in history have been forced to see. And, in case we missed it the first time around or in the event we weren't even born when it transpired, we must see such images again and again and again. Ten thousand times we will see Kennedy's brains vaporized. Ten thousand times we will see Oswald jackknife in mortal agony, murdered Jews stacked like cordwood, the terrifying miracle of nuclear fission assaulting the heavens, the executions, the wars, the Chernobyls and Fukushimas, the Twin Towers heaving their great sigh. We have been there and revisited endlessly. And if we somehow miraculously missed the mayhem itself, we will be privileged to have it meticulously reenacted for us in a Movie of the Week. And the upshot of this front row seat? Perhaps a universal loss of innocence? A numbing of the soul? A surfeit of tragedy and a deep, unacknowledged hopelessness.

Yes, Lincoln was murdered, 23,000 men were ripped apart at Antietam in one day, Jack the Ripper struck, but we were not bludgeoned by incessant reruns for decades thereafter, for the duration of our lives. It happened, we read about it or heard it on the radio, we mourned, but we could only imagine the event itself. It happened, but it happened dimly, behind a scrim, a photograph faded with time.—

The question is then, how does one maintain courage in the face of the slow-motion pan when every horrendous act in the world is endlessly repeated on television? How does the good soul not falter in the blast, not succumb before the implacable onslaught of evil?

Well…could it be we gather in a Merrie Band in the fastness of the forest? We gather courage from our fellows and, when we're ready, we strike and strike again.

And Sherwood Forest? Why, it's the internet, of course.

- *Watch out Monsanto!*

84

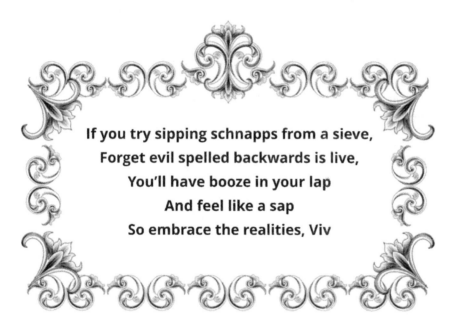

If you try sipping schnapps from a sieve,
Forget evil spelled backwards is live,
You'll have booze in your lap
And feel like a sap
So embrace the realities, Viv

And the reality? Here's my own personal revelation in a nutshell, here's my awakening: ***Those of lowest consciousness seek and attain the very highest levels of power***. Buddha ain't never gonna run for president. Jesus is not a Republican. Or a Democrat for that matter. But 99% of those on the Throne of Power? Scavengers. Predators. Those of lowest consciousness. Need proof? Simple. Watch any presidential debate. Down and dirty guaranteed.

- *And another thing:* ***THE DEAD SOULS NEVER QUIT!***

If you're Lancelot and you somehow just passed some really neat legislation about school lunches, reproductive rights, gay marriage, help for single mothers, reducing the appropriations for more war...just wait. The bad guys'll be back. Count on it. Makes no difference how long, how expensive, how difficult, theeeey'll be back.

But just today, I finally got that these scumbags can't serve the greater good, are incapable of compassion, of Truth, in fact, couldn't acknowledge the Truth even if it would save their own lives, would lie to enrich their sorry asses if they were standing before the Throne itself, right hands raised, looking straight into the eyes of God Almighty Herself.

Scumbags? Yeah, ok, I'm sorry, I'm from Brooklyn. But if a rose is a rose is a rose then a scumbag is a scumbag is a scumbag! So next time you're wondering about your elected public servant, wonder deeper.

- *Looking for reality? You got reality.—*

85

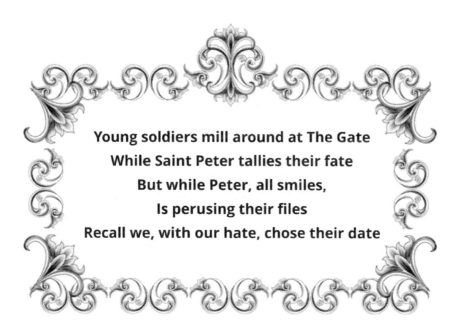

Young soldiers mill around at The Gate
While Saint Peter tallies their fate
But while Peter, all smiles,
Is perusing their files
Recall we, with our hate, chose their date

The *U.S. News and World Report* dated 12-9-96, in its cover story, a Special Report entitled Weapons Bazaar, tells the bizarre story of U.S. "aircraft, weapons and weapons parts worth billions of dollars" are sold to all comers as "military surplus." The most sophisticated weaponry as well as "fully operational encryption devices, submarine propulsion parts, radar systems, electron tubes for Patriot guided missiles, even F-117A Stealth fighter parts" were all presumably destroyed but, in fact, all are on the auction block brand new, frequently in their original packing crates.

Items for sale by the Pentagon receive a "demilitarization code" that is supposed to determine how the item is sold. A desk should be coded "A," a machine gun "D" for destroy. Investigators found, however, that "45 percent of the demilitarization codes were wrong and that about half the items were coded too leniently..."

A man in Montana who repairs helicopters had Cobra attack helicopters "fully armed." "I had rockets on it and machine guns. I was out there shooting coyotes with them," said one Ron Garlick. This of a weapon described in the article: "When armed, the Cobra is one of the deadliest military attack vehicles ever invented."

The Pentagon, downsizing because the Cold War had ended, was also interested in making profits, so everything was for sale and the more fully operational an item was, the more it fetched in the marketplace. So, there was a rather powerful incentive not to bung up a perfectly good missile if you were looking for top dollar.

Furthermore, like everything else the government touches, the scale of the surplus sales is gargantuan. There is even a website that lists "every piece of equipment that has entered the surplus inventory." Its address is: www.drms.dla.

- *Need something to kill something? Boot up, Baby.*

There is so much for sale at sites around the country by the Defense Logistics Agency (the office in the Pentagon responsible for surplus sales) no one can possibly keep track of it all. Besides, programs like this never work (always a nasty problem) - in fact, they cannot work - because people are operating them, and people just don't do it by the book. People don't care. People take shortcuts. People want to make money scamming on the side. People want to appear more successful than they are and cook the books to hype themselves. They're stupid or angry or resentful or have other fish to fry. And it's really just all about death anyway and what happens to the minds and hearts of people who are always dealing in that commodity? I mean, we're not talking about mixing decorator colors at a paint bar.

It so happens, I have an army story of my own about how it doesn't work. After induction, I was shipped first to Fort Dix, New Jersey and then to Fort Bliss, Texas, there to go through eight weeks of Basic Training before an additional eight weeks of specialized training in "Fire Control" which sounds like hoses and ladders and shiny brass poles but, in fact, meant operating a system that controlled four 90 millimeter Howitzer anti-aircraft guns. I was in the artillery! Without getting into endless detail, the truth is we didn't give a damn about

228

what we were learning. To us (395 mostly Jewish kids from Brooklyn) it was a big, stupid joke. We learned nothing. And when, for our final exam, an old World War Two bomber (I think it was a B15) was towed along as a target at about 12 miles an hour at very low altitude, we couldn't hit the thing to save our lives. Or anybody else's life for that matter. Not only that, but by the time we had "learned" to operate the system on which we'd been trained, a new system was in place and our "training" was already obsolete.

And weapons have become infinitely more sophisticated since that time so I find it impossible to believe the grunts who are operating them today aren't just as dumb as we were and couldn't give less of a damn just like us.—

The whole structure of military preparedness is supported by rage and fear...not a great foundation on which to raise an edifice. It doesn't work, it's incredibly costly in every imaginable way, it harms the soul of a nation and all its citizens and reeks of death. But the bottom line is it doesn't even work. We're told it works, but it does not.

- *Sorry, Junior, sometimes mommy and daddy tell fibs.*

86

Now Arise! Now Arise! Arise!
Let's awaken and open our eyes
Know, because we are human,
We *can* illumine
Ignorance, hatred, and lies

There is, in my mind, no question we languish in the profound sleep of an all-encompassing ignorance. It's not that we're stupid. All of us have great native intelligence, compassion, and humanity. But we're born into a web of lies and fear. Bombarded from the get-go with falsehood and deception, there seems to be no escape.

One morning, I experience an interesting juxtaposition. I visit the home of an insurance salesman who wants to sell me a long-term care policy. While he's smoking his Camels on his patio and pitching his various ideas to me, I have to go to the bathroom. And there I see, on his sink, a book by an East Indian spiritual leader named Adi Da who, according to the back cover, is the "incarnation of God." I'm fascinated. Not by Adi Da, but by a chain-smoking 53-year-old insurance salesman who has this book in his bathroom.—

When I return, I mention the book and he proceeds to show me a whole bookcase filled with spiritual literature. In the course of this conversation, he happens to mention that there's a branch of the Theosophical Society in Ojai, a small town in the Ojai Valley about 15 minutes from where I live. Since I'm somewhat conversant with Theosophy and years ago visited branches in LA and New York, I decide to check it out.

That afternoon, I make my first stop at an archery store in Ojai. I used to love archery when I was in the Boy Scouts and I shot again for a while in the early 70s under the tutelage of a much older man who, back in the late 30s, had been Errol Flynn's archery instructor and stand-in in the classic movie *Robin Hood!* But I haven't touched a bow since '72 or '73 and now I have this idea that I'm going to get back into target archery because it looks like maybe I'm retired. (Remember, acting is the only profession where you're retired but nobody bothered to tell you.) The owner of the shop goes hunting in Montana every year and he's got a little target range in the back where cutouts of animals pop up. When I'm just about to leave, a band of bow hunters comes in to buy various supplies and to practice killing something. So, I leave my arrows to be fletched, buy some things Bob tells me I need and head out to find the Theosophical Society five minutes up the road

It's called The Krotona Institute, named after Crotona, Italy where the great genius Pythagoras was said to have had his school in ancient times. A little soft-spoken lady named Laksmi shows me around, turns on the lights so I can sit in the Meditation Room, and allows me to browse in their wonderful library. Before I head out, Laksmi gives me some literature to take home so I can decide if I want to return (I already know I do). There are pamphlets entitled "What Is Theosophy," "Theosophy and Vegetarianism," "Theosophy and Christianity," "Cults, the Occult, and Theosophy," "The Power of Thought," and "The Art of Meditation." On the first page of a little booklet I'm given, I read:

Fundamental Ideas

"For thousands of years, from Egypt to Einstein, human minds, when confronted by the mysteries of existence, have sought a spiritual basis for the understanding of the living universe and the relationship of human consciousness to it.

"In this attempt to probe the mysteries of existence, the following fundamental ideas have been used as a basis because without them the development of a spiritual point of view does not seem possible.

- Matter is not limited to the perception of the five senses.
- Energy is indestructible.
- Consciousness can exist independently of the physical body.
- There is no proof consciousness ends at death...and much evidence that it continues.
- Life is a continuing process.
- Every human being has the potential to create for himself or herself and for humanity a future whose splendor has no limit."

Before I go home, I walk over to their bookstore and wander through the gardens on their beautiful grounds. And I'm struck once again, powerfully, by the almost totally disconnected mindsets in our world. Back at the archery shop, a group of hunters who love to stalk and kill and eat animals is honing their skills to do just that. Five minutes up the trail, another group is engaged in the quiet search for the ineffable experience of God.—

And the opportunity to once again rediscover this inexplicable discontinuity is given to me by a bleary-eyed, divorced, conservative, chain-smoking life insurance salesman who's covered his walls with "Impressionist" canvases he bought from an artist selling them door to door!

- *Wow.*

87

It's tempting to toss in the towel
Abandon the field, holler "Foul"
To flee to Tahiti
And leave this graffiti:
"Come step in the mound from my bowel"

I'm in a Safeway in Everett, Washington, a town of 65,000 about a half hour north of Seattle. I look around at the people and the products for sale on the shelves and I get the idea that this Safeway could be seen as a tiny microcosm of America two weeks before Christmas. Carols wash reassuringly over us, the gigantic store is well lit, the products on the shelves are all lined up like little soldiers waiting for inspection. Tinsel hangs everywhere. People stroll up and down the aisles. It's 6 o'clock in the evening, a Tuesday and, outside on Broadway, traffic is steady and heavy on the grey, wet street. All's well chugging towards the Nativity, eh?

Not so. Many of the shoppers look poor and unhealthy: tired, overweight, dull-eyed. The shelves are filled with quantities of foodless foods, dead, artificial, and huge quantities of booze. The produce department is colorful, but I know too much about chemical fertilizers and pesticides to believe that what I see, though attractive, is packed with high-class nutrition.

I've been in Everett for three days. It's been cloudy the whole time. I'm told in the winter it can remain cloudy and rainy for weeks on end. And I stand in this bright pool of fluorescent light, Christmas music gurgling, the soft swish of the wet pavement just outside and I think of the image of Gauguin's people on the beach in Tahiti and I think about the paradise the Earth was before we got hold of it. And I look at what I see in the bodies and faces around me and where I am, and I think, "Man, we really did a serious job here."

And I'm tempted to run like hell to see if there's any beach left in the whole world that doesn't have a high-rise hotel, a mansion or a billboard. Any place at all where I might just glimpse once, before they vanish forever, Gauguin and his lovelies lazing in the sun with blossoms in their hair.—

Because I know one thing, whatever it is I'm seeing around me this cold, wet evening in Everett, WA this 10th day of December...so sorry Safeway...this ain't it.

- *Merry Christmas*

88

I lay back in the web, in the nexus
Connected to All in that plexus:
We spin and we wheel
With astonishing zeal
Towards the new age that's dawing, the Next Us

At the heart of all the mischief is the perennial belief that we are separate from all about us. The thought is, I'm me and you're you and unless we choose to have a relationship, we are completely separate and unconnected. Or, this is my property, that is yours. You have nothing to say about what is mine, and I nothing to say about what is yours. Humans are humans, animals are animals - no connection. — Plants are low, people high. Phylogeny is destiny. My tribe is better than your tribe. Thus, I am better than you. Bigger than you. Stronger than you. More beautiful than you. Smarter than you. More deserving to be alive than you. Cows exist to provide milk for humans. Bulls exist to impregnate cows to provide milk for humans. Or to be steaks. Trees exist to provide lumber for houses for humans. Entrepreneurs make more money than workers do. Entrepreneurs are rich. Rich is better. I'm taller, you're shorter. I'm at the top of the food chain, everything else is beneath me. Everything below me is inferior to me and exists at my pleasure.

When I return from a short walk with my little pal Gorby, I notice he's not following me up the driveway. I stop and turn. He's looking at me expectantly. He says to me, "Let's keep walking, I don't want to go in just yet." I say, "OK, I'm in no hurry, let's push on." He says, "Oh, wow, that's cool, I'm happy, let's go." And off he goes on the next leg of our adventure. We're connected. We have a very familiar relationship. Very intense. Lots of companionship. Good talk. Close friends. No secrets. Connected.—

- *And Gorby's a dog.*

In fact, we are all connected all the time, we've just mostly forgotten. Whole cultures have been based on celebrating the web of life into which we are all plugged all the time. Mystics get it and at the moment they "awaken" that's what they say they get. But, tragically, most of us have now forgotten. And the culture that's fast becoming the world culture - the culture of international big business - is founded on amnesia, individuality, competition and separation from the web.

The good news is that we can't step off the wheel, even if we want to. We're spinning, like it or not. Old people wonder why young people are so taken with drugs. Why would anyone do that to themselves, they wonder with pointed disdain? Well, Mr. and Mrs. Christian Right, Mr. and Mrs. Middle America, the answer is that drugs remind us for a moment that we're all part of a vast skein of something so beyond our ordinary consciousness, so ubiquitous, we can't even see it. Like air, it connects every living thing to every other and to the living earth. Shhhh! Sometimes illegal drugs help us wake up.

And, check it out: that's *why* they're illegal. Waking up is not good for business. I mean, you better believe there are zero mystics stuck in that traffic on the 134.

The New Age dawns, a thin bright line on a black horizon. Perhaps there really is a slow awakening. Perhaps, since we can't escape the web, it makes no sense to try. Perhaps the way to go is simply to relax and fall backwards into the great pool of being.

Remember the guy in a Lipton Tea commercial a while ago? He's standing on the edge of a pool on a hot summer day and he just falls backwards. Just smacks his back into that pool with a big smile on his puss.

- *Splash.*

89

If crises of conscience garrote you
Quotidian rituals besot you
Then give her a tickle
She'll wiggle your pickle
And teach you that crises are not you

I'm thinking of Vermont long ago. Late summertime, early fall. Warm fields with golden haystacks. I'm thinking of that lovely idiomatic phrase, "a roll in the hay." Of course, a roll in the hay implies there is hay which suggests a warm barn nearby with an even warmer hayloft (heat provided by the fifty cows talking softly below) or a haystack in a field dusted with September sun and time to roll and laugh and forget for a moment the daily careworn rituals. It implies freedom from deadlines and money and contacts and email and cellphones and the Internet and CNN and Washington and scandals. A roll in the hay assumes zero concern with Human Immunodeficiency Virus and condoms and conception, religion and rules, strictures, pronunciamentos, encyclicals, mandates, *ex cathedra* imperatives, morality and the trillions of guilt trips fashioned by sick men (and women) to foil freedom and pleasure. A roll in the hay has nothing to do with listening to the voice of a disapproving God.

It *is* God. Here's Wordsworth:

> The world is too much with us; late and soon,
> Getting and spending, we lay waste our powers:
> Little we see in Nature that is ours;
> We have given our hearts away, a sordid boon!
> This Sea that bares her bosom to the moon;
> The winds that will be howling at all hours
> And are up-gathered now like sleeping flowers;
> For this, for everything, we are out of tune;
> It moves us not...

And Wordsworth was still 50 years away from a telephone when he wrote that!

Near the end of *Intimations of Immortality*:

> What though the radiance which was once so bright
> Be now forever taken from my sight
> Though nothing can bring back the hour
> Of splendor in the grass, of glory in the flower;
> We will grieve not, rather find
> Strength in what remains behind...

Even though a roll in the hay might not have been what Bill was talking about, "splendor in the grass" *is* a lovely way to say it.

- *Nevertheless, with apologies to WW, I do grieve.*

You know, there still used to be haystacks back in Vermont in the '50s and early '60s when I was there. Unfortunately, I didn't know a milkmaid at the time.

- *Pity.*

239

90

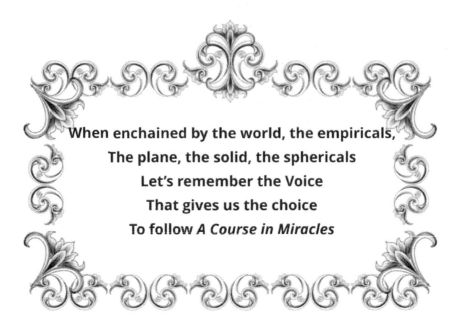

When enchained by the world, the empiricals,

The plane, the solid, the sphericals

Let's remember the Voice

That gives us the choice

To follow *A Course in Miracles*

The book is *A Course in Miracles (ACIM)*. It begins, "This is a course in miracles. It is a required course. Only the time you take it is voluntary." It then goes on to lay down a path of study which, if followed, offers the possibility of throwing off the chains of perception which bind us.—

It was transcribed by a middle-aged professor of medical psychology at Columbia University named Helen Schucman. In her seven-year collaboration with a colleague, Professor William Thetford, they produced this book. Professor Schucman was attuned to the promptings of an inner voice and transcribed the information the voice imparted to her. The following day she would read the material she received to Thetford while he typed it. She has said these communications were a spontaneous, "channeled" (my word, not hers) series of step-by-step lessons.

It is not difficult for me to believe her because the book is an amazingly detailed, densely reasoned, highly literate voyage over the various hills and vales, rivers, canals and locks of the human mind and spirit. It does not seem possible to me that an ordinary human being could have written it. I cannot even imagine all the renowned modern psychologists together, the Freuds and Jungs, Reiks and Adlers - all of them collaborating - could have written this book. From my point of view, *ACIM* makes the Bible look like a scary children's story.

In a book of poems by the great Persian poet Rumi, entitled *Rumi, In the Arms of the Beloved*, translations by Jonathan Star, there is a passage in the book's introduction from the Sufi philosopher Ibn Arabi:

> My heart holds within it every form,
> It contains a pasture for gazelles,
> A monastery for Christian monks.
> There is a temple for idol worshippers,
> A holy shrine for pilgrims;
> There is the table of the Torah,
> And the Book of the Koran.
> I follow the religion of Love
> And go whichever way His camel leads me.
> This is the true faith;
> This is the true religion.

These lines offer us a more profound, a more inclusive way to see the world. They offer us the possibility of awakening from our long and restless slumber. Zen Buddhism teaches us this possibility exists. Theosophy teaches it. Ridhwan teaches it (www.ridhwan.org). All the great mystics and enlightened beings over the ages have taught us there is another world hidden within the world of everyday reality, like a *trompe l'oeil* picture, a Magritte: the witch becomes a fine lady combing her hair; the stairs go down until suddenly they go up. After glimpsing the alternate picture just once, one is thereafter able to see both at will. Before that, one is trapped in a universe essentially unreal.—

At the end of the book, *ACIM* asks us this question:

241

"Why would you wait for this and trade it for illusions, when His love is but an instant further on the road where all illusions end? — Nothing real can be threatened. Nothing unreal exists."

- *Looking for a guidebook?—*

- *Here's the Baedeker.*

91

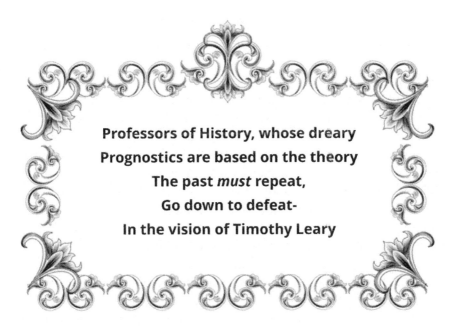

Professors of History, whose dreary
Prognostics are based on the theory
The past *must* repeat,
Go down to defeat-
In the vision of Timothy Leary

Timothy Leary died on May 31st, 1996. He died of prostate cancer discovered during a routine physical. I knew him slightly through my wife who had been his good friend for many years and who spent the last months of his life, at his behest, living in his house, sometimes sleeping in his bed, helping to coordinate his care, nurturing him to his end. Her fingers were on his throat when he breathed his last and his pulse ceased.

- *Those who are aware of how he chose to die know he went out as he had lived, with verve and panache.*

It was that great patriot Richard Nixon who once called Timothy Leary "the most dangerous man in America." And Nixon, without knowing why he was right, *was* right. Leary threatened the very foundations of patriarchal, acquisitive, militaristic, soulless society. In the '60s, "Tune in! Turn on! Drop out!" became the rallying cry of millions. As young people (and some older ones, too) woke up to bigotry, discrimination, the Vietnam War, the savaging of the environment, they tuned in to Rock and Roll, Dylan and Baez, Woodstock, sex and joy. And they did it non-violently. Bad news for Business As Usual.

- *But the Status-Quoers got it and went after Leary big time!*

Dr. Leary was one of the most intelligent men of the century. When I studied Marriage, Family and Child Counseling at The California Family Study Center, (at that time the largest training institution for MFCCs in the country), the text used to teach personality was written by Timothy Leary. And it was brilliant. It wasn't by accident he had been a Harvard professor. But Leary strode through (to use Aldous Huxley's phrase) "the doors of perception," looked around, and beckoned us all to follow him. Millions did. He was busy mapping - along with other Harvard profs - the coastline of the New World he'd discovered when Harvard freaked and fired him.—

Because mind-expanding drugs can be incredibly powerful and sometimes overwhelming to the uninitiated, Leary understood they were to be used in peaceful settings under the supervision of experienced guides. They were not to be used casually, frequently, or profanely. Tragically, in its inability to comprehend the potential salvation such drugs offer, the government did the predictable and criminalized them. They are still illegal.

But times they are achangin'! Back in the Bush years, the U.S. Supreme Court upheld the decision of a lower court to allow physicians in California and other states with Medical Marijuana laws to counsel seriously ill patients about the potential benefits of pot and actually prescribe it if it was thought it would be beneficial. This ruling must have given the then Attorney General, poor John Ashcroft, a conniption fit. In fact, this sad man and the administration he shilled for vowed at the time to prosecute violators of their insane drug laws *despite the Supreme Court ruling*! And even as recently as 2016, Pres. Obama faithfully pandered to the frightened right by maintaining his administration's puritanical, unenlightened posture vis a vis pot. Never mind a number of states have now even made the sale of *recreational* marijuana absolutely legal.

Consider: Carlos Castaneda writes a series of successful books recounting his training and experience with the *nagual* Don Juan and the only people who can really understand what the hell he's talking about are those who've taken the drugs Don Juan used to wake up Castaneda. To see that mind-numbing drugs like alcohol and nicotine are perfectly legal and universally available, while the use of drugs capable of waking people up earn long prison terms must either drive one to madness or laughter.—

Leary - awakened, brilliant as he was - laughed. And that *really* pissed them off! When I think of Leary, I inevitably think of the great opening lines of Sabatini's great novel *Scaramouche*: "He was born with a gift of laughter and a sense that the world was mad. That was all his patrimony." But, of course, they haven't yet burned his books (their mistake) so laboratories still manufacture LSD and Ecstasy, the Sacred Mushroom still grows lovingly nurtured in damp basements, peyote hangs drying in warm attics, a stash hidden in the pantry awaits the bong. —

And courageous souls on silent Saturday nights still listen to angels whispering...

- *felons on the ceaseless search for Dr. Leary's outlawed Gods.*

92

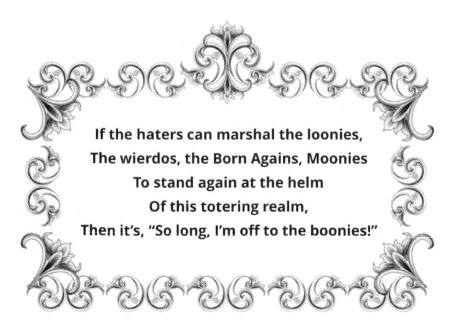

If the haters can marshal the loonies,
The wierdos, the Born Agains, Moonies
To stand again at the helm
Of this totering realm,
Then it's, "So long, I'm off to the boonies!"

- *Nothing more to say. Anyway, I'm packing.*

93

You skeptics who openly chortle
May yet wish to stride through the Portal,
Hear heavenly voices
Sing praise for your choice, Sirs,
See names on the Roster: IMMORTAL

A few times on Saturday mornings when I was a kid in Flatbush in Brooklyn, I had a mystical experience. I didn't call it that at the time, of course, because I didn't know there was such a thing. It's only now, as I look back, that I think, Wow, I'll bet those were sublime states, actual experiences of a presence.

I'm playing stick ball on Hawthorne Street. It's 1946. I'm 14. The war is over. We've won. I can't hit the ball to save my life, but Tommy Connors can hit it two sewers. And I can catch. It's Saturday morning. The whole weekend's ahead. Although Sundays are awful because you can't play on Sunday and you have to be quiet. But Sunday is a long way off. Now it's Saturday morning and tonight Granma will make hot dogs and sauerkraut with buns and mustard and maybe Gramps will give me a taste of his beer. And Joey and Bob and Lenny are on my team. It's Saturday morning and there's the whole warm interminable afternoon ahead of us. There'll be a Tarzan movie at the

Patio on a bill with some boring grown-up movie and there'll be a chapter and three cartoons, the Movie Tone News narrated by Lowell Thomas and a documentary short subject. And it's '46 and they're saying atomic energy is going to be the greatest boon to humankind since the sun: cheap and perfectly safe.

And suddenly I'm in another dimension. I'm looking out at my friends, I'm seeing the few cars on the street, (the Green Dodge is first base, the sewer is second and the fender of my mother's $600 blue Plymouth is third) and it's all quiet and full of wonder and I know absolutely that everything is perfect and I'm going to be all right and I'm filled with joy. This happens to me maybe four times in the course of my young life. Then never again. Until last week. For one second, there's a momentary harkening back to the old block, a reminder of those few Saturday mornings I've never forgotten. Only a second, but it's enough to make me certain once again that there exists another world within this world.—

Have you been there? Or perhaps you're skeptical. Well and good. — Only remember, our word comes from the Greek *skeptikos* which means "thoughtful, inquiring." So be thoughtful. Inquire. No matter. But, been there or not, I know we're immortal and heavenly choirs will lift their voices when we pass through the membrane of perception separating us from that world I saw for a moment so long ago before the Tarzan movie.

- *Wherever you are Tarzan (aka Johnny Weissmuller), thanks for those great Saturday afternoons.*

94

Men fiddle around like mad Neros:
Plan torching the Earth! Say, will heroes
Dare stand to protect Her
Not gloat to have wrecked Her?
Ah, but most are not heroes, they're zeros

Yesterday the most amazing thing happened. Two men – four-star generals - stood up at the National Press Club weekly luncheon and said all nuclear weapons must be removed from the face of the earth. The one whose excerpts I heard spoken on the radio (in a piece on NPR's show All Things Considered) was Gen. Lee Butler, former Commander-in-Chief of the Strategic Air Command and, later, Chief of U.S. Strategic Command, positions that placed him in charge of all of America's strategic nuclear forces. As far as our nuclear posture is concerned, Gen. Butler is the horse's mouth. The man who stood beside him, Gen. Andrew Goodpastor, was the former commander of NATO, the Commander of the famed 8th Infantry Division, Superintendent of the U.S. Military Academy, Commander of the National War College and advisor to presidents from Ike to Clinton.

I elaborate their credentials at some length to make the point that both men have borne weighty military responsibilities. Of course, it would have been better if both men were still on active duty. As it is, when they spoke out, they'd both recently retired. It is common that, when high-ranking military officers speak out (aka telling the truth), we see that little "(Ret.)" after their names. But, God knows, better late than never.

Again, according to NPR, the day after their appearance at the Press Club, 80 more generals and admirals joined Butler and Goodpastor in their statement. The reported reaction of the White House was predictable. It said something to the effect of, "Well, the generals make good points but a change in this nation's nuclear strategy can't be envisioned for the foreseeable future - certainly not until the Russians agree to the next step in arms reduction from 6,000 to 3,500 nuclear weapons."

- *Figures.*

But this utterance from the generals is earth-shattering. Two men from The Club stood up and broke the unwritten rule of conformity. And I heard some of what Butler said. He spoke eloquently.

He talks about his "long and arduous intellectual journey from staunch advocate of nuclear deterrence to public proponent of nuclear abolition." He says, "We have yet to fully grasp the monstrous effects of these weapons, that the consequences of their use defy reason...poisoning the earth and deforming its inhabitants." He asks us, faced with "the obscene power of a single nuclear weapon...to accept that the Cold War is in fact over, to break free of the norms..." The force and poetry of his message and the power of his revelation is contained in phrases like "nuclear war is a raging, insatiable beast whose instincts and appetite we pretend to understand but cannot possibly control."

- *The point is, they said it. They stood up. They became heroes.*
- *There is hope.*

NPR's Morning Edition has a follow-up piece on the previous day's event. The late retired Admiral Eugene J. Carroll, Jr. - then Deputy Director of the Center for Defense Information and a sane voice regarding military issues - is on the line with Bob Edwards, the host of the show, and Richard Perl, a former Asst. Sec. of Defense and a leading hawk.

Admiral Carroll applauds the statement of Generals Butler and Goodpastor. Perl says essentially, "Yeah, eliminating nuclear weapons would be dandy but both those generals know it can't be done." And, as an example, Perl says we need nuclear weapons to deter terrorists. When he says this, I'm screaming at him in my kitchen, "You stupid son of a bitch, how can nuclear weapons deter terrorists? You can never even know who committed what terrorist act. Who ya gonna bomb? You sick moron, you can't even deter terrorists with crummy conventional weapons." I'm going nuts. And then Admiral Carroll, bless his dear, courageous soul through all eternity, pops in as cool and quiet and reasoned as can be and blows Perl out of the intellectual water: "But the twin towers in New York could have been blown with a nuclear device that would have taken out most of Manhattan and who would you have used your nuclear deterrent on? No target. No deterrence."

But what can you say to the Perls of the world? They're very stupid men. Perl himself works at someplace like the Heritage Foundation or the American Enterprise Institute and he's undoubtedly considered a feather in their cap.

- *Double duh.*

(Gen. Butler's speech is so important I've included it in an appendix.)

95

A sport from Olympus named Zeus
Got blitzed on unusual juice
And ever since then
The model for men
Has their beak up some Leda's sweet sluice

Somebody once asked the wonderful comic actor Buddy Hackett why he got into show business. He said, "Because that's where the pretty girls are."

If we're going to be honest, it's not money or power on the bottom line, it's sex. Money and power are sought because rich and powerful men get the prettiest girls and the prettiest girls are desired for two reasons. Their beauty confers status on the man who has the wherewithal to "possess" such currency (think Onassis and Jackie). And, because beauty is a powerful aphrodisiac, it conjures better orgasms.

The arena where wealth and power do not necessarily coincide is politics. A man can have great power - Bill Clinton in Arkansas is an example - and not be extremely wealthy. So, despite modest wealth, in Clinton's case his power was sufficient to dip his beak in beautiful

Gennifer Flowers all those years. Of course, being rich as well doesn't hurt. JFK was getting it on with Marilyn. Bobby, too. And is there anyone in the continental United States over the age of three who believed Mary Jo Kopechne was taking dictation on Chappaquiddick? Though, on second thought, she probably was taking "DICKtation" on Chappaquiddick. Why quibble? In case you're too young to remember the details of the incident with Mary Jo and Ted Kennedy, get online and be amazed.

Washington is awash in booze and sex. Visiting dignitaries are wined and spine-ed, lobbyists provide the means for clients to relax as the deal goes down, congressmen are whisked away on jaunts to play golf and stretch their joints. I have it on unimpeachable authority that a certain well-known congressman actually maintained a line of call girls to assist his colleagues in their "deLiberations."—

It should come as no surprise that sex is what makes the world go round but, as Oliver so plaintively sings,

- *"Where, oh, where is love?"*

PS: I wrote this before Harvey Weinstein and the boys got their beaks busted by a whole lotta gutsy ladies.

96

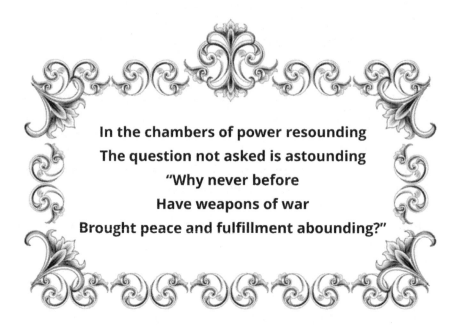

In the chambers of power resounding
The question not asked is astounding
"Why never before
Have weapons of war
Brought peace and fulfillment abounding?"

Werner Erhardt used to say in the then-popular *est* training, "If you want to know what your intentions are, look around you."

It's good. Barring accidents, your life as it is now is what you intended. Not fate. Intention. Your career? Intended. Your spouse? Intended. Your financial situation? All of it. You're responsible for who and where you are. Those are your hands on the wheel.

- *It's really a bit of a pain in the ass to have to accept absolute and complete responsibility. —I mean, isn't it?*

And for us collectively, the same. If men intended peace, there'd be peace. If women intended men to be peaceful, they would not collaborate in sending their sons and daughters to war. There is strife and conflict and continuous war because that is not only what we accept, it's what we intend.

When we manufacture weapons of war around the clock, purvey them to the world, now even urgently plan to weaponize space with Trump's new Space Force as a separate arm of the U.S. military (talk about Nutsville) we must accept that we are the "connection" for the world's fix, the pusher for the world's habit. Arming every nation to the teeth may be intended to further our "security" but its result is War. As Michael Moore documents in his Academy Award-winning film *Bowling for Columbine*, the National Rifle Association fights ferociously for our constitutional right to bear every kind of weapon without restriction but the result is a shamefully high murder rate. In Japan, where guns are absolutely forbidden, there is virtually no murder by gunshot or by any other means. I can only be tempted to shoot you if I'm able to. I can only send my planes and tanks against you if I have them.

I watch guys at the gym with mountainous bodies working ever harder to add yet another weapon to their arsenal of muscle and I think, "Man, I wouldn't want to mess with that guy." Which is exactly the thought every nation hopes its neighbors have when peering across the border. After all, national leaders, and most of us as well, have exactly the same brains as the hulk at the gym. The problem is that somebody always comes along to see if they can knock you over when you're the biggest dude on the block; to see if they can draw quicker if you're the fastest gun in Dodge. And, sooner or later, somebody can. What's more, you've spent so much time, effort, and money being the biggest, toughest, meanest dude on the block that it flushes every other aspect of your life down the toilet. Yeah, you're King of the Hill, but you're as dumb as a rock. For example, we may be the most pumped up nation on earth, but the libraries in our towns are only open three days a week and every year the National Endowment for the Arts faces extinction from the same lumphead legislators who're getting their pockets tickled by the NRA.

And the only social skill you have is constantly peering at your own reflection in the mirror, staring in fascination at your own image, incessantly repeating the mantra, "I'm number one, the biggest, baddest sob or corporation or nation in the world." But worse yet, the little guys who have no hope of ever stacking the kind of muscle you have, find wimpy, cowardly ways to sneak up behind your back and whack you while you're admiring your own invulnerability. They blow up your barracks in suicide bombings, they drag your dying soldiers through the mud on TV so the whole world can see, they lust to incinerate your cities with some of the tons of fissionable materials lying around for the buying, they blow up your school buses, they plan to poison your water supplies with one of the billions of biological weapons canisters stacked to the moon, their deadly contents copulating within, dreaming of the light of day. And occasionally, for the price of a few plane tickets, they get lucky Big Time.

The other way? Drop it, enough already, get real. Intend peace. Work for peace. Stand for peace. No longer say, "Well, if *we* don't sell Chile our sophisticated jets, the French or the British will sell her theirs." Which is what the U.S. has said again and again regarding our massive arms sales. Well, let them have the sale. Instead of that old, boring song, stand up and say, "Hey world, we're out of the war game, we stand for peace. We could do it technologically, we *could* put weapons in space if we wanted to, but we're not gonna do it. We're gonna go into space peacefully and provide more jobs and profits that way and more benefits to Mama Earth than would ever devolve from the old weapons game!"

Second Order Change: raise statues in the park to honor men and women of peace, for heaven's sake. Have parades honoring great peaceful events. Go with what former Rep. Dennis Kucinich attempted: create a Department of Peace. In fact, why not transform the Department of Defense (sneaky: it used to be called the "War Department") into the Department of Peace? Teach peace in kindergarten. Fund peace. And now that that great American Pete Seeger has died, honor him with more songs about peace. Have a national poetry competition on Peace. As Kucinich once said, "Make war archaic."

When I was a Boy Scout, you were supposed to do good deeds for people every day. And, if you did your good deed for that day, you were entitled to tie a knot at the end of your kerchief to honor yourself for your action. A sort of tiny symbolic badge you gave yourself for being the kind of person you wanted to be that day. Sort of a medal you gave yourself. So: medals to honor peace? None to honor war?—

256

I'm sitting here thinking again about Lew Ayres. I was thinking about how angry the nation was at him when he refused to be conscripted to fight and kill. He told me he was on the beach on some Pacific island and the Japanese were shelling the American troops with everything they had and a GI he was pinned down with said to him "Jesus, this is horrible." To which Ayres responded, "Oh, this is nothing, Hollywood makes this look like a picnic." Even as a kid, I understood what it took to face the opprobrium of an angry nation. If you haven't figured it out already, Lew was my Hero. In my heart, what this man did, a movie star, standing up before the whole world for what he believed, putting his entire career, his entire life on the line, going into battle as a medic not a soldier, when he could have been making propaganda films for the Army Signal Corps on Long Island like a lot of other stars...that's guts. That's valor. *He* deserves what should be a new Congressional Medal of Peace. Sadly, for Lew, now bestowed posthumously. That would mean a lot to me. I would feel proud of my country that day. I would go to the park and place a rose at the base of that statue.

Helen Keller said, "Security is an illusion. It does not exist in nature." The word "security" meant "carefree" in the original Latin.

- *Ask yourself: have the trillions the U.S. has spent on "security" made you feel carefree?*

97

We search for our Heroes: let's be 'em

No excuses that rarely we see 'em

Live our lives like the Gods

Not contemptible clods

On our flag blaze the words *"Carpe Diem!"*

Robin Williams made a film called *Dead Poets Society* in which he played a teacher at a private school for boys who changes the lives of his students by awakening them to a richer, more passionate experience of life. The motto of the group of young men he gathered together was *"Carpe Diem"*: "Seize the Day" in Latin.

At the time I saw the film, it so happened I had just discovered the phrase *carpe diem* while wandering in the dictionary and, because I had rarely seized the day and because the euphony of the phrase pleased my ear, I memorized it. People used to have mottoes and stuck them on their flags or their coats of arms and then presumably tried to live by them. —No one does that anymore. At least no one I know. The closest thing I can think of resembling a coat of arms today is a license plate. But having "The Sunshine State" on your automobile's rear end along with a few million others can hardly be considered a call to anything but possible skin cancer. Or, I suppose "The Land of

10,000 Lakes" might appeal to a fisherperson or a water-skier. Of course, there are vanity plates. These are license plates on which, for a fee, one can emblazon one's own message for everyone to see. — Some of these are unique but, at least in California, you only get seven letters to say your piece. *Carpe Diem* misses by two. Although much clever abbreviation takes place on vanity plates, it somehow seems wrong we should have to truncate a statement that attempts to abbreviate our entire life's guiding principle.

Instead of poring over ancient tomes to ascertain whether our forebears had coats of arms in the 16th Century or thereabouts, though such a search would undoubtedly be interesting, perhaps we should create anew such crests for ourselves. Then we'd be forced to distill the meaning of our lives into symbols we wanted to appear there, and we'd choose words that would announce to the world who we are and what we stand for. I mean, the Founding Fathers had to come up with something for the National Seal that would tell other nations who we were going to be. And they did it neatly with *E Pluribus Unum*...Out of Many, One. Perfect for what they were trying to say. Naturally they all knew Latin, probably even spoke it, so they could fancy up our nation's motto with a dead language. Though, mind, it wouldn't have fit on a license plate.—

Imagine if each of us had a motto that was emblazoned on a banner that fluttered over the roofs of our homes or was painted on the doors of our apartments. We'd all have something clearly stated to live up to. And, although you could change it as you went along, as you grew, it wouldn't be that easy to do. You'd have to do a lot of soul searching beforehand and it would be costly to get your flag changed and people might take notice your apartment door had been repainted and you'd have to explain to them either that you'd grown, or you'd copped out.—

When I was in college, I came on the Latin phrase "*ad astra per aspera*" which means "to the stars through difficulties" and I decided to memorize it and take it as my motto. (It should be the motto of NASA but it's really the motto of Kansas!) I probably wouldn't have adopted it as my motto if I'd known Kansas was already using it. Anyway, over the years I forgot about it. Though, as I look back on my life, it seems to me that perhaps I didn't forget it, that perhaps I took it more seriously than I imagined. It *has* been difficult, and I have continued to reach up. And when I think of how many times I've sung "The Impossible Dream" from the great musical *Man of La Mancha*, first as Richard Kiley's original understudy in the very first production of the show that opened on November 22nd, 1965 – the second anniversary of JFK's assassination - and later in other productions around the country, and sometimes at events where I thought it would give people strength or hope...a song that ends

> And the world will be better for this
> That one man scorned and covered with scars
> Still strove, with his last ounce of courage
> To reach the unreachable stars.

- *I am stunned at this moment, as I write, appreciating the aptness of my early motto!—*

But I'm changing my motto as of this moment. *Ad astra per aspera* no longer pleases me and this change has nothing to do with Kansas. It's too much about the future and the difficulties of getting there. Like the end of The Impossible Dream...who wants to go after stars that are "unreachable"? Too intimidating and, as the song warns, "impossible." I want something I can do now, today. Something that, when I lay down at night, will allow me to say to myself, "I didn't wimp out, I didn't lie or cheat or postpone, I faced what needed to be done today and I did it." I'd rather be a hero than a pussycat.

My new motto, therefore, is *Carpe Diem.* —I intend hereafter to seize the day.—

- *So, if it appeals to you, get out your flag and start the needlepoint.*

- *And, if you felt you wanted to share my new motto Carpe Diem with me, it would be my honor.*

98

If singing these songs could connect you
Their lilt and their message cathect you
Then I'll say my *adieus*
With positive news,
I'm delighted they moved you not decked you

I sit here at the beginning of 2018 in Ashland, Oregon thinking how different the world is this evening than it was in June or July of 1987 when I woke up in the middle of the night and began writing down the first five of these limericks that had just come to me in my dream. I was rehearsing the musical *Peter Pan* at the Kansas City Starlight Theatre. I was going to play Captain Hook.

Since '87, the world's most famous political prisoner, Nelson Mandela, was not only freed but became president of his country. The Soviet Union collapsed. The Berlin Wall is gone. Germany is reunited. The U.S. invaded a sovereign country, Panama, and imprisoned its leader in the United States. We have fought two wars in the desert over oil and killed perhaps several hundreds of thousands of people doing it. American troops were in Bosnia and Kosovo; Sarajevo, one of the most beautiful and cosmopolitan cities in the world, was utterly destroyed by a stupid internecine war. The

Japanese stock and real estate markets collapsed and interest rates in Japan are still today at -0.1%. Wall St., not to be outdone, soared to historic heights, subsequently crashed and burned twice and is now in the stratosphere, the Dow at 26,000!!!. Before that, the Savings and Loan industry in the U.S. collapsed taking real estate prices with it. Then real estate prices soared because interest rates were at historic lows; then real estate collapsed again. A democrat lived in the White House for two terms for the first time in fifty years. Republicans and Democrats don't speak. There was something called The Tea Party. Cute, huh? It was very right wing. The 85 richest people on Earth have, between them, as much wealth as the poorest half of the world, according to shocking new statistics from Oxfam. *Hill Street Blues* and *Major Dad* are ancient history. There was a hit show on CBS whose leading characters were all angels. Terrorism stalks the world.

James Redfield, who wrote the enormously successful *The Celestine Prophecy*, talks about the revolution that took place in the Middle Ages in which science threw off the Church's yolk. He says science and religion made a tacit pact wherein each agreed to stay out of the other's bailiwick. This pact, which forced science to remain rigidly committed to the tangible world of physical laws, has now been violated by the revelations of subatomic physics that seem to lead inexorably towards realms once exclusively belonging to religion. Could we be seeing the re-spiritualization of the world?—

- *I hope so. —I hope this book will have contributed to that.*

99

On the sidelines you're merely a flunky
A post neither dory nor hunky
Snap out of your daze
Start calling the plays
There's a chance you're the One Hundredth Monkey

An Englishman named Rupert Sheldrake has a theory that we all reside in "morphogenetic fields" in which we are biologically each connected to the other. As I understand it, it's been observed scientifically that, if you teach a rat to run a maze, succeeding generations of rats will learn to run it faster even though there is (or seems to be) no physical way for the information to have been transmitted to the next generation. Ken Kesey wrote a popular allegory about this phenomenon called *The Hundredth Monkey*. He tells the story of an isolated island in Japan where all the monkeys dig sweet potatoes from the ground. One young monkey gets the brilliant idea that, if she washes her potato in the river before eating it, she will not get sand in her mouth. She teaches this innovation to her mother who then proceeds to teach it to others of the tribe. At the point where the hundredth monkey learns to wash their potato, all the monkeys suddenly get the message...even the monkeys on other islands who have no contact with the original band of innovators.

The idea is that, at the point when a sufficient percentage of any population - a "critical mass" - gets a certain idea, that idea becomes unstoppable.

It is possible we have already achieved critical mass on the most important idea of our era: that we are, in fact, spiritual beings existing in a great interconnected wheel of life so vast it is beyond the capability of all but the most enlightened souls to comprehend. We are not separate. We are One.

Since I am not an enlightened person, I do not know if this is true. However, based on my reading of some of the advanced souls who *have* experienced this reality and have told us of their awakening to this reality, I believe it.—

My first year in college at the University of Vermont, I had to take a required course called Introduction to Philosophy or Philosophy 101. It was a subject in which I was not at all interested. I mean, who cared about Leibnitz and Kant and Spinoza? As it turned out, the teacher, Professor Duikhuisen, not only introduced me for the first time to the joy of learning, but he said something which in this present context may be important. He said he was not sure if God existed, therefore he had two options: to live his life as if He *did* exist or as if He did *not* exist. If God did exist it would have turned out that he, Duikhuisen, had lived correctly. And if God did not exist, he would simply have played it safe and lived a virtuous life.

I'm not sure the theory of morphogenetic fields is correct; I am not sure we are all One, or that there is or can be a Hundredth Monkey with its unstoppable idea. But is it not better, like Professor Duikhuisen, to live *as if* the idea is so? Because if it is, then anyone of us, when we finally stand before the Throne, may discover *we were the one that tipped the scale towards love.*

- *We were The Hundredth Monkey who made Peace and Love the unstoppable ideas they must become.*

THE END

PS: I left the hundredth limerick for you to write. *Carpe Diem*, friend, and make sure you scrub all the sand off your sweet potato.

APPENDIX ONE

Speech of Gen. Lee Butler at the National Press Club, Washington, D.C. December 4th, 1996

Thank you, and good afternoon, ladies and gentlemen. —Let me say first that I am both professionally honored and intellectually comforted to share this rostrum with General Andrew Goodpaster. He has long set the standard among senior military officers for rigorous thinking and wise counsel on national security matters. He has been a role model for generations of younger officers, and most certainly was for me. His views on the risks inherent in nuclear weapons and the consequences of their use have long been a matter of public record. I found them very compelling as I made the long and arduous intellectual journey from staunch advocate of nuclear deterrence to public proponent of nuclear abolition.

- *This latter role is not one that I ever imagined nor one that I relish.*

Far from it. I have too much regard for the thousands of men and women who served under my command, and the hundreds of colleagues with whom I labored in the policy arena, to take lightly the risk that my view might in any way be construed as diminishing their service or sacrifice. Quite to the contrary, I continue to marvel and will always be immensely gratified by their intense devotion and commitment to the highest standards of professional discipline.

I would simply ask them to understand that I am compelled to speak, by concerns I cannot still, with respect to the abiding influence of nuclear weapons long after the Cold War has ended. I am here today because I feel the weight of a special obligation in these matters, a responsibility born of unique experience and responsibilities. Over the last 27 years of my military career, I was embroiled in every aspect of American nuclear policy making and force structuring, from the highest councils of government to nuclear command centers; from the arms control arena to cramped bomber cockpits and the confines of ballistic missile silos and submarines. I have spent years studying nuclear weapons' effects; inspected dozens of operational units; certified hundreds of crews for their nuclear mission; and approved thousands of targets for nuclear destruction. I have investigated a distressing array of accidents and incidents involving strategic weapons and forces. I have read a library of books and intelligence reports on the Soviet Union and what were believed to be its capabilities and intentions...and seen an army of experts confounded. As an advisor to the President on the employment of nuclear weapons, I have anguished over the imponderable complexities, the profound moral dilemmas, and the mind-numbing compression of decision-making under the threat of nuclear attack.

I came away from that experience deeply troubled by what I see as the burden of building and maintaining nuclear arsenals: the increasingly tangled web of policy and strategy as the number of weapons and delivery systems multiply; the staggering costs; the relentless pressure of advancing technology; the grotesquely destructive war plans; the daily operational risks, and the constant prospect of a crisis that would hold the fate of entire societies at risk.

Seen from this perspective, it should not be surprising that no one could have been more relieved than was I by the dramatic end of the Cold War and the promise of reprieve from its acute tensions and threats. The democratization of Russia, the reshaping of Central Europe...I never imagined that in my lifetime, much less during my military service, such extraordinary events might transpire. Even more gratifying was the opportunity, as the commander of U.S. strategic nuclear forces, to be intimately involved in recasting our force posture, shrinking our arsenals, drawing down the target list, and scaling back huge impending Cold War driven expenditures.

Most importantly, I could see for the first time the prospect of restoring a world free of the apocalyptic threat of nuclear weapons.

Over time, that shimmering hope gave way to a judgment which has now become a deeply held conviction: that a world free of the THREAT of nuclear weapons is necessarily a world DEVOID of nuclear weapons. Permit me, if you will, to elaborate briefly on the concerns which compel this conviction.

FIRST, a growing alarm that despite all of the evidence, we have yet to fully grasp the monstrous effects of these weapons, that the consequences of their use defy reason, transcending time and space, poisoning the earth and deforming its inhabitants. SECOND, a deepening dismay at the prolongation of Cold War policies and practices in a world where our security interests have been utterly transformed. THIRD, that foremost among these policies, deterrence reigns unchallenged with its embedded assumption of hostility and associated preference for forces in high states of alert. FOURTH, an acute unease over renewed assertions of the utility of nuclear weapons, especially as regards response to chemical or biological attack. FIFTH, grave doubt that the present highly discriminatory regime of nuclear and non-nuclear states can long endure absent a credible commitment by the nuclear powers to eliminate their arsenals. And, FINALLY, the horrific prospect of a world seething with enmities, armed to the teeth with nuclear weapons, and hostage to maniacal leaders strongly disposed toward their use.

That being said, let me hasten to add that I am keenly aware of the opposing arguments. Many strategists hold to the belief that the Cold War world was well served by nuclear weapons, and that the fractious world emerging in its aftermath dictates that they will be retained...either as fearsome weapons of last resort or simply because their elimination is still a Utopian dream. I offer in reply that for me the Utopian dream was ending the Cold War. Standing down nuclear arsenals requires only a fraction of the ingenuity and resources as were devoted to their creation. As to those who believe nuclear weapons desirable or inevitable, I would say these devices exact a terrible price even if never used. Accepting nuclear weapons as the ultimate arbiter of conflict condemns the world to live under a dark cloud of perpetual anxiety. Worse, it codifies mankind's most murderous instincts as an acceptable resort when other options for resolving conflict fail.

Others argue that nuclear weapons are still the essential trappings of superpower status; that they are a vital hedge against a resurgence of virulent, Soviet-era communism; that they will deter attack by weapons of mass destruction; or that they are the most appropriate choice for response to such attack. To them I reply that proliferation cannot be contained in a world where a handful of self-appointed nations both arrogate to themselves the privilege of owning nuclear weapons, and extol the ultimate security assurances they assert such

269

weapons convey. That overt hedging against born-again, Soviet-style hardliners is as likely to engender as to discourage their resurrection. Those elegant theories of deterrence wilt in the crucible of impending nuclear war. And, finally, that the political and human consequences of the employment of a nuclear weapon by the United States in the post-Cold War world, no matter the provocation, would irretrievably diminish our stature. We simply cannot resort to the very type of act we rightly abhor.

Is it possible to forge a global consensus on the proposition that nuclear weapons have no defensible role; that the broader consequences of their employment transcend any asserted military utility; and that as true weapons of mass destruction, the case for their elimination is a thousand-fold stronger and more urgent than for deadly chemicals and viruses already widely declared immoral, illegitimate, subject to destruction and prohibited from any future production?

I am persuaded that such a consensus is not only possible, it is imperative. Notwithstanding the uncertainties of transition in Russia, bitter enmities in the Middle East, or the delicate balance of power in South and East Asia, I believe that a swelling global refrain will eventually bring the broader interests of mankind to bear on the decisions of governments to retain nuclear weapons. The terror-induced anesthesia which suspended rational thought, made nuclear war thinkable and grossly excessive arsenals possible during the Cold War is gradually wearing off. A renewed appreciation for the obscene power of a single nuclear weapon is coming back into focus as we confront the dismal prospect of nuclear terror at the micro level.

Clearly the world has begun to recoil from the nuclear abyss. Bombers are off alert, missiles are being destroyed and warheads dismantled, former Soviet republics have renounced nuclear status. The Non-Proliferation Treaty has been indefinitely extended, the Comprehensive Test Ban Treaty is now a de facto prohibition, and START II may yet survive a deeply suspicious Duma. But, there is a much larger issue which now confronts the nuclear powers and engages the vital interest of every nation: whether the world is better served by a prolonged era of cautious nuclear weapons reductions toward some indeterminate endpoint; or by an unequivocal commitment on the part of the nuclear powers to move with much greater urgency toward the goal of elimination of these arsenals in their entirety.

I chose this forum to make my most direct public case for elimination as the goal, to be pursued with all deliberate speed. I firmly believe that practical and realistic steps, such as those set forth by the Stimson Center study. Or by the Canberra Commission on the Elimination of Nuclear Weapons, can readily be taken toward that end. But I would underscore that the real issue here is NOT the path—it is the willingness to undertake the journey. In my view, there are three crucial conditions which must first be satisfied for the journey to begin, conditions which go to the heart of strongly held beliefs and deep-seated fears about nuclear weapons and the circumstances in which they might be used.

First and foremost is for the declared nuclear weapons states to accept that the Cold War is in fact over, to break free of the norms, attitudes and habits that perpetuate enormous inventories, forces standing alert and targeting plans encompassing thousands of aim points.—

Second, for the undeclared states to embrace the harsh lessons of the Cold War: that nuclear weapons are inherently dangerous, hugely expensive, and militarily inefficient; that implacable hostility and alienation will almost certainly over time lead to a nuclear crisis; that the failure of nuclear deterrence would imperil not just the survival of the antagonists, but of every society; and that nuclear war is a raging, insatiable beast whose instincts and appetite we pretend to understand but cannot possibly control.

Third, given its crucial leadership role, it is essential for the United States to undertake as a first order of business a sweeping review of its nuclear policies and strategies. The Clinton administration's 1993 Nuclear Posture Review was an essential but far from sufficient step toward rethinking the role of nuclear weapons in the post-Cold War era. While clearing the agenda of some pressing force structure questions, the NPR purposely avoided the larger policy issues.

Moreover, to the point of Cold War attitudes, the Review's justification for maintaining robust nuclear forces as a hedge against

271

the resurgence of a hostile Russia should now be seen as regrettable from several aspects. It sends an overt message of distrust in an era when building a positive security relationship with Russia is arguably the United States' most important foreign policy interest. It codifies force levels and postures completely out of keeping with the historic passage we have witnessed in world affairs. And, it perpetuates attitudes which inhibit a willingness to proceed immediately toward negotiation of greatly reduced levels of arms, notwithstanding the state of ratification of the START II Agreement.

There you have, in very abbreviated form, the core of the concerns which led me to abandon the blessed anonymity of private life, to join my voice with respected colleagues such as General Goodpaster, to urge publicly that the United States make unequivocal its commitment to the elimination of nuclear arsenals, and take the lead in setting an agenda for moving forthrightly toward that objective.

I left active duty with great confidence that the imperative for this commitment, and the will to pursue it, were fully in place. I entered private life with a sense of profound satisfaction that the astonishing turn of events which brought a wondrous closure to my three and one-half decades of military service, and far more importantly to four decades of perilous ideological confrontation, presented historic opportunities to advance the human condition.

But now time, and human nature, are wearing away the sense of wonder and closing the window of opportunity. Options are being lost as urgent questions are unasked, or unanswered; as outmoded routines perpetuate Cold War patterns and thinking; and as a new generation of nuclear actors and aspirants lurch backward toward a chilling world where the principal antagonists could find no better solution to their entangled security fears than Mutual Assured Destruction.

Such a world was and is intolerable. We are not condemned to repeat the lessons of forty years at the nuclear brink. We can do better than condone a world in which nuclear weapons are accepted as commonplace. The price already paid is too dear, the risks run too great. The task is daunting, but we cannot shrink from it. The opportunity may not come again.

APPENDIX TWO

The Treaty on the Prevention of the Placement of Weapons in Outer Space

The Treaty on the Prevention of the Placement of Weapons in Outer Space establishes a framework and procedures to assure that space will be a neutral realm from which all classes of space-based weapons are banned and from which no hostile action shall be taken toward beings or objects on Earth or in space from space.

This Treaty invites Nation States to become Signatories to this Treaty and invites all Nation States, with recognition to Indigenous Nations, to commit to plan and assist in the orderly development and implementation of a framework and procedures that will assure and verify that space is and will remain to be a peaceful neutral realm from which all classes of space-based weapons are banned in perpetuity. Peaceful international cooperative space exploration, research and development can continue as now is the time to replace strategies and technologies of violence with strategies of Space Age cooperation that solve problems instead of creating new ones.

The Parties to this Treaty:

Reaffirm the urgency of preventing a destabilizing, threatening, and costly arms race in space,

Recognize that an agreement by Treaty to create a weapons-free space domain to ensure universal cooperation in space will save huge sums that would otherwise be expended for a dangerous and provocative space arms race,

Recognize that eliminating space-based weapons is more easily accomplished by agreement before any further investment is made to place them in permanent positions based in space,

Confirm that it is the obligation of all State leaders to ban all space-based weapons including the intention to weaponize space, the moon

273

or any celestial body or to use any space-based technology as a space-based weapon, using the foundation of all relevant previous, current and proposed treaties now with a focus specifically on space-based weapons,

Reaffirm the urgent need for international agreements on concrete proposals and projects deriving from confidence-building, world cooperative space ventures which will replace and prevent an arms race in outer space,

Recognize that information and data gained from cooperative space exploration and development will provide unlimited benefits and opportunities to all humankind in areas of health, education, the economy, mutual security, energy, and the environment,

Acknowledge that all Nation States will be important allies to each other for real security and development, and that our national and international space ventures and policies must reflect this reality,

Realize that the demonstrated capability of missiles or nuclear and other possible weapons technologies are threats to all including all agreements on Earth if they are permanently based in space with no treaty law to ban the weapons technologies and this reality serves notice of our limited understanding of physics and of the clearly dangerous consequences of continuing to escalate destructive technologies into space that could be intended to be weapons of control and domination or that could be intended to cause harm to any object or being on Earth or in space from space,

Affirm that the possibility of reclaiming and initiating a real peaceful future for humankind in a safe environment on Earth is intimately linked with curbing our violence toward each other and Earth, and with preparing to survive as Earth heals herself after decades of suffering and destruction that it is now time to stop,

Note that every class of space-based weapons, including weapons of mass destruction or precise destruction, is a symbol of fear for which violence provides no remedy,

Recognize that space must forever be free of man-made hazards, and must be a passageway to open the secrets of our past and the new challenges and opportunities of our future,

Inspired by the great prospects of Earth taking its rightful place in the Cosmos as all world citizens share the fruits of their cultures with respect for each other and all humankind,

Reaffirm that preventing placement of space-based weapons will avert otherwise inevitable resulting consequences, risks, and dangers to the commitment to establishing real and possible peace on Earth and peace in space now,

Believe that world cooperation in space will contribute to developing mutual understanding and to strengthening security based on a new form of verification and enforcement that applies the latest tools of technology for observation and information sharing because cooperative relations and projects in space already build more trust and transparency and can be enhanced for all,

Understand that this space Treaty is now verifiable and enforceable via applying cooperative monitoring, observation, and information sharing techniques both existing and forthcoming in the context of a new frequency of consciousness that commits to keeping space free of the intention to turn technology based in space into weapons to be used against beings or objects on Earth or in space are inspired by the great peace time prospects, benefits, and opportunities for stimulating the economies, jobs, profits, products and services applied directly to solve urgent and potential problems of humans and the rest of the biosphere,

Recognize that every country's space assets can be protected only by mutual cooperation and verification, and that this Treaty will accomplish this objective,

Realize we are one interconnected and interdependent human species on our home planet, and we are determined now to live in peace with all our neighbors,

Affirm that it is the policy of Signatories to this Treaty to permanently ban all space-based weapons and to proceed into space cooperatively, and that all Signatories are convinced that this Treaty will further the purposes and principles of the Charter of the United Nations.

The Nation States Signatories to this Treaty agree to the following Articles:

ARTICLE I

Each Nation State signing and ratifying this **Treaty on the Prevention of the Placement of Weapons in Outer Space** shall:

1. Implement a ban on the research, development, testing, manufacturing, and deployment of all space-based weapons;

2. Implement a ban on the use of space-based weapons the purpose of which is to destroy or damage objects or beings located in space or on Earth;

3. Terminate any current research, development, testing, production, manufacturing, and deployment of all space-based weapons;

4. Each Nation State Signatory to this Treaty shall support and encourage other Nation States to sign, ratify, and implement the **Treaty on the Prevention of the Placement of Weapons in Outer Space**. Nothing in this Treaty shall prohibit the following space-based ventures that are not activities related to space-based weapons:

a. Space exploration;

b. Space research and development;

c. Testing, manufacturing, production or deployment of non-weapons systems not prohibited are commercial, civil, entrepreneurial or military space-based ventures that are confirmed to not be any part of a space-based weapon system or to have no intention to become or support for a space-based weapon or system;

5. Cooperative space-based ventures with all peoples are encouraged;

6. Upon signing of this Treaty, cooperative research and development of verifiable defenses specifically against impacts from space debris, natural celestial asteroid and meteor bodies will be permitted.

After the first nine (9) Nation States sign and ratify the **Treaty on the Prevention of the Placement of Weapons in Outer Space**, the Secretary General of the United Nations shall submit to the General Assembly of the United Nations the official recognition of this Treaty henceforth as ratified law.

ARTICLE II

Each Nation State Signatory to this Treaty shall not base any weapon on any object or celestial body located in space. Permitted is the establishment of space-based related military bases or operations, including for communication, navigation, reconnaissance, early warning, remote sensing, and surveillance that does not interfere with operations of any other satellites, with living and working in space, or with space ventures, provided that it can be verified that there is no intention to use any space-based technology or system as a space-based weapon.

The use of military technology or personnel for peaceful space-based purposes is not prohibited. The use of any equipment or facility in space related to the research and development, testing, manufacturing, production, deployment or application of space-based weapons is prohibited.

ARTICLE III

1. Nation State Signatories to this Treaty agree to the establishment, equipping, and organizing of a United Nations Peace in Space Office;

2. This Peace in Space Office shall be composed of representatives from diverse areas such as commercial, civilian, entrepreneurial and military sectors that will check registration of space ventures and determine methods for monitoring compliance, including verification and enforcement measures that will be based on cooperative ventures and enhanced communication that will maintain the permanent commitment of all Nation State Signatories to this Treaty;

3. The Peace in Space Office is mandated to monitor outer space to verify and to enforce this Treaty using the latest tools of technology and information sharing;

4. The Peace in Space Office will identify any entity or program that engages in activities contrary to the provisions of this Treaty and will work with all Signatories to correct this situation via cooperation, not confrontation.

ARTICLE IV

1. The term "space" and "outer space" is defined as the space extending above the earth at an altitude of 100 kilometers above sea level. Weapons banned by this Treaty are considered to be space-based if they are located at or above 100 kilometers above sea level;

2. Space-based weapons are defined as being anything that is based in space that can be used with intention to damage or destroy objects or beings in space or on Earth from a location based in space;

3. This Treaty bans all space-based weapons, including the dual-use of any space-based object or technology when it is located in space with the intention to be used as a weapon that could damage or destroy any object or being on Earth or in space;

4. Weapons launched from the Earth that travel through space but are not based in space are not banned by this Treaty;

5. The terms space-based weapon and space-based weapons systems are defined for the purpose of this Treaty in order to identify weapons, devices, or systems that are based in any space location for the purpose of damaging or destroying, from space, any object or being that is located in space or on Earth;

6. This Treaty prohibits:

a. Firing one or more weapons based in space that would be intended to collide with any object or being in space;

b. Detonating any explosive device based in space in close proximity to any object or being in space;

c. Directing any space-based source of energy offensively against any object or being in space or on Earth;

d. Basing controls or systems of any space-based weapons that are or could be intended to collide with or inflict damage upon objects or beings in any location in space including on the moon, any celestial body, on a satellite, craft, or on any form of space station.

ARTICLE V

1. The United Nations Office for Outer Space Affairs shall be responsible to coordinate the first meetings between members of the United Nations and representatives of Signatory Nation States and Indigenous First Nations;

2. A permanent Liaison for earth and space communication will be available to the United Nations Security Council to answer questions and to provide counsel on issues of security and development of earth and space;

3. The Liaison will assist in identifying and neutralizing any attempt to deploy or use any space-based weapon.

ARTICLE VI

1. The provisions of this Treaty that ban all space-based weapons shall apply to all Nation States, whether or not they are Signatories to this Treaty;

2. This Treaty shall enter into force upon the signing and ratification of the first nine (9) Nation State Signatories.

ARTICLE VII

1. This Treaty shall be open to all Nation States for signature. Any State that does not sign this Treaty before its entry into force may accede to it at any future time;

2. This Treaty shall be subject to ratification by Signatory Nation States. Instruments of ratification or accession shall be deposited with the Secretary General of the United Nations;

3. This Treaty shall enter into force upon the deposit of instruments of ratification by nine (9) Governments. For any Nation State whose instruments of ratification or accession are deposited subsequent to the entry into force of this Treaty, their ratification shall enter into force on the date of the deposit of their instruments of ratification or accession;

4. The Depositary Governments shall promptly inform all Signatory and acceding Nation States of the date of each signature, the date of deposit of each instrument of ratification of and accession to this Treaty, and the date of its entry into force and other notices;

5. This Treaty shall be registered by the Depositary Governments pursuant to Article 102 of the Charter of the United Nations;

6. This Treaty shall be of unlimited duration.

ARTICLE VIII

1. Any Nation State Signatory to the Treaty may propose amendments to this Treaty;

2. Amendments to the Treaty shall enter into force upon acceptance by a majority vote of the Nation State Signatories;

3. The text of any proposed amendment shall be submitted to the United Nations Depositary who shall promptly notify all Nation State Signatories.

ARTICLE IX

This Treaty, of which the English, Arabic, Russian, French, Spanish and Chinese texts are equally authentic, shall be deposited in the archives of the Depositary Governments. Certified copies of this Treaty shall be transmitted by the Depositary Governments to the Governments of the Signatory and the acceding Nation States.

IN WITNESS WHEREOF the undersigned, duly authorized by their respective governments, has

Signed this
Treaty_____

At the location of

_____

On this date of

_____

TELL YOUR COUNTRY LEADER TO SIGN THIS TREATY

For more information about the Treaty on the Prevention of the Placement of Weapons in Outer Space go to: peaceinspace.com.

The book below was written to raise funds for the Treaty and Children's charities. It conveys my wife Carol's story and may explain her unrelenting commitment to this worthy cause.

FOR THE CHILDREN

By
Suzzan Babcock
With contribution from Craig Babcock

For
Dr. Carol Sue Rosin

"There is no guarantee due to the human ego."

As I wrote:

"We're at the Big Crossroads. Peer into the crystal ball and what do we see? Which path do we take? Less civility, more barbarism? Are we whistling in the dark? Crossing our fingers and praying angels or ETs will swoop down to rescue us and somehow save the day? In Search of Peace: *FOR THE CHILDREN* blazes a different path that leads to a new world. Through my wife Carol, and Suzzan and Craig's life journeys, the book reveals how our ancestors may have known more than we do!!!: that the modern "discoveries" of Noetics and the deeper functions of the mind are not innovations at all, but are a part of sacred teachings known as the Mysteries. We learn that the Fall of Humanity that is in all the world's sacred writings may identify a different enemy: one hiding in the background behind the archetypes of the various incarnations of the Devil. The authors say the problem is this "enemy" has a partner actually living inside us, our ego. They show how the ego is no friend to our true selves or spirit because it wrecks all our good intentions as often as it can. In Search of Peace: *FOR THE CHILDREN* explains how we can identify this villainous saboteur within through its everyday actions in our lives. Once we understand the real lie of separation, we can then dispel the Great Illusion and embrace our true roles. This book is one of hope."

Jon Cypher

SUMMARY OF IMPORTANT
—TALKING POINTS—
A NEW WIN-WIN VISION

I call on all world leaders to sign and ratify the World Space Preservation Treaty as quickly as possible, because this ban of all space-based weapons makes it possible to:

*Prohibit the research and development (R&D), testing, manufacturing, production and deployment of space-based weapons and systems, and the use of weapons to destroy or damage objects in space that are in orbit (i.e. satellites). — This prohibits the introduction of all operational weapons in space, and the escalation of war on earth from space and in space.

*Permit space exploration, R&D, testing, manufacturing, production and deployment of civil commercial and defense activities (including communication, navigation, surveillance, reconnaissance, early warning or remote sensing, including asteroid and comet hazard mitigation) that are not related to space-based weapons or systems.

*Transform the war industry into a space industry and other industries by removing the mandate to weaponize space while simultaneously allowing the inexorably linked military-industrial-entrepreneurial-lab-university-intelligence-NASA (and other space agencies and organizations)-government(s) complex to continue to expand into space, but without space-based weapons.—

*Stimulate a new economic stimulus package based on creating a new marketplace as we evolve from earth into space with more jobs and training programs, and more profits and contracts than during any hot or cold wartime. Space R&D and exploration programs are the foundation for a win-win platform that will produce clean and safe Space Age technology, products and services that will be applied, with focus and intention, directly to solving urgent and potential problems of human needs, new energy, and a sustainable environment. We can transform the war-based economy, industry, and mindset into a Space Age economy, industry, and mindset. This is a new Space Age vision that includes what IS in space and what CAN BE in space,

*Build a strong national defense and a global security system based on bringing the world's leaders to agree to 1) ban all space-based weapons and 2) apply civil, commercial, military/defense, and entrepreneurial Space Age technology and information services to enhance worldwide cooperation in communication and information exchanges about all vital issues of human needs, new energy sources, and our environment. Space-based technology will no longer be used as "force multipliers" to enhance war capabilities but will now be used to observe earth so that we can preserve our common environment and protect all life. Security will be based on cooperation with respect for our unity and diversity and on our coming together to reap the abundance of benefits and opportunities that will better life as we recognize we are an interconnected earth-in-space species in the universe(s). Peace on Earth as it is in Space = real security.

*Provide a new role for the military and military budgets, and for corporations and corporate profits, in order to focus their R&D, technology, and info services to protect humanity, produce alternative energy and lifesaving resources, and to preserve our environment in the context of a whole new Space Age paradigm. A new way of thinking and acting will emerge as war on earth becomes archaic and as humans evolve and transition into a higher state of consciousness as we live, work and travel in space. This is

the time to create an exciting action program with a grand new vision with and for the people in the Complex in order to replace the war industry and replace the old mindset of war.

*Verify and enforce agreements, because when the first twenty U.N. Member Nations sign and ratify this World Space Preservation Treaty it will become law and a new entity forms: an international/world cooperative Outer Space Peacekeeping Agency will be established and equipped to monitor outer space and enforce the space-based weapons ban. This same equipment can and will be applied with intention not to enhance war fighting capabilities, but to verify agreements including the reduction and elimination of missiles (thus eliminating the need for "missile defense"), nuclear weapons, and other dangerous, toxic, and polluting technologies.

*Free budgets, brains, hearts, and souls to live, work, and travel joyfully together on earth, as well as peacefully in space while creating space habitats, schools, hotels, resorts, farms, labs, industries, elevators, and spacecraft instead of space-based battle stations, space-based weapons, and space bombers. Instead, imagine happy lives filled with culture, music and the arts. We can evolve our intelligence, think and act in the context of a new Space Age paradigm with understanding, compassion, peace and justice for all, and with respect for our diversity and different perspectives, while acknowledging our interconnectedness, with a love and caring that will provide a wonderful, healthy future for our children, for all the children and their children…and for all sacred life.

*Provide the time and place, in 2005, yes, in our lifetime (!) when world leaders will come together to sign the World Space Preservation Treaty, and the U.S. Congress and

Administration will pass the companion Space Preservation Act. This will awaken and shift consciousness. This will have a positive impact on all issues and peoples because this will cause "second order" change, real change. Not only will the truth be revealed but it will be officially acknowledged, paving the way to the establishment of an Outer Space Peacekeeping Agency that will shepherd us to peace on earth and in space.

There shall be Peace on Earth as there is in Space.

A PERMANENT BAN ON SPACE WEAPONS — STATEMENTS OF SUPPORT—

UN Secretary General Kofi Annan
April 12, 2001:

At United Nations headquarters in New York, Secretary-General Kofi Annan used the occasion to urge that space exploration be devoted to peaceful pursuits such as environmental monitoring, not to waging war.

"Without mentioning the United States by name," Annan said, 'we must guard against the misuse of outer space, and, in particular, against the creation of an arms race in outer space.'"

Foreign Minister John Manley of Canada
July 25, 2001:

"I don't know what to make of some of these comments that are coming out of Washington that there are some in the United States' administration that want to develop space-based weapons," Manley said Wednesday in a telephone conference call from Hanoi. "I've made the point as strongly as could possibly be made that Canada is unalterably opposed to the weaponization of space."

The minister said the opening of the international space station offers another avenue for the use of space. "It's the largest engineering project ever undertaken by humanity," said Manley, noting the involvement of the U.S., Russia, the Europeans, Japan, and Canada. —"That's entirely for peaceful purposes and the advancement and encouragement of scientific research and discovery and we think that's the appropriate thing to be doing in space," said Manley. "We have to persuade them [the United States] that unilateralism ultimately will lead to confrontation."

Foreign Minister Igor Ivanov
September 28, 2001:

"Russia invites the world community to start working out a comprehensive agreement on the non-deployment of weapons in outer space and on the non-use of force against space objects,"—Russian Foreign Minister Igor Ivanov told the UN general assembly this week.—

Ivanov said nations should commit to not placing in the Earth's orbit any kind of weapons or deploying them on the moon, planets or space stations. —"As the first practical step in this direction, a moratorium could be declared on the deployment of weapons in outer space pending a relevant international agreement," he said. —"Preventing the deployment of weapons in outer space forms an important part of the set of measures designed to ensure strategic stability."

China's UN ambassador Wang Yingfan September 28, 2001:

China's UN ambassador Wang Yingfan echoed Russia's concern about the planned US missile defense system.—

"The success of international disarmament and nonproliferation efforts depends on the maintenance and observance of this treaty," he said. "The ABM treaty not only involves the signatory countries, but also bears critical importance and relevance to maintaining global strategic balance and stability as well as promoting international disarmament and nonproliferation process."—

China's position papers to the UN Conference on Disarmament
Feb. 9, 2000 & June 6, 2001:

"China is dedicated to promoting the international community to negotiate and conclude an international legal instrument on the prevention of the weaponization of space and an arms race in outer space."

"What should be particularly emphasized is that the Powers with the greatest space capabilities bear a special responsibility for preventing the weaponization of and an arms race in outer space and ensuring the use of space for peaceful purposes. Pending the conclusion of a new multilateral legal instrument on the prevention of an arms race in outer space, all countries concerned should undertake not to test, deploy or use any weapons, weapon systems or components in outer space."

Canadian Nobel laureate John Polanyi, representing 105 Nobel laureates
December 7, 2001:

More than 100 Nobel laureates have signed an appeal criticizing the climate change and missile defense policies of the United States under President Bush. —Among the appeal's signatories are exiled Tibetan spiritual leader the Dalai Lama, South African bishop Desmond Tutu and Mikhail Gorbachev, the last leader of the former Soviet Union. Several U.S. winners also signed.—

"It is time for the industrialized world to take responsibility for being a member of the world community and stop thinking in terms of nations," said Canadian John Polanyi, who won the 1986 Nobel Prize in Chemistry and initiated the appeal.

"We must persist in the quest for united action to counter both global warming and a weaponized world," the appeal stated. —It added that the 105 signatories supported international agreements including the Anti-Ballistic Missile (ABM) Treaty and the so-called Kyoto Convention on Climate Change. In an indirect reference to the National Missile Defense (NMD) system planned by the United States as a shield against attacks from what it has called rogue states, the appeal said it was time to "turn our backs on the unilateral search for security in which we seek shelter behind walls."

Member Nations of the U.N. General Assembly voted 156-0 to stipulate on January 3, 2001 that it:

1. *Reaffirms* the importance and urgency of preventing an arms race in outer space and the readiness of all States to contribute to that common objective, in conformity with the provisions of the Treaty on Principles Governing the Activities of States in the Exploration and Use of Outer Space, including the Moon and Other Celestial Bodies;

2. *Reaffirms its recognition*, as stated in the report of the Ad Hoc Committee on the Prevention of an Arms Race in Outer Space, that the legal regime applicable to outer space by itself does not guarantee the prevention of an arms race in outer space, that this legal regime plays a significant role in the prevention of an arms race in that environment, that there is a need to consolidate and reinforce that regime and enhance its effectiveness, and that it is important to comply

strictly with existing agreements, both bilateral and multilateral;

3. *Emphasizes* the necessity of further measures with appropriate and effective provisions for verification to prevent an arms race in outer space;

4. *Calls upon* all States, in particular those with major space capabilities, to contribute actively to the objective of the peaceful use of outer space and of the prevention of an arms race in outer space and to refrain from actions contrary to that objective and to the relevant existing treaties in the interest of maintaining international peace and security and promoting international cooperation...."

Astronaut Dr. Edgar Mitchell, Sixth Man to Walk on the Moon; Chairman, ICIS Board of Advisors

"As an Apollo astronaut, and long term advocate of banning weapons in space, I urge that all of us, as individuals, and at each level of government, recognize the critical nature of this issue. —If, as the leading spacefaring nation, and the world's only superpower, we fail to stop the spread of weaponry into this frontier, and do so by example and self-restraint, civilization's hope to end war will be forever lost, and the eventual destruction of life on Earth assured, as weaponry becomes ever more destructive."—

Dr. Charles Mercieca, President, International Association of Educators for World Peace and NGO-UN, Professor Emeritus, AAMU-USA

"Weapons in space must be banned forever, otherwise the tragic consequences would soon reach a point of no return to the detriment of our own children and their posterity. I am writing in support of the —Space Preservation Act and the Space Preservation Treaty."

PERSONAL NOTE FROM JON CYPHER

With great appreciation for your having joined me on this personal journey, may I now suggest that you go to www.peaceinspace.com where you will find real news updates that are relevant to our many issues of concern.

Contact Jon Cypher

spacetreaty@gmail.com

JON CYPHER BIO

Brooklyn-born Jon Cypher is a Broadway, TV, and movie actor. For seven seasons, Jon was the Chief on the show that changed TV, *Hill St. Blues*. As Gen. Craig on the hit sit-com *Major Dad*, he brought big laughs into our homes. He was Joan Collins' nemesis for two seasons on *Dynasty*. He's starred in a number of Broadway shows: *Night of the Iguana, The Disenchanted*, he was Dr. Carrasco in the huge hit *Man of La Mancha* (and, as Richard Kiley's understudy, he played Quixote many times in N.Y. and to rave reviews in productions around the country). He was Jefferson in the hit musical *1776*, the Dist. Att. in Tony Award-winner *The Great White Hope*, Kate Hepburn's dad (!) in *COCO, Sherry,* and in *Big, the Musical* (based on Tom Hanks' movie). In eight seasons of repertory and stock, he played dozens of major roles, from Macbeth to El Gallo in *The Fantasticks*. Among his five soaps are *As the World Turns, General Hospital,* and Emmy winner, *Santa Barbara.* He's starred in 22 feature films: *Strictly Business, Masters of the Universe*, in the Western classic *Valdez Is Coming* (opp. Burt Lancaster) and with Hayley Mills and David McCallum in *The Kingfisher Caper*, and Leigh Taylor Young in *Accidents* (the latter two made in So. Africa), *Spontaneous Combustion, Blade,* and *Believe in Me.* He's guested on series from way back when TV was live: *Bonanza* (Jodie Foster's dad!), *The Kaiser Aluminum Hour, U.S. Steel Hour, Kraft Theatre, Armstrong Circle Theatre.* up to the more recent *Murder She Wrote* and *Law and Order.* He was Robt. Loggia's boss in the highly successful mini-series *Favorite Son*, and Priscilla Presley's dad in the hit mini-series *Elvis and Me* based on her book. He was in *Knotts Landing* for a season and was Joan Collins' nemesis for two seasons on *Dynasty*. In the mini-series *Malice in Wonderland*, he was

Liz Taylor's husband and was Doris Day's lover on her TV series. Jon is well known as the original Prince Charming opposite Julie Andrews' *Cinderella* (the original Rodgers and Hammerstein made-for-TV spectacular). For over two years, Jon played Peron in the record LA production of *Evita* and, again at the Shubert Theatre, he starred in the hit musical *42nd St*. He was *Sweeney Todd* in the hit production at the Pittsburgh Civic Light Opera and, again at the CLO, he was Fagan in *Oliver*. As an activist for animals, the environment, and peace, Jon works with his wife, Dr. Carol Rosin, to prevent the placement of space-based weapons. This is his first published book.

Contact Jon:

spacetreaty@gmail.com